BRING YOUR
FICTION
TO
Life

KAREN S. WIESNER

WD

WRITER'S DIGEST BOOKS

WritersDigest.com
Cincinnati, Ohio

For more resources for writers, visit www.writersdigest.com.

21 20 19 18 17   5 4 3 2 1

Distributed in Canada by Fraser Direct
100 Armstrong Avenue
Georgetown, Ontario, Canada L7G 5S4
Tel: (905) 877-4411

Distributed in the U.K. and Europe by F+W Media International
Pynes Hill Court, Pynes Hill, Rydon Lane
Exeter, EX2 5AZ, United Kingdom
Tel: (+44) 1392-797680, Fax: (+44) 1626-323319
E-mail: postmaster@davidandcharles.co.uk

Library of Congress Cataloging-in-Publication Data

ISBN-13: 978-1-4403-4982-9

Edited by Cris Freese
Designed by Alexis Estoye
Production coordinated by Debbie Thomas

BRING YOUR YOUR FICTION TO *Life*

ACKNOWLEDGMENTS

This book wouldn't be complete without the mention of several people I want to publicly acknowledge for all they did to see this book through.

First and foremost is Linda Derkez, my sister and fellow author since our teenage years when we mass-produced chapters of our individual Works-In-Progress during long, daily writing sessions that always included a little coffee with our creamer and long breaks where we walked, listened to very loud music, and verbally brainstormed together. It was during this time our mutual love of writing became solidified. Quite frankly, this writing reference would never have seen the light of day without her encouragement, critiques (through every single last draft of it, which, incidentally, started out as a four-thousand word article I couldn't sell that I somehow turned into a full-fledged book), and sound kicks in the pants that definitely motivated me. I gave up more than once, insisting I just couldn't get any of this to work the way I wanted it to. She never let me stop there because she believed this book needed to be published, and absolutely had to get into the hands of struggling writers. Additionally, she gave this book the badly needed perspective of *new, unpublished writer* it lacked previously. *Bring Your Fiction to Life* is dedicated to her with all my gratitude for her willingness to believe in me without wavering.

Next, another writing partner and soul sister from the other side of the world: Chris Spindler. Together, we write the Falcon's Bend Series, and Christine has always been in my corner, whether it's been to defend me because she believed I had valuable advice to offer other writers, or to critique anything I asked of her, even when it was down to crunch time and I needed it done ASAP. She did that with this book, and her feedback improves everything I produce. Thanks, Chris.

Also, thanks to my son, who read the article version of this book when the idea was in its infancy and seemed impressed even then and was proud of me when I sold the title to Writer's Digest Books (top dogs!). Your expert feedback, as a fellow writer and copyeditor, and your respect for my career in general mean more to me than I can express.

Gratitude also goes to my nephew, who inadvertently gave me the idea for this topic while I was reading one of his amazing works of short fiction.

A farewell to my previous editor, Rachel, whom I loved working with on my last project. Thanks for passing me into such capable hands. To that end, thanks to my new editor, Cris. A good editor does his job, smoothing out all the rough edges; but a great one makes a book infinitely better for having a hand in the project. Thanks for making this project such an enjoyable process.

Finally, I just want to thank all the writers who benefit from the writing reference books I've offered over the years and send me nice notes of gratitude or with questions. I love hearing from each of you, and love helping in any way I can. That's the main reason I keep offering these titles. Happy writing, and keep the notes coming. We're in this together.

ABOUT THE AUTHOR

Karen Wiesner is an accomplished author with 120 titles published in the past nineteen years, which have been nominated/won 134 awards, and who has thirty-six more contracted releases. Her books cover such genres as women's fiction, romance, mystery/police procedural/cozy, suspense/thriller, paranormal/supernatural, futuristic, fantasy, gothic, inspirational, thriller, horror, chick-lit, and action/adventure. She also writes children's books, poetry, and writing reference titles, such as *First Draft in 30 Days* and *From First Draft to Finished Novel* (out of print; reissue available now under the title *Cohesive Story Building*). Her third offering from Writer's Digest Books was *Writing the Fiction Series: The Complete Guide for Novels and Novellas*. For more information about Karen's fiction and many series, consult her official companion guide *The World of Author Karen Wiesner: A Compendium of Fiction*. Visit her website at http://www.karenwiesner.com. When she isn't writing or brainstorming, she can be found reading from any conceivable genre of fiction or nonfiction, playing video games, or visiting her son—also a writer and copyeditor—where he attends college. She lives in Wisconsin with her husband and stuffed animal pets.

Check out Karen's author page on Facebook: http://www.facebook.com/KarenWiesnerAuthor. If you'd like to receive Karen's free e-mail newsletter, Karen's Quill, and become eligible to win her monthly book giveaways, send a blank e-mail to KarensQuill-subscribe@yahoogroups.com.

TABLE OF CONTENTS

Introduction

WHAT IS THREE-DIMENSIONAL WRITING?

Three-dimensional: Of, relating to, or having three dimensions; giving the illusion of depth or varying distances; having or appearing to have length, breadth, and depth; having volume; describing or being described in well-rounded completeness; true to life, lifelike; having different qualities that are like the qualities of a real person; solid, concrete, vivid, realistic, rounded; sufficiently full in characterization and representation of events to be believable; simulating the effect of depth by presenting slightly different views of a scene.

Applied to writing, the word *three-dimensional* is easy to define as solid, realistic, rounded, and lifelike, even living. The hard part for authors comes in translating these concepts into the craft of writing. Most writers know what is *not* three-dimensional writing. Simple words and phrases convey what's lacking: flat, cardboard, paper doll, archetypal, convenient to the story, lacking history with loose and undefined ties, predictable, unrealistic, unremarkable, undeveloped or underdeveloped, dead.

Writing that is three-dimensional seems to have length (essentially the foundation of a story), width (structure), and depth (the completeness of fully fleshed-out characters, plots, and settings, as well as multiple layers and rich, textured scenes). Length and width are story basics, and generally even novice writers grasp these concepts. Depth is where complications arise.

Three-dimensional writing is what allows a reader to step through the pages of a book and enter a fictional world, where plot and characters are in that glorious, realistic realm that starts with little more than a line and progresses into shape and, finally, solid form. Once three-dimensionality is within reach, all things are possible: direction, motion, focus, vivid color, texture, harmony, and variety in which change is attainable and value becomes concrete.

But three-dimensional writing is also so much more than this. Three-dimensional writing has three aspects that need to occur to bring about the potential for truly three-dimensional, living fiction:

1. three-dimensional characters, plots, and settings
2. complex, three-dimensional scenes
3. multilayered storytelling

Once we come into a project with the necessary preparation for crafting three-dimensional characters, plots, and settings, we're left with the hands-on process of translating these dimensional foundations into opening and closing scenes, along with those all-important bridge scenes. That's where three-dimensional writing becomes sketchy and requires an examination of step-by-step technique. A multilayered approach to storytelling is also required for authors who intend to make writing their careers. We'll explore all of these in detail in the pages that follow. I'll also provide aids that can be used to ensure three-dimensionality for each story.

THE PURPOSE OF THIS BOOK

The purpose of *Bring Your Fiction to Life* is to show writers at every stage of their careers the distinctive layers of a story and how to build three-dimensional aspects through all stages in the process. Three-dimensional thinking needs to start immediately, even during the brainstorming phase, and it's crucial that three-dimensionality be maintained throughout the writing and revising of your story. Every work of fiction needs three-dimensionality. It doesn't matter if the story in question is two pages or two thousand. It's a mistake to believe that a shorter length means the story doesn't have to be well developed. It's more than possible to express a tremendous amount in just a few words, but readers can't connect with your characters, plots, or settings if those aspects of your story aren't fully fleshed out. So, regardless of length, do everything you can to ensure that you build in the potential for three-dimensionality.

This book is broken down into seven chapters followed by two appendices, with bonus material online.

Chapters one through three explore the three core elements of character, plot, and setting, and how to create three-dimensionality with each. The provided Character Sketch Worksheet will ensure that your characters, plots, and settings are all three-dimensional.

Chapter four covers the anatomy of three-dimensional scenes, namely, opening, resolution, and bridge scenes. The furnished Present, Past, and Future (hereafter referred to as P/P/F) Scene Worksheet should remove any doubt as to whether you've properly set *up* and set *out*, anchored and oriented readers before leading them with purpose through your story landscape; examined the past in careful increments to fill in realistic layers; and made certain there's a whisper of what's to come.

Chapter five offers two additional techniques for ensuring your story has the required depth. First, we'll learn how to construct back cover blurbs with P/P/F Dimensions. Next, we'll talk about evaluating an outline or manuscript with a P/P/F Dimension Development Chart. Although this book assumes you'll be using the method described throughout for a brand-new project, the technique can also be used for projects that are in a second draft or revision stage. The chart contained in this section will help you pinpoint the exact scene where a lack of three-dimensionality may plague your story.

Chapter six focuses on the crucial need to write in stages to create the layers necessary for three-dimensional writing.

The conclusion sums up what we've learned about the vital role three-dimensionality plays in producing multilayered, complex stories readers can step into interactively.

The two appendices and online material contain all the supplemental materials you'll need to work your way through the three-dimensionality process:

- **APPENDIX A** contains blank worksheets, checklists, charts, and additional aids you can use to build three-dimensionality into your story.
- **APPENDIX B** provides exercises to help develop your three-dimensional writing muscles by using back cover blurbs and chapters from published novels.
- **THE ONLINE MATERIAL** offers a detailed example—using a published novel—of all the three-dimensional aids presented in this reference, including the Three-Dimensional Character, Plot, and Setting Sketch Worksheet; the Three-Dimensional Scene Worksheet; the Three-Dimensional Back Cover Blurb Breakdown; the P/P/F Dimension Development Chart; and an excerpt from the published novel I mentioned here to see how the three dimensions were brought to life. When analyzed in this manner, you'll see for yourself how three-dimensionality is created and layered through progressing scenes in a story.

Some clarifications about the examples from published novels I've used that you'll find in this book: I didn't feel comfortable fabricating material for published books to fit into sections of my worksheets. Therefore, I could only use what was found in the text, and there may not have been much to find since the authors weren't using my worksheets or methods when writing their books. Needless to say, it's not easy to "work backwards" with something published (not even in using my own, as you'll see in the online material). The work's already done, and I can't speculate what might have been done during the writing of the book. For that reason, I've used direct quotes from the text when citing specific examples from published books. As you're filling out your own worksheets, you'll be using a different technique—summing up what's needed in each worksheet section into a handful of focused sentences. I've provided "simple examples" that include random pieces of story (all using a basic theme so you can see definite development), as yours probably will be when you use the worksheets. These show a succinct way of filling out the worksheet. If you've read my book *Cohesive Story Building*, you may recognize this "simple example," titled here "Dark Places," from the Story Plan Checklist Exercise provided in Appendix D of that reference.

HOW TO USE THIS BOOK

Virginia Woolf said, "As for my next book, I am going to hold myself from writing it till I have it impending in me: grown heavy in my mind like a ripe pear; pendant, gravid, asking to be cut or it will fall." This precisely describes how a story should grow in the author's mind until it absolutely *has* to be written. The best-case scenario is always, always, always to start a story only *after* you have a lot of story ideas, vivid characters, setting, plots, etc., to work with. The three-dimensional writer starts with a solid story that's ready to drop into his hands like ripe fruit. While you can do the same for an idea that's not ready, it'll be a *lot* harder. In fact, it might take the author decades to get an unripe story off the ground.

To get a story ripe enough to carry you through the beginning stages of the project, we need to have a method for growing those story ideas, especially if you have multiple ideas vying for your attention at one time. In chapter six, we'll talk about creating story folders that will not only help you develop all your ideas but will prevent you from getting distracted from your current work-in-progress.

A couple of other notes: Throughout this book, for consistency, I'll refer to *characters* in the female point of view. To offer distinction, I'll refer to *readers and writers* in the male POV. Clearly, characters, readers, and writers can be of either sex, but to prevent an erratic jump from one to the other, I've chosen this method.

Also, I'll be referring to dimensions in terms of present, past, and future, which may sound out of order since we're used to hearing them in a more linear grouping (i.e., past, present, and future). In nearly every story, the most important dimension of self is present, obviously, because you're telling the current story in present tense, in the here and now. That doesn't mean past and future aren't also critical—far from it, as we'll see. It's simply that stories are almost exclusively (and probably wisely) told in the present with carefully orchestrated reaches into the past and future.

One other thing to take notice of is that a great number of the examples used throughout this book are from movies. The reason for this is because the motion picture medium is so much more visual and, sadly, there are more moviegoers than readers these days. Statistics from a 2014 study conducted by the Pew Research Center pointed out that nearly one quarter of Americans failed to read a single book during the year, while more than two-thirds of the population went to the cinema at least once during the year; and frequent moviegoers attended at least once a month. Safe to say, the fiction in movies may be better known than that in books, although those reading this reference probably read more books than they watch movies. Ultimately, all the examples are fictional, so I saw no reason not to use some from each medium.

Additionally, I'll note up-front that I believe a series name is part of its branding (see my book *Writing the Fiction Series*). Not only should the series title be included everywhere the name of a book is spoken or written about, but the word *series* or *trilogy* should be capitalized in order to further solidify the branding. In other words, I never refer to my series Family Heirlooms as simply that. Always, I refer to it as the "Family Heirlooms Series" because that's the full title and the most effective way to brand it to my readers. That's why you'll see every series mentioned within this book with the word *series* or *trilogy* capitalized.

One final note of clarification: Keep in mind that you don't have to perform every step in this—or any other—writing method. Every author is different, we all think and perform differently, and ultimately it makes no sense to do more work than we need to. The goal for each writer should be to find what works for *him* personally. Most of the time that means finding what *doesn't* work first.

My motto is, "Utilize what works for you; discard the rest." The point of sketches, worksheets, and checklists is to give help in pinpointing problem areas. If you're not having a problem in a certain area, go ahead and skip the in-depth processing. In my writing methods, in particular, my goal is to make sure authors have everything needed to learn to write instinctively. What I mean by that is that through copious amounts of practice, usually over the course of several years, your brain begins to grasp the basics of crafting characters, plots, and/or settings, and even some of the harder concepts of writing, like writing three-dimensionally. This means you can do a lot less prewriting before you write a story, as in, you may not have to do endless character or plot sketches, etc. You may instinctively inject just the right amount of setting description that has purpose beyond simply depicting locations. After having more than one hundred books published, I write instinctively; so my story crafting (including building P/P/F Dimensions into every scene) is done in the course of outlining each and every book. It comes automatically, without the need for worksheets. If you feel like some (or any) of this isn't instinctive for you, go through the steps as I've listed them. Every author's endgame is and should be instinctive writing.

GETTING STARTED

If your characters, plots, settings, and the scenes made up of each of these are truly three-dimensional, your book will be so vivid it'll be as real as the physical world to your readers when they step into the pages and experience your words. My hope is that *Bring Your Fiction to Life* gives you a solid plan of action from start to finish through in-depth discussions, examples, and exercises, with leave-no-stone-unturned aids and a layering process that allows you take the three-dimensionality plan into your own writing.

⊙ Download bonus online material at
www.writersdigest.com/bring-your-fiction-to-life.

THREE-DIMENSIONAL CHARACTERS

"Complexity is an indispensable ingredient of life, and so it ought to be with the characters we create in our stories."

—STAVROS HALVATZIS, PH.D.,
"HOW PARADOXES DEEPEN CHARACTER"

The word *three-dimensional* translates well into the craft of writing. Writing that's three-dimensional is complex and multilayered, vivid and realistic, tailored specifically for the story with unique histories threaded in deep and definable roots, unpredictability, and individuality that's fully developed and *alive*.

In preparation for writing this book, I read everything I could get my hands on concerning three-dimensional writing. There's a fair amount out there, but all contained only small pieces of the whole three-dimensionality package, focusing just on sketches for character, plot, and/or setting—the three core elements of any story. Few went from explanation to hands-on technique. The one thing missing from such material is that *layers* are crucial in the creation of the core story elements, as the length, width, and depth of every solid story. Using sketches to develop the necessary multidimensional layers of character, plot, and setting is the technique that comes closest to reaching our three-dimensional goal. However, the biggest problem is that only *one* dimension of character is generally sketched out on these worksheets, namely, the "present self" character. What's lacking are the other two dimensions of self. Each major character in a book needs a present self (the person she is in the here and now of the active story), a past self (who this individual was before), and a future self (who she'll be in the future, refined and shaped by current situations, conflicts, other characters, and her settings). If you want three-dimensional protagonists and antagonists with heartbreakingly realistic conflicts set in a world so vivid readers can actually enter it alongside the characters, you need to have all three "self" dimensions.

However, some clarification is called for at this point: First, your goal as a writer is to get to know your characters thoroughly. Not everything you come up with in your sketches will (or should) be used within the story, but it's still important to figure out all you can. The more you know before you start writing, the easier you can convey a fully fleshed out character with the words you write. Also, don't expect to come up with substance or something brilliant immediately. Work on these sketches over time, develop and layer them; remain aware that the rich imagery, textured sentences, and clever turns of phrase will all come later in the writing and revising. The goal right now is to get started. You also do *not* need to work in the presented order. Feel free to mix up the items on the worksheets in this book in whatever way makes the most sense to you—or in whatever order the ideas come to you. Work steadily on the one area you're inspired to get going on at the time. When you finish that, look through the rest of the items and see what you're inspired to develop.

Next, the Three-Dimensional Characters, Plots, and Settings Sketch is streamlined with only the absolute necessities about each main character. This sketch is presented in one worksheet in Appendix A with the dimensions side by side so you can compare the developments between the dimensions and ensure cohesive, deep, logical progressions. You'll find character, setting, and plot sketches galore online—just type "character sketches" or "plot sketches," etc., into any search engine and you can take your pick from what comes up if you want to go roots deep with yours. Feel free to add anything you'd like to the basic Three-Dimensional Characters, Plots, and Settings Sketch worksheet in order to explore your characters' three-dimensional selves in-depth.

Additionally, when you're first learning the craft of writing, inspiration will play a huge role in your accomplishments. Constant brainstorming is the most important part of writing and should begin long before you start work on a story. During this time, you should be jotting down notes as ideas come to you and storing them in individual story folders (more about this in chapter six). Write down everything that comes to you, no matter how trivial. The sketches will help you dive into the depths of your characters, your plots, and your settings from a three-dimensional viewpoint. Work on your three-dimensional sketches only after you've developed strong story ideas—when you're most inspired—and do everything you can to keep yourself brainstorming while you're fired up about it. If you don't have the ideas or motivation, this process becomes like pulling teeth.

Finally, fix this axiom in your mind: Character reveals plot and setting, just as plot and setting reveal character, and setting reveals character and plot. This trinity is vital to the dimensionality of your stories. They work together to unearth, connect, and layer a story. So a Three-Dimensional Plot Sketch is going to be ascribed to each major character, just as a Three-Dimensional Setting Sketch will be. In your sketches for each dimension of self, try to think of *cohesive* connections between them, since these connections are what you'll ultimately highlight in the writing of your book. The strongest stories are the ones in which *every* part of the story—the characters' role, physical descriptions, personalities, strengths and weaknesses, relationships, skills, conflicts, goals and motivation, and settings—becomes cohesive and fits together organically. We've all read stories in which the parts didn't merge naturally. Maybe we didn't notice a specific problem, but we knew *something* was off; that something lacked logic or didn't quite fit with the rest of the story, and the imbalance frustrated us. There's a chance you never finished reading the story. The books that you absolutely cannot put down, the stories that stay with you every minute of the time you're reading them and for years afterward, are the ones in which every aspect is so intricately connected that separating the threads is impossible.

Cohesion needs to start with the first spontaneous spark of a story in your head. Characters must blend naturally with the settings you've placed them in, just as plot must become an organic part of your characters and settings. If a story doesn't work, it could very well be because your character, plot, and setting elements aren't blending naturally. It could also be that your story isn't following one of the cardinal rules of writing: Everything that happens at the beginning of the book must be linked to something that happens later on. Characters must blend in naturally with your setting, just as your plot must be an organic part of your character and setting. Story elements need to be cohesive and progressive, layering and building up and bringing *together* all aspects within the book until the resolution. Chapter four goes in-depth into introducing, developing, and concluding story elements. If you're not sure whether your core elements are truly cohesive, you'll find a Cohesion Checklist you can use after you've finished your first draft of a story in Appendix A. My book *Cohesive Story Building* explores this theme in-depth.

Finally, you might wonder specifically *which* characters you should sketch. One thing that's extremely important to note for authors of all genres is the *point* of introducing characters in a story. A character can be main, secondary, or even minor, but *all* characters *must* be important to the story. A character who fits the role and achieves the goal you set for her, however small, is an important character. If not, why include her at all? You might want to use the following criteria for deciding whether to do the sketches for a particular character:

1. Will the character play a major role throughout the book? If the answer is no, it's up to you to decide to include that particular character in the sketches. If the answer is yes, then that character definitely needs to be included.
2. If you use a simple designation for the character (like "Argus Filch, Hogwarts caretaker"), is that all that's needed to explain the character's role in the story? If yes, you don't really need to do more than that, but you can if you want to. The sketches are for your own use.

3. Is there a lot of background on the character that needs to be told even though the character won't play a major role in the book? If the answer is yes, then that character may require a P/P/F sketch as a secondary character. If the answer is no, there's little need to do an in-depth P/P/F sketch. Go with your gut instinct.

DIMENSIONS: PRESENT, PAST AND FUTURE

Regardless of whether a writer is character, plot, or setting oriented, the fact is that character is the most important of the three. Without characters, settings are barren landscapes, regardless of how beautiful, breathtaking, or life changing. In a story, after all, whose life changes? You got it: the characters'. Without characters, plots are a series of actions that happen without context, consequence, or emotional reaction. Settings and plots never realize their own worth. Readers love or hate characters; they root for or decry the individuals populating the story, not the setting or plot so much. And nothing makes a reader put down a book faster than realizing at any point that the author doesn't know his own characters in all stages of life.

Now, I absolutely feel that main (point of view, referred to as POV from this point on) characters must be addressed here. Most books these days include many POV characters ... many, *many*. I've said frequently in interviews, my classes, and my books that the trend of including so many characters in a single book isn't one I can get on board with. The biggest reason for that is because every main character *has* to be three-dimensional. How can so many characters be three-dimensional when the only way to effectively cover the three dimensions of each is to write a 200,000-word novel?

Bottom line, main characters rarely become three-dimensional when there are too many in one (average-size) story. And that is the crux here: In most stories written today, the main characters *aren't* three-dimensional because there simply isn't room to make them so, unless you're George R.R. Martin, for instance, who does a thorough job of creating three-dimensional characters, specifically because he writes massive, sprawling, here's-Lady-Catelyn-Stark's-grocery-list *sagas* with every single title.

Martin can get away with such stories because he's extremely skilled and has editors and readers who justifiably cherish every last written word. Most authors *can't* do this because publishers will be wary about releasing an expensive one-thousand-page novel for new or midlist authors without proven sales records. Editors crop (sometimes unwisely) when a book gets too big to be profitable. The word count they'll allow will prohibit in-depth characterization if the cast in your book is huge. There's simply no way to do it unless you've achieved the level of popularity of Martin, Gabaldon, Rowling, Brown, King, or other big name authors who write impressive tomes. Quite frankly, if there's any chance the story can't be three-dimensional (because there isn't room, the word count prohibits it, your editor is asking you to crop ruthlessly, or you grow lazy developing some of the characters), then you might want to reconsider having a gazillion characters in the book.

This leads to the obvious question you may be wondering: Is it even *necessary* to do these sketches for each dimension of self? That question, fundamentally, points to the main reason writers don't usually provide P/P/F Dimensions: They don't believe much will change from present to past to future. The purpose of this book is to shatter the illusion that any of the dimensions can be cropped, foregone, forgotten, or neglected, whether deliberately, inadvertently, or justifiably (when an editor decides too much is too much). Remember, even if you don't include everything you come up with concerning P/P/F, you need each dimension in some capacity in every scene, and you as the author need to know all the dimensions thoroughly for every main character.

Characters wouldn't be growing and developing if they remained static throughout their lives. Think of it this way: Are you the same person you were when you were born, two months old, sixteen, twenty-five, fifty, seventy-five years old? Of course not. You can be sure you won't be exactly the same person you are now ten years—or even *one* year—from today. Everything you go through in your life, whether it's traumatic, evolving, or even constant, will change you in big and subtle ways. It's the nature of a human being. In the same way, to create layered, developing characters, you have to see where they are currently, where they came from, and where they may be heading.

That said, it is true that not too much may—or even *should*—change, depending on the circumstances and story material, from one dimension to the next. A radical shift in character, plot, and setting is possible, but usually only in extreme cases, and only with solid justification. Alterations between the dimensional sketches will likely be subtle rather than drastic, but allow development and growth to flourish. Out of these sketches, your story should begin to evolve organically.

Let's talk more about all of this within the distinct dimensions.

Present Self

In sketching the present dimension, you're essentially starting every character in the middle of her story. However, starting your sketches with the present dimension makes the most sense. Present character is always the person she is currently and sets the focus of the story you're writing in the *here and now*. The more you get to know the character through present dimension, the more development you'll gain in sketching her past and future dimensions. After all, a character's reaction to her experiences has a direct bearing on who she is and becomes, the choices she makes, and the actions she takes all through her life.

Maybe it's true that most people do have an innate way of being, conceivably born to act in a certain way; but in a work of fiction, a genetic disposition is of limited use. Instead, we focus on the universal truth that—like real people—almost all of a character's traits in the present are the result of the coping strategies used (good, bad, and everything in-between) and lessons learned (again, these reflect choices that are easy, hard, and all the nuances between) in every situation faced and the behavior that results. These are layers of that person's entire makeup. These change subtly over time. Naturally, the deeper you go into someone's past and psyche, the more you understand all that's shaped her growth.

In Scott O'Dell's *Island of the Blue Dolphins*, twenty-four-year-old Karana and her younger brother (the children of the tribe's chief), whom she's very motherly toward, are digging roots that their village needs for food in the spring when they see a ship on the ocean—an event that can be as exciting as it can be fearful, since in the past, visitors brought harm to the tribe. In the present dimension, life on the island for the Ghalas-at tribe (and Karana specifically) is built around the seasons and the tasks that must be done for them to survive. There are very few visitors to the island to stir up the daily routine. In the time since the last ship came to the island, the tribe has learned to be fearful of the hunters that come, demanding rights and making promises they don't intend to keep. At this point, they have no way of knowing who these visitors are and what they want, but there's good reason to be wary.

When sketching the present dimension, you're creating a character who's worth following all the way through to the end of a story. A good present dimension character will convey in a creative way what she's learned in life, what matters most to her in her current situation, and how she'd like her life to change or how she fears it will change. This is probably the easiest dimension, the one few authors would leave out since there would be no true story without it.

Past Self

Detailing the present dimension of your character is only the beginning. You need to weave pieces of the past throughout a story to flesh out the character's past dimension. You can't truly understand who someone is until you've seen her developmental years, what she's been through, and where she's come from. I love how K.M. Weiland describes this in "Improve Your Character Instantly: Just Add a Ghost" when she says that what all characters have in common are the depths of their backstories. "They arrive at the beginning of their stories with baggage already in tow." (Incidentally, the "ghost" here is something from the past that haunts the character. Brilliant!) Baggage can be another term for the past dimension, a character's backstory.

The dictionary definition of backstory for fiction is the history or background created for a character *that impacts the current events of the story*. Backstory is everything that occurred before the current story that *directly impacts* what will happen in the story. But it's only necessary to include backstory that's relevant to current choices, decisions, or events. But, as I've said, the author needs to know backstory in advance to authentically layer his characters.

It's been said that backstory shouldn't be placed at the beginning of a story, but that's only partially true. While front-loading a story with huge chunks of backstory isn't ideal (it could get incredibly boring or hard for the reader to digest if too much comes at once), we need to enlighten and engage readers, not overwhelm and crush out any interest with overkill. The true issue is that *pieces* (not great chunks) of backstory are needed at *all* stages of a story. Fragments of backstory need to be placed carefully throughout a story from the beginning all the way through to the end. Doing this will reveal character, plot, and setting in all dimensions.

Building on our previous example from *Island of the Blue Dolphins*, the last visitors to the island were a group of hunters who asked the tribe to hunt sea otters almost to their extinction. Karana's father, the chief of the Ghalas-at, doesn't remember this event fondly and is wary of the new group of hunters that has arrived abruptly to disrupt the tribe's regular routine. These new visitors make the same promises the last hunters did and their unwillingness to be forthcoming about the tribe's share of otter skins increases the underlying threat.

While it's popular to crop out the past dimension to meet a limited word count, too much shearing will prove detrimental to the three-dimensionality of any story. On the other hand, there is a point where too much can be overkill and would be better placed in the notes of an annotated version of the book, should your popularity ever warrant such a thing. With the three-dimensional worksheet we'll talk about soon, you'll give yourself the means to produce multidimensional characters, plots, and settings.

In sketching the past dimension for your character, you need to consider what fits in terms of the physical descriptions, personality traits, strengths and weaknesses, and skills she's acquired; the relationships she's had; the internal and external conflicts she's faced; and the environment she grew up in. What resulting goals and motivations are in line with who this character was, is, and justifiably will become? Your character's past dimension should inspire more development of her present, as well as the future dimension waiting in the wings.

We don't often consider the past dimension of a character like Sherlock Holmes, but the knowledge of doing so adds to his long-standing appeal. Holmes is best known for his observation-based inferences and his supreme, borderline arrogant confidence in his intellectual abilities, tempered by his humility in not actively seeking fame. He first developed his methods in university as an undergraduate taking on the cases of his fellow students (how's that for logical origin?), where he no doubt learned that his deductive methods rarely failed. After meeting a classmate's father, he was inspired to pursue detective work as his profession. Financial difficulties following graduation led him to advertise for a fellow lodger, hence his beginning with the chronicler of his most interesting cases, Dr. John Watson. The past dimension of this character creates another layer of intrigue.

These dimensions of self work together to form the basis for three-dimensionality. Who your character is in the present should be a direct result of many of the things in her past dimension. If she was a geeky girl teased relentlessly all through school, it wouldn't be hard to establish that friends and romantic relationships were all but nonexistent for her past self. If her present-day character has had a dramatic change in appearance, that's cohesive with her past self because she developed her appearance as a result of her experience. Her current internal conflicts need to reflect the ones she dealt with in her past, and her goals and motivations *now* should be in line with her coping mechanisms *then*.

Future Self

In contrast to backstory, the future we're talking about in respect to "future dimension" (future self, future setting, future conflicts, etc.) throughout this book is *not* specifically referring to actual future events of the fictional characters we create. Nor is it a "futuristic" way of looking at what's going to happen at some point in the story of this character's life. In other words, we're not trying to show the character in a setting or situation decades in the future of the current story. Instead, the future self is about projecting forward to what *may* come in the future, what resolution may result at the conclusion of the story, based on the ever-evolving development of current events.

Ask yourself these questions:

- What does your character want in life?
- What will it take to get that?
- What might change if she gets it?
- Just as important, what would happen if she doesn't get it?
- What's at stake?

If you don't give characters fully fleshed out situations, conflicts, and goals and motivations for the future, you essentially leave the reader with nothing to hope for or look forward to. He won't be inspired to rage when it looks like the character might not succeed in her goals, nor will he be held in suspense waiting for the worst to happen. Whispers of the best and the worst that *could* happen are the very things that keep the reader engaged in the story. Don't underestimate the importance of including this in each and every scene of your story. Without an undertone of what's ahead, a reader will read each page wondering *Where is all this going? What's the point of this? Is it worth reading?* These hints are the very things that keep the reader engaged scene by scene.

To show future dimension of self is a way of allowing readers something to either anticipate and/or dread in terms of where the characters and story are going, as well as project possibilities, expectations, apprehensions, and anxiety about what might happen in the future at each stage in the storytelling. You want to produce suspense and outright tension, excitement, and trepidation. Bottom line, you want to create an *uncertainty of outcome* in every stage without creating an illogical or unsatisfactory resolution. The future dimension anchors and deepens the context for a resolution because the reader needs to be aware from one scene to the next where this story is (or may be) going, in what direction events are unfolding, and where it may (or may not) conclude.

Obviously this is something that is constantly evolving in response to the character's own direction throughout the story. It's often been said that the beginning of a book should resonate at the end of the story. An opening scene or scenes should include, in some capacity, a hint of the character's ideal goal, what she ultimately wishes for her future. The bridge scenes that carry the middle of a story will gradually reflect or challenge this ideal as plots develop in reaction to internal and external conflicts, and as the character's goals and motivations transform. The resolution scenes will also mirror that objective, though it's unlikely that "The End" is exactly what the character envisioned at the beginning. In fact, that initial outcome is usually undesirable by the time the last scene comes, because all writers should strive for a logical—but unpredictable—ending.

The point is, without that future dimension that looks ahead toward the possible outcomes of a story, the reader won't be grounded in knowing exactly what he should be hoping for and rooting to happen. A reader who isn't engaged is one you'll lose sooner or later. For that reason, future dimension is as pivotal as the present and past.

All main characters need a fully fleshed-out future dimension of a character, woven in throughout scenes. Human beings desire purpose; Maslow's Hierarchy of Needs is at the heart of the reader's hope/dread response as a story is being told.

self-
actualization
morality, creativity,
spontaneity, acceptance,
experience purpose,
meaning, and inner potential

self-esteem
confidence, achievement, respect of others,
the need to be a unique individual

love and belonging
friendship, family, intimacy, sense of connection

safety and security
health, employment, property, family, and social stability

physiological needs
breathing, food, water, shelter, clothing, sleep

We all have strengths and weaknesses, dreams and regrets, vices and virtues, failures and accomplishments, boundaries to set and hurdles to overcome. In combination, these will begin in our formative years. They will be the foundation of the person we currently are, and shape who we become in the future. Weaving this future dimension of self throughout a story is vitally important. Without it, there can be no satisfactory, logical—yet unpredictable—ending. If you can't create a longing in readers for the main character to reach her story goal right from the start, to resolve with fierce motivation her conflicts and fulfill her goals, there's no reason to read (or for the author to write) the book.

Island of the Blue Dolphins includes the future dimension in the very first scenes when the new group of hunters wants to parley with Karana's people: They'll hunt the sea otters and give the tribe one part of the goods, keeping two parts for themselves. The chief insists the parts must be equal, since the sea that surrounds the island—where the otters live—belongs to the tribe. When the captain of the hunters insists they can come to an agreement about the split later, Chief Chowig refuses and demands an equal share. After looking at the tribal members standing at the ready to defend the people and land, the captain agrees—perhaps only because his own men haven't yet arrived to back up his argument. This scene implies the captain's potential for deceit.

CHARACTER DIMENSIONS: 3-D CHARACTER SKETCHES

In creating a three-dimensional character, you have to realize how much that character needs you, the author. Any character you create will have your unique spin, your originality, a tiny sliver of your essence. Without you, that character wouldn't and couldn't exist at all, and the importance of this becomes very clear during character, plot, and setting sketching. Your particular slant makes any story you write unique. Don't underestimate how crucial that is in story building.

Drawing on your own life experience and that of the people around you, you surely realize that no one is who they seem on the surface, in real life or fiction. That's the very reason writers create character sketches—to find out what's lurking beneath a character's exterior presentation. If the writer doesn't know what lives under the skin, neither will the readers.

The best character sketches are done in a two-step process. The first step is a story spark—something that intrigues and ignites a story scenario that you can carry toward fruition. Initially, it's that aha moment that a writer has when something completely captures his imagination. He must brainstorm to see how this story develops and concludes. The next step is to take that story spark you brainstormed and bring it to *three-dimensional* life through written sketches. Many authors start a story on a strong note because the idea that initially fascinated them guides them naturally into creating dimensions. Give yourself time to daydream about your character's three dimensions of self, about her settings and conflicts. Remember that all characters must have purpose in every scene, or there's no reason to include them. If the story is one you've been growing for a long time, chances are you won't have to force the character into scenarios to reveal dimensionality. The process of developing her should come organically.

Once you've spent sufficient time doing what I call "dimensionalizing your character" through adequate brainstorming, you can formally begin the second step of sketching characters using worksheets that include areas that will highlight items that provide particular focus. This is what we'll do now, with a strong emphasis on developing all the dimensions of your character. A simple character sketch worksheet that covers the most crucial aspects follows.

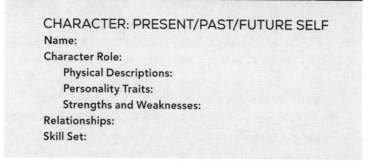

CHARACTER: PRESENT/PAST/FUTURE SELF
Name:
Character Role:
    Physical Descriptions:
    Personality Traits:
    Strengths and Weaknesses:
Relationships:
Skill Set:

Defining characters in three-dimensional sketches allows you to know main characters entirely. Remember the difference in three-dimensional writing is that you'll have a separate sketch for each main character that includes her present, past, and future selves. So take the previous basic sketch and duplicate it three times across a landscaped page with three columns, labeling the sketches: "Present Self," "Past Self," and "Future Self." You should end up with something that looks like this:

CHARACTER: PRESENT SELF	CHARACTER: PAST SELF	CHARACTER: FUTURE SELF
Name:	Name:	Name:
Character Role: (hero/ heroine, other main character, secondary character, villain) Physical Descriptions: Personality Traits: Strengths and Weaknesses:	Character Role: (hero/ heroine, other main character, secondary character, villain) Physical Descriptions: Personality Traits: Strengths and Weaknesses:	Character Role: (hero/ heroine, other main character, secondary character, villain) Physical Descriptions: Personality Traits: Strengths and Weaknesses:
Relationships: Parents: Other important family: Friends: Romantic interests: Enemies:	Relationships: Parents: Other important family: Friends: Romantic interests: Enemies:	Relationships: Parents: Other important family: Friends: Romantic interests: Enemies:
Skill Set: Occupation(s): Education: Hobbies: Interests:	Skill Set: Occupation(s): Education: Hobbies: Interests:	Skill Set: Occupation(s): Education: Hobbies: Interests:

You'll find a blank worksheet for your use in Appendix A. As I said previously, you can add anything to this worksheet, if it helps you, but these are the pivotal areas that need to be fleshed out in all dimensions of the self.

Let's break out each section on this worksheet and discuss what you're looking for in completing the dimensional sketches. First, some notes of clarification. In our discussion of the sections on this worksheet, I'll include examples to illuminate. The first will be set down in a "simple scenario," henceforth referred to as "Dark Places," which is never more than a few sentences long, all following a basic theme. This is provided to give a concise example of what's needed in this section of the worksheet, and it'll most resemble what you'll have in the sections of your own worksheet.

The main example will be from *A Christmas Carol* by Charles Dickens. Remember what I said in the Introduction about the awkwardness of "working backwards" in using examples from published works to fill out these worksheets. Finding exactly what was needed from *A Christmas Carol* for the specific sections of the worksheet wasn't easy and may not seem exactly "on point." As I said before, many of these are quotes taken directly from the text, which will differ from what you'll do on your own worksheet. As you're filling out your own worksheets, you'll be using a different tone—a less refined one—and probably won't include more than a sentence or two for each section. I specifically chose *A Christmas Carol* for a handful of reasons: 1) It's a short story (only five short chapters), 2) It's in the public domain and therefore the in-depth usage doesn't require permission, and 3) This well-known story affords a close study that readers of all ages, cultures, and genres are familiar with. It's widely read and will be more easily understood because most readers will already know the basic theme and therefore can concentrate on the development of dimensions throughout the examples. However, you may see the story characters, plots, and settings in a way you've never considered before in the framework of three-dimensionality.

Present/Past/Future Name

Your character's name is important, but doesn't (and may not need to) necessarily imply memorability. Think of some of the most exciting characters in the literature we love. Many don't have names that instantly intrigue us. Harry Potter. Tom Jones. Dr. John Watson. Tom Sawyer. James Bond. Through popularity, these names have become larger than life and more compelling than they actually are. Would the authors of these stories have changed the names if they'd known in advance how big these characters would become? Honestly, who knows, and I'm not sure a perpetually memorable name is a requirement. The more important question is, does the name fit the character?

One way to try to tailor your character's name is by finding a picture of your character from whatever source you'd like. A fuzzy mental picture of a character doesn't usually make you feel like you know her as well as you should; nor can you adequately ascribe a name to someone you haven't seen. It's easier to marry a name to a photograph because, if you can picture your character clearly, if you can actually see her, the chances are you'll write about her in a more intimate, comfortable way. For me, a picture of a character is like a three-dimensional infusion each time I look at it. I desperately want to know that person's name, where she came from, what makes her tick. My characterization development deepens by ascribing a name to an actual face.

In this section of the worksheet, simply list the name of the character you'll be sketching P/P/F Dimensions for. Since you're sketching each dimension of self, the name will be the same on all (unless the character changed or changes her name at some point, or has one or more aliases).

The names of the main characters in our two examples remained the same throughout the P/P/F Dimensions:

"DARK PLACES"

CHARACTER: PRESENT, PAST, AND FUTURE SELF
Name: Jason Delaney

A CHRISTMAS CAROL

CHARACTER: PRESENT, PAST, AND FUTURE SELF
Name: Ebenezer Scrooge

Present/Past/Future Character Role

A role, quite simply, is the function a character assumes in a particular situation. In the world of fiction, roles are fairly well-defined. Depending on the size and genre, there may be one hero and one heroine (protagonists), or many of both (i.e., other main characters). You may also have secondary characters and villains (antagonists). Essentially, all these roles are defined by the reader response the author wants to develop in his story.

To understand the underlying concept of role, we have to ask a basic question: What makes a reader root for a character? Sympathy. At times, even empathy. Everyone has strengths and weaknesses, virtues and flaws. Everyone commits both acts of altruism and sin. Everyone far exceeds expectations and falls short of ideals at various times in her life. A combination of a protagonist's strengths and weaknesses draws sympathy because a reader is likely to identify with a problem everyone struggles with, and this makes the character flesh and blood instead of a paper doll on a static page. However, the struggle with downfalls have to be balanced with heroisms—noble traits—in order for the main character to be a true hero in the reader's eyes.

When we talk about nobility, we think of excellent, redeeming, moral qualities, as well as honor and motives. A character without nobility is generally considered the story's villain. Keep in mind that a lot of writers, usually inexperienced ones, have a tendency to create protagonists without heroisms, and this makes them unlikable and difficult to root for.

In essence, the only difference between a hero and a villain, from a reader's standpoint, is *forgiveness*. Both characters are human (unless you're writing supernatural fiction) and both have a unique combination of redeeming, weak, or unsavory traits, and both should be filled with polarities of good and bad. This makes them real to the reader. The difference lies in variations on the basic flow chart governing reader response to the character:

CHARACTER'S FLAWS → **READER'S RESPONSE** →

CHARACTER'S BEHAVIOR → **READER'S RESPONSE**

With a hero, the flow chart will follow this course:

CHARACTER'S FLAWS → READER'S UNDERSTANDING →

CHARACTER'S GROWTH → READER'S FORGIVENESS

With a villain, the flow chart will follow this course:

CHARACTER'S FLAWS → READER'S UNDERSTANDING →

CHARACTER'S LACK OF GROWTH → READER WITHHOLDS FORGIVENESS

Note that if your villain doesn't inspire reader understanding, she's one- or only two-dimensional. There has to be some level of understanding to make all characters realistic, even bad guys, as we'll find out. In the same way, if your hero isn't particularly likeable and/or one that readers can root for, try putting her into the hero equation above—is she acting more like a villain? Then you know what you need to do to fix her character. The flow chart paves the way. If the character doesn't have flaws the reader can sympathize with and the character fails to grow as a person, the reader won't forgive and therefore won't want to see this character's journey to redemption.

A hero's flaws need to be balanced by the reader's understanding of what she did and why she did it. In many fictional cases, the crime is a noble one, or the character redeems herself for past sins through her current and future actions. The hero's outward conviction will carry her on what may seem like a self-destructive course, but she'll give away hidden pieces of herself that contradict her crime or, at the very least, prove her regret. The reader will sense a dual conflict—he'll comprehend that something terrible has happened, is happening, and may happen again to this character he's championing. And, despite any semblance of wrongdoing or ruthlessness on the hero's part, the reader will feel sympathy for her. The reader will bestow forgiveness on the hero because, throughout the course of the story, the hero grieves, repents, mends her ways, and performs gallant deeds worthy of applause. Dwight V. Swain says "only the character who cares about something, finds something important, is worth bothering with."

Heroes we love are classic: Luke Skywalker, Peter Pan, Sherlock Holmes, Van Helsing, Clarice Starling, Harry Potter, Beowulf.

In the same way, a villain should have a complex, identifiable reason for her crime. In "Maybe Your Bad Guy Is RIGHT!" K.M. Weiland says, "Even if you find the bad guy generally repulsive, you need to be able to put yourself so thoroughly into his shoes while you're writing him that, just for those moments, you almost believe his slant yourself." A villain's reason is rarely noble, nor can it be justified, however, she should never be portrayed as evil through-and-through (unless you're writing supernatural fiction and the villain *isn't* human). The most effective villain is the one who rouses almost as much sympathy in the reader as she does revulsion. This is a direct result of *three-dimensionality of role*, because we understand who she is, what made her that person, what she went through, where she's been, and (because three-dimensionality is crucial) see hints about how she'll be different and more noble in the future.

In contrast, the villain almost never repents and, in fact, goes on to commit even worse crimes. The reader can't go beyond his own sense of morality to forgive this character, no matter how sympathetic he may be toward her, because the character shows no evidence of growth, no indication of nobility. Though the villain may intrigue us, the reader can't accept her goals. Few people root for Darth Vader (though he does become a good guy in the end), Captain Hook, Moriarty, Dracula, Hannibal Lecter, Voldemort, or Grendel and his mother.

On this portion of the sketch sheet, you list the character's role in the story as a hero or heroine (main characters), another main or secondary character, or a villain. And here's one other thing to be aware of: Obviously, you don't want to become so fixated by "role" in three-dimensional character development that you create superficial, stereotypical characters in your fictional world. Stick figures are two-dimensional at best. More likely, they're one-dimensional. Keep in mind, though, that all living people assume different roles when interacting with different people; fictional characters shouldn't be an exception to this rule. Your characters will act differently with the various people who populate their worlds; but fictional characters shouldn't be an exception to this rule, provided they remain consistent. After all, if one person describes your main character in the present as "Clark Kent" and someone else considers him "Al Capone's twin," your characterization needs work, or you have to provide justifiable reasons for this duality. If your character was an "Al Capone" in the past and is now a "Clark Kent," we need to see the motivation and circumstances that allowed this radical transformation to take place.

This scenario is unlikely in fiction, just as it is in reality; though nothing is impossible or inconceivable. There are definitely situations where a "good guy" might be in a bad situation that keeps her from realizing or living up to her "good" potential, and vice versa. For example, in the Harry Potter Series, Professor Snape is believed to be evil throughout the books until the last one, where he proves to be a good man with honorable motives. At the opposite extreme, Chancellor Palpatine in *Star Wars* was a respected political leader in Episodes I and II, and most of III, but revealed himself to be the ultimate villain by the end of Episode III.

As for the future dimension, remember, our goal in including this is to look ahead at the possibilities (good and bad) about what might happen in the future at each stage in the storytelling. Radical changes between P/P/F Dimensions are unlikely, and nowhere is this truer than in the future dimension. While you want to produce suspense and tension, dread and hope, and uncertainty of outcome throughout the story, a story's ending shouldn't be completely illogical—as it would be if a character role did a one-eighty from hero to villain or the opposite. Although there are very definite situations in a story where this could make sense (*How the Grinch Stole Christmas* proves that), for the most part, you won't see any extreme shifts, at least not ones that don't make perfect sense in light of the story. Reader/viewer reaction to any degree of shift between dimensions should be similar to what we experienced in *Indiana Jones and the Last Crusade*: Shouldn't we have known from the start that Elsa and Walter Donovan were traitors? All the clues were there … weren't they? The two of them know entirely too much and lead Indy right where they needed him to go. The reaction shouldn't be outrage, disappointment, or confusion.

As an example of the more subtle changes between the dimensions of self that we're likely to see in most stories, think of Peter Pettigrew in the Harry Potter Series. If I had to define his role with an adjective, it would be as a spineless (not good, nor truly evil) secondary character. Because of his own weaknesses, he was drawn away from the good side to the bad, betraying his friends for the possibility of power and protection. In the course of his lifetime, I believe his failings as a human being filled him with regret—because he betrayed his friends. He'd placed himself in a dangerous, morally skewed situation where he lived in desperate fear and silent grief on a daily basis. While there was some ambiguity built into the actual writing, I think in the end Peter calmly accepted his death in the last book in order to atone for his lifelong sins. That explanation is warranted and logical. If he'd joined Harry's side, no one would have bought the radical shift of allegiance. If he'd outright killed Harry, this action wouldn't have fit what we'd come to believe of his defined role over the course of the series. This is what all shifts in dimension should strive for: A perfect, logical fit.

Our first example of role includes the same information carried over for all three sections:

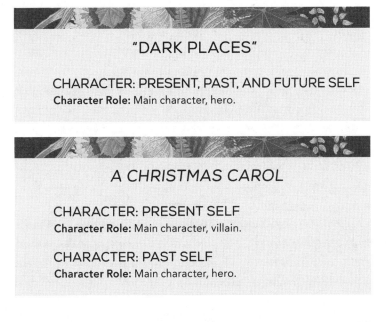

"DARK PLACES"

CHARACTER: PRESENT, PAST, AND FUTURE SELF
Character Role: Main character, hero.

A CHRISTMAS CAROL

CHARACTER: PRESENT SELF
Character Role: Main character, villain.

CHARACTER: PAST SELF
Character Role: Main character, hero.

Present/Past/Future Physical Descriptions

Physical appearance of a character serves a purpose in every story, providing its own kind of characterization. I don't believe these things should ever be chosen randomly or indiscriminately. Character appearance should reveal personality traits as well as strengths and weaknesses do. Additionally, appearance may define relationships and possibly even suggest skill sets. (A twist on this can also be intriguing: How does a slight woman fit into the all-male world of firefighting, for instance?). Physical descriptions can also be influenced by the dimensions of plot (internal conflicts and certainly goals and motivations) and setting, since how a character looks and feels about her appearance can be vastly influenced by where she lives. For example, a ninety-pound male weakling in Los Angeles will feel the effects of his differences among the tanned, buff bodybuilders on the beach, just as a bucktoothed Rubenesque-size scientific type of a woman would on the same beach.

If you're using a third-person POV, chances are that your main characters will be described by other characters. Although this kind of description can include physical appearances, it should always incorporate the *impressions* that your characters make. Very few people describe themselves the same way others describe them. That makes it even more important for main characters to describe themselves, since the reader gets a strong sense of who your players really are with both outside and self-descriptions. In Sarah Langan's suspense novel *The Keeper* the first chapter is all about the impressions characters have of Susan Marley, who was once the local beauty, but—through a series of unfortunate events—became the town slut.

P/P/F Dimensions for physical appearances are very likely to change from one dimension to the next—dramatically—except in cases where your character is very young and has little "past" to draw upon. In Rachel Lee's third book in the Conard County Series, *Miss Emmaline and the Archangel*, the hero Gage Dalton is a former DEA agent whose wife and children were killed in a car bombing meant for him. He was nearby when the bombing happened, and it left him with scars, a limp, and almost constant pain from damaged nerves. His physical appearance from past to present is definitely changed. Alterations don't have to be this dramatic, of course. A character could deliberately change original hair color, grow to over six feet after being of short stature as a child, or go from a wallflower to a beauty, the way my heroine, April St. Clair, did in *Taming April*, Book 4 of the Cowboy Fever Series: (see comments in brackets and italics)

> **Past Dimension (in her own POV):**
> The last time anyone in Fever, Texas, had seen her, she'd been a waif of a shy girl, taller than almost everyone her age, and certainly ganglier. She'd been all straight, blond hair and awkward, skinny, long limbs. Most probably didn't even know what she'd looked like without her nose buried in a book—library book. She'd never owned a book until she went off into the world on her own. [*A lot is conveyed about the heroine's appearance, her personality, as well as the financial difficulties of her youth in this paragraph.*]
>
> Pretty? No. She'd been far from it. She'd also never worn makeup until she'd left this place. No boy had ever looked at her, and she hadn't had a single friend to call her own.
>
> *When Mama was gone, all I ever wanted to do was escape this place. The ragged clothing and boots that I never knew how many other people had worn before me. The broken fingernails and split ends because I could never get a haircut, let alone a manicure. Daddy never had any money for that. For anything.* [*Another way to include past dimension is through introspection or internal monologue. We get to see inside the character's thoughts and these are fully clothed in emotional conveyances in a way that simple narrative may not adequately achieve.*]
>
> The day she'd graduated high school, she'd been beyond petrified to have to deliver the valedictory address—by virtue of having the highest rank in a graduating class, in fact the highest rank in nearly thirty years—at the commencement exercises. She hadn't believed she could be more agonizingly self-conscious than in doing that, but she'd been wrong about that being the worse of it. As she'd returned

to her seat after her speech, Shawn Jacobs had stuck out his leg at the last minute and she'd gone sprawling like the gangly filly she'd been. The entire school had broken into wild laughter. Even to this day, the thought of that incident mortified her. Shawn had only compounded the problem by trying to help her up. She'd slapped him away. She'd never wanted him to touch her again, and she wasn't sure she'd ever be able to forgive him for ending her time in town as the laughingstock. It was probably what everyone remembered best about her. [*The heroine's past, growing up in this small town, is developed. Now we moved into the present dimension: As a contrast that fleshes out what we've read about her, we'll next see her in the hero's POV.*]

Present Dimension (as described by the hero, Shawn):
Suddenly, the shiny, all-but-new car parked in the ranch clearing lost its appeal when Shawn noticed what was standing next to it. This honey was at least five foot ten inches tall, slim but beautifully shapely with long, silky, butter-blond hair, wispy bangs, brilliant green eyes, wearing a designer skirt suit that showed just a hint of cleavage and mile-long, tanned legs. Those legs tapered down to four and a half inch stiletto heels with peep toes.

Shawn reached up instinctively to shove his hat back so he could get a better look at her, but he must have lost the worn, raffia straw hat out in the pasture when he'd been dragged by his own horse after trying to rope a blind calf. *She's gotta be hotter than hell dressed like that in hundred-degree weather. And, God help me, she does look hotter than hell.* [*This peek into the present description of the heroine is supported by some setting details that reflect the developing details.*]

Defying the fact that he could barely move and, come tomorrow, he'd be all but paralyzed for the next week or more and the fact that he couldn't stink worse if he'd actually taken a bath in manure, he decided he would have had to be dead not to react to this woman. She looked like a porcelain doll, too beautiful to touch let alone look at without hurting his eyes. But her face was as immobile as a doll, too. He wondered if her full, shapely, Michelle Pfeiffer mouth would actually crack if she tried to smile. Unfortunately, the memory of his old girlfriend Racquel was too close, and he couldn't stop remembering how she'd always dressed wrong, too fancy, for every location and occasion—and she'd done it on purpose. She'd wanted to be the movie star among hicks. [*The hero's past collides with the present as he compares the heroine to a former girlfriend he'd had a bad experience with. Future tension is effectively implied.*]

Don't neglect your future dimensions when you sketch physical descriptions, though there's a tendency to. But consider that there isn't a person alive who doesn't dream about making changes to physical appearance. This, in itself, is a way to develop dimensions. If you have a heroine who's constantly talking about being on a diet, going on a diet, doing something radical to change her weight, but does the exact opposite at every turn (professing that the multiple donuts on her plate are the absolute last before she buckles down), projecting a future self dimension of characterization here isn't difficult. However, insert a strong motivation (meeting up with her old flame at the ten-year class reunion) and results may be in the offering. Another way to come at this to avoid predictability in the scenario is that the weak-willed heroine doesn't lose a pound—maybe even gains it—before the reunion, yet her still gorgeous old flame falls in love with her anyway.

There's always a way to inject a future dimension into your characterization to give readers something to hope for, as well as to dread. In our *Island of the Blue Dolphins* example, Karana's worry for what the future will bring for her tribe after the hunters come to the island (supposedly to hunt seals and then leave) affects every part of her life. Suddenly her normal life is anything but ordinary and routine with these outsiders on the island. The feeling of uncertainty that's introduced from the beginning produces a natural desire in the reader for Karana's life to go on normally, without any damage. But external events create trepidation, which produces equal amounts of tension in anticipation of the worst.

Physical description P/P/F Dimensions of Self are included below:

"DARK PLACES"

CHARACTER: PRESENT SELF

Physical Descriptions: Jason is twenty-eight years old, tall, muscular with unkempt black hair. His dark attractiveness is at odds with his moodiness which makes him appear dangerous, sometimes even menacing.

CHARACTER: PAST SELF
Physical Descriptions: When Jason was eight years old, he was gangly, skinny, tall, with greasy black, unkempt hair. He was a social misfit, an outcast who was teased ruthlessly because he was weak and unattractive.

CHARACTER: FUTURE SELF
Physical Descriptions: Jason refuses to play the victim ever again. He's become as toned as a soldier and is now a cop who works out on a daily basis. So he's strong, imposing, dark, intense, and frequently off-putting to those around him.

A CHRISTMAS CAROL

CHARACTER: PRESENT SELF
Physical Descriptions: "The cold within him froze his old features, nipped his pointed nose, shrivelled his cheek, stiffened his gait; made his eyes red, his thin lips blue; and spoke out shrewdly in his grating voice. A frosty rime was on his head, and on his eyebrows, and his wiry chin. He carried his own low temperature always about with him; he iced his office in the dog-days; and didn't thaw it one degree at Christmas."

CHARACTER: PAST SELF
Physical Descriptions: Solitary, lonely, neglected, forgotten as a boy. Later, during his internship as a young man—a man in the prime of life—whose "face had not the harsh and rigid lines of later years; but it had begun to wear the signs of care and avarice. There was an eager, greedy, restless motion in the eye, which showed the passion that had taken root, and where the shadow of the growing tree would fall."

Present/Past/Future Personality Traits

Who we are (and will be) is largely determined by who we were and by what we've been through. Think nurture and nature, environment and experience, likes and dislikes, fears and areas of confidence, secrets both known and hidden. Consider specifically where a person comes from in terms of how setting shapes personality: the size of that setting and living conditions there; social or economic status (and also race and gender); customs and traditions; even "voice" (how a person sounds, the way she communicates, and her dialogue choices can be a direct result of where she comes from). To create believable characters, all these things have to be developed through the P/P/F Self sketches.

Unfortunately (or fortunately), human beings are full of contradictions. It's engrained in our nature to experience the world both as we would like it to be and how it actually is. What we believe, what we know, what we stand for, and what we end up doing can all be completely at odds and yet exist side by side. Think of Sherlock Holmes, who's an absolute study in contradictions (great detective, lousy human being; methodical mind, yet complete slob). What about James Bond, who can save the whole world, but never himself? This is a man who will never find true peace or lasting happiness in his life.

How do we translate all this into our characters without creating a chameleon, convenient to whatever we need in our story? Human beings, and characters, are absolutely infused with so many flexible, dimensional facets. It's not surprising that it can be hard to figure out what to focus on when it comes to personality traits. The only, albeit generalized way, to incorporate so much into our characters without being confusing or unrealistic is by doing what Marshall J. Cook advises in *Leads & Conclusions*: "If you want to capture the general, focus on the specific. If you want to describe something huge and inanimate, begin with someone small and human." To create a truly unique character—and what writer doesn't want this?—we need to focus on specific parts of a personality that include both *enhancements* and *contrasts*.

Enhancements are the subtle, balanced, or extreme elements that complement what the writer has already established as characteristic traits for that character. They're personality traits that make that character uniquely memorable. A writer can't create a truly ordinary Jane, because she would bore the reader. In the fictional world, an author may present a hero who at first glance seems ordinary. Even so, there must be something about her that makes her stand apart. This something may not be revealed until later, when her quality is tested. Faramir, Boromir's brother, in J. R. R. Tolkien's *The Lord of the Rings* comes to mind. Faramir spends most of his life in the shadow of his older brother, whom his father always compares him to. He never lives up to the larger-than-life hero that his glorious sibling is ... yet, when tempted to take the ring from Frodo, Boromir gives in to evil desire (later repenting before his death). When Faramir comes face-to-face with the ring, he considers giving his father this mighty gift to gain the standing his brother has always had. In the end, he chooses to forgo this honor—a lifetime of craving that's created a voracious hole in his heart—to do the right thing in letting Frodo (and the ring) go. In this way, Faramir is an extraordinary hero, regardless of how he'll personally suffer for his selfless sacrifice.

A contrast, which can also be subtle, balanced, or extreme, is an element that's in opposition to what the writer has already established as "characteristic" traits for that character. A contrast in a personality is one of the best and most often used ways of making a character rise to the spotlight. Readers want baffling contrasts. They want to see a high school dropout spouting Byronic poetry, a bleeding heart paired with an otherwise unmovable hero, the wounded warrior rescuing a stray dog, the uptight virgin wearing six-inch stiletto heels. They want to watch a character rebuild and rediscover her dignity, her self-respect, her inner moral compass.

BRING YOUR FICTION TO LIFE

Any character who's so hard and jaded that she almost seems untouchable will need a soft contrast—something that makes readers like and sympathize with her, and forgive her. Readers need to be touched or moved by what's beneath her mask in some way. For example, consider a hardened cop who's seen the worst in her fellow man, yet she never fails to visit chronically ill children in the hospital. This makes a poignant impact on readers. The contrast proves that she's human, and that there's still vulnerability buried deep inside her that will surely rise to the surface in other ways, given time, circumstances, and opportunity. An emotionally guarded, straightlaced woman, who's cold in her manner to co-workers, sits in the shadows of a smoky jazz bar and closes her eyes, swaying while she listens to the sensual saxophone. She's a woman who's obviously not as uptight as she wants her fellow employees to believe. *Her sensual vulnerability breaks free in the dark of a nightclub—where else might it show? And what makes her feel she ever has to hide?* The reader wants to know more.

An interesting example of a complex, at times contradiction-ridden (in a totally believable way) character with enhancements and contrasts is from the TV series *Alias*. While the heroine Sydney might not say outright that she wants to be a hero, the predisposition is in her blood. When she's approached by a supposedly covert branch of the CIA called SD-6, she joins … only to discover much later that she's been working for the bad guys all along. This isn't the kind of organization you can submit a resignation to and walk away. But she can't get herself to blindly continue working for the enemy, so she becomes a double agent, working for the real CIA to bring down SD-6, while letting them think she remains loyal. Her enhancements are the people she loves, forever her downfall in the course of this series, as she battles with her loyalty for her country and her own ingrained morality. She isn't totally altruistic though. She takes risks, occasionally displaying a naiveté that's at odds with everything she's been through: She sometimes foolishly trusts that fate isn't out to get her, and she tries to have a normal life and deep, genuine relationships amidst all this chaos.

Think of some of the most unique characters in history, on the big screen and in literature. Indiana Jones, dashing adventurer and ambitious scholar, is truly a study in contrasts. He'll enter any dangerous situation to retrieve an artifact, yet he's terrified of snakes. He's a sedate college professor and equally a reckless, ambitious adventurer. Everything about him *fits him*. All the things that make up his personality enhance his character and make him unforgettable.

Take the character of Westley in William Goldman's unforgettable *The Princess Bride*. An acquiescing farm boy quietly in love with his mistress goes off to seek his fortune to become worthy of her hand in marriage. He comes back a notorious, invincible pirate who kidnaps her, then repeatedly rescues her even after he's dead … or "only mostly dead." He's charming, tenacious, forgiving, and an unshakeable believer in true love. Pair him with a princess who's not sure of anything, but who comes around in the end, plus two lovable rogues, and this is a story that has multidimensional building blocks from start to finish. Westley has enhancements and contrasts that fit him consummately.

Consider Heathcliff, the dark, tortured hero in Emily Brontë's classic, *Wuthering Heights*. He is an unwanted orphan who—in contrast to his emotionless, humble beginnings—becomes violently obsessed with Catherine, the daughter of his benefactor, to the grave. Everything about him is extreme, and it enhances him in a way that makes him stand out—perhaps not positively, but nevertheless irrevocably—in a sea of ordinary men. Every other man is in violent contrast to him. No wonder Catherine could never forget him.

What about Éowyn, the daughter of Theoden of Rohan, in *The Lord of the Rings*? A caretaker by nature, and yet not content to stand by while the men of Rohan ride off to war. She puts on battle armor and marches to war beside them. Though she's soft and vulnerable, she's also the very warrior who defeats the immortal Witch-king.

All of these characters have enhancements and contrasts that make them breathtakingly memorable.

Another effective means of developing a character with a memorable personality is to give her some sort of *symbol* that defines her, defines the situation she's in, or does both. Whether you make symbols subtle or well-defined, they take on layers of meaning each time they're mentioned, becoming an integral part of the story. As a general rule, each character should have only one associated symbol, but if you have two total in the book, one of them should be subtle while the other is well-defined. The point is to enhance or contrast, not to allow a symbol to become the focal point.

The symbol can certainly be tangible, in the form of something that defines the character, plot, and setting in some way—a piano, pet, flower, key, map, or necklace. Let's consider an example from the first Indiana Jones movie, where the heroine, Marion, carries around a sentimental artifact for years. She wears it around her neck as a means to remember her father, who gave it to her. Later, she finds out that this artifact is the headpiece of the Staff of Ra that Indiana Jones needs in his search for the long-buried vault containing the Ark of the Covenant. This kind of symbol is used a lot in fiction because it so effectively adds character, plot, *and* setting enhancement.

But your symbol doesn't *have* to be tangible. It can be a trait or mannerism the character uses frequently that says something about her and/or develops the character, plot, and setting in some way. It could also be a hobby, vice, or a character disability or disfigurement, like a scar. This tangible or intangible symbol must make sense for this character and can't be something thrown in for the fun of it. One way or another, it has to enhance or contrast, and thereby develop the core story elements in deeper ways.

In my inspirational romance *Wayward Angels*, the heroine has many unique personality traits that, at first, seem off-the-wall. She makes up a personality and history for a cat featured in the story. Readers learn from this that she's reticent about talking about her own past and, by making up a history for the cat, she can tell the hero about herself. The cat's history is actually her own, and she's revealing pieces of herself when she speaks through the pet. This oddity is the heroine's symbol, and it hints at something deeper than what the reader sees on the surface. Each time the symbol is mentioned, it takes on more meaning and advances the plot. In the course of the story, the reader eventually learns that the heroine is bipolar and this oddity with cats is indicative of her unwillingness to accept her condition.

In the same book, I wanted to subtly show how the hero has left behind the things that have previously led to his downfall. Several times in the book, I've mentioned that the only colors in his house are black and white (this is true even of the shelter for troubled boys he runs), and there are absolutely no decorations to be seen. He shrugs this off by saying he's never had much time to do any decorating or fixing up. However, this unwillingness to make a house a home becomes an indicator that the hero has a black-and-white fear in his life—the apprehension in letting color back in, and thus the trouble that came with it before. This lack of color is a symbol with deep dimensional character, plot, and setting connotations.

In personality, P/P/F Dimensions are likely to transform subtly, rather than radically change from one dimension to the next. The exception is when your character is very young and has little past to draw upon. It's true that most every middle-aged person that you talk to will say they've changed dramatically from when they were children. But have they really? Examine closely. Taking one mild, but specific, area of my own life, I read so many books as a child I was usually the star of the school or library who won any bookworm prize offered. If someone else my age read a book, I'd read twenty-five to his one, and in less time. Nearly every free moment I had, you'd find me with my nose buried in book. From day to day, that book might have changed (even the genre—I've always been an eclectic reader), but this was my personality. Some thirty-five years later, not much has changed in this regard, though I might not have as many of those free moments. Still, not a single day goes by that I don't read a book. What do I foresee for my future? More of the same, though I project that my failing eyesight might make it harder and harder, and in that case I'll find inventive ways to do what I love. This is, admittedly, a mild example (and certainly too boring to put in a book). The point is, in past, present, and future, there are no radical shifts in this particular personality trait of mine, and that's true of people/characters and their personalities in general. Subtle is more likely than radical in this regard.

Another example of personality, again in the iconic character of Indiana Jones, is that, from past to present (in the first three movies),

Indiana was a boy who chased adventure and found trouble from his Boy Scout days. He continues that into every facet of his adult life as a full-time professor of archaeology and part-time treasure hunter. In the fourth Indiana Jones movie (the "future") he's quite a bit older, possibly wiser, but he's still following adventure—and trouble—like a bloodhound. Viewers want to follow this intriguing path instead of the (possibly more realistic) predictability of the character teaching full-time in his stuffy, cloistered academic world where he only dreams about the good old days.

Our example personality traits for P/P/F Dimensions are:

"DARK PLACES"

CHARACTER: PRESENT SELF
Personality Traits: Whether or not he realizes it, Jason distances himself from other people with the intimidating way he looks (hard and muscular) and his withdrawn nature—dark and moody and incredibly intense. No one understands him except his partner at the police department, whom he often thinks may be the only person on the planet who actually knows him.

CHARACTER: PAST SELF
Personality Traits: Withdrawn, lonely, friendless, wanting only to be ignored because attention always leads to merciless teasing and cruelty from the others around him.

CHARACTER: FUTURE SELF
Personality Traits: Jason realizes that he'll be lonely for the rest of his life if he doesn't allow people to get close to him, especially his partner (and sometimes love interest) Sharon, who still hasn't surrendered hope that he might someday open up. After his childhood, he doesn't know how to trust.

A CHRISTMAS CAROL

CHARACTER: PRESENT SELF

Personality Traits: "A tight-fisted hand at the grindstone, Scrooge! a squeezing, wrenching, grasping, scraping, clutching, covetous, old sinner! Hard and sharp as flint, from which no steel had ever struck out generous fire; secret, and self-contained, and solitary as an oyster."

CHARACTER: PAST SELF

Personality Traits: Work and profit weren't all Scrooge focused on in his youth. He loved family (Fanny), longed for home (instead of the boy's school he was forced to attend), and as an intern, when Fezziwig tells them to "clear away" for their Christmas celebration, Scrooge obliges enthusiastically: "It was done in a minute. Every movable was packed off, as if it were dismissed from public life for evermore; the floor was swept and watered, the lamps were trimmed, fuel was heaped upon the fire; and the warehouse was as snug, and warm, and dry, and bright a ballroom, as you would desire to see upon a winter's night... There were more dances, and there were forfeits, and more dances, and there was cake, and there was negus, and there was a great piece of Cold Roast, and there was a great piece of Cold Boiled, and there were mince-pies, and plenty of beer."

CHARACTER: FUTURE SELF

Personality Traits: When his employee Bob toasts Scrooge as the founder of the Christmas feast, his wife rebukes him because they both know that such an odious, stingy, hard, unfeeling man shouldn't have his health toasted. By the time the Ghost of Christmas Future appears, Scrooge "revolves in his mind a change of life, and thought and hoped he saw his new-born resolutions carried out in this."

Present/Past/Future Strengths and Weaknesses

In "Getting to the Core of Character Motivation," Becca Puglisi says, "The one common thread in all of the books that are falling apart on my shelf? Characters—flawed ones with desires and needs who spend most of the story tripping over their weaknesses in an effort to get what they want."

Ask yourself what people admire most about heroes, or even villains. The hero who's optimistic to a fault, whiter than snow, and perfect in every way is dull. Flawed (but likable) characters are the ones readers want to champion because a character without vices or fears or hidden secrets is a character without conflicts and is, consequently, devoid of intrigue. There's no way for her to improve and grow if she's already perfect. Readers instinctively realize that true courage for a character is facing what she fears most, even if that means her own failures and regrets. And when she pursues goals, she refuses to give up because her motivation for acting means something to her passionately. Even when failure is on the line (and looks inevitable), defeat is never really an option.

Readers go crazy for a rough and raw, imperfect hero with more baggage (of the emotional kind) than a pampered socialite. True heroes are almost always eternal *pessimists* who want nothing to do with the "hero" title, let alone the job. She's only forced into it by an oft-buried sense of nobility or justice, or because something or someone she deeply cares about is in danger. One example of a very reluctant hero can be seen in the movie *Arachnophobia*. Dr. Ross Jennings has a deep-seated fear of spiders—a very pronounced, debilitating, paralyzing terror. Yet when his family and an entire town is threatened by a giant, poisonous spider from Venezuela that started a monstrous family of deadly web spinners in Dr. Jennings' new hometown, he has to get past his extreme arachnophobia and put himself in heartbeat-close contact with the eight-legged creatures to save everyone.

Think about reluctant heroes this way: If a character is perfect and has no trouble acting or succeeding, there's no challenge and, ultimately, there is no honor in an effortless battle. Glory comes from difficulty, from overcoming obstacles that originally seem too big and impossible to face. In a well-known example, Simba runs away from home in *The Lion King*, believing he's to blame for his father's death. Even though he has a moral responsibility to take his place as the ruler of the savannah, he checks out and starts a whole new life: one without worries, far away. Even when he's called back because his lion pride needs him, he resists. His weaknesses prevent him from taking up the title of hero and king, and only dire internal and external conflicts force him to overcome his weaknesses to become who and what he's meant to be. This is a character rife with strengths and weaknesses, and he's reluctant to be the hero others know he is deep inside.

Strengths and weaknesses give the fictional people populating your world the opportunity to grow in a believably anguishing way over the course of a story, just like in real life. And that's where characters are brought to three-dimensional life. Our characters' P/P/F strength and weakness dimensions are in some ways ones they're born with, but events (plot, external, and internal) and environment (setting) play a large part in shaping them. From one dimension to the next, the same thing we said for personality is true here. The transformation may appear radical simply because it's instinctive for people to assume changes are major. It's certainly possible that they might be, too. But it's more likely that, upon close examination, the changes have been a subtle shift from past to present, just as they might be in the future dimension of strengths and weakness in character traits. What fits your story best? What makes the most sense from one dimension to the other?

The following example shows the strengths and weaknesses for P/P/F Dimensions.

"DARK PLACES"

CHARACTER: PRESENT SELF
Strengths and Weaknesses: Jason goes after bullies and criminals ruthlessly in his line of work, with a particular focus on helping children. While he's a reluctant hero, a dedicated soldier, he's good at his job as a detective, and he puts everything into bringing bad guys to justice. He's established himself as a threat to known criminals in the city he lives in, and it's a rare week that he doesn't get a death threat or two from an enemy he's made.

CHARACTER: PAST SELF

Strengths and Weaknesses: As an eight-year-old child, Jason was kidnapped and held captive in the woods for ten days until he was rescued. This horrible event is what led him to vow to become strong—never again a victim—and also to do everything in his power to help other kids who are abducted. His past set him on his career path. He started in the Marines right after high school and excelled, but ultimately chose to go into law enforcement after his discharge.

CHARACTER: FUTURE SELF

Strengths and Weaknesses: When an eight-year-old boy is kidnapped in the town where Jason grew up, he knows there may be a connection to his own kidnapping; the scenario is similar and his captor was never identified and caught. He can't allow another child to go through what happened to him.

A CHRISTMAS CAROL

CHARACTER: PRESENT SELF

Strengths and Weaknesses: "External heat and cold had little influence on Scrooge. No warmth could warm, no wintry weather chill him. No wind that blew was bitterer than he, no falling snow was more intent upon its purpose, no pelting rain less open to entreaty. Foul weather didn't know where to have him. The heaviest rain, and snow, and hail, and sleet, could boast of the advantage over him in only one respect. They often 'came down' handsomely, and Scrooge never did."

Additionally, Scrooge is afraid of ghosts. "To say that he was not startled, or that his blood was not conscious of a terrible sensation to which it had been a stranger from infancy, would be untrue."

CHARACTER: PAST SELF

Strengths and Weaknesses: During the whole of this time, observing himself when he was younger, "Scrooge had acted like a man out of his wits. His heart and soul were in the scene, and with his former self. He corroborated everything, remembered everything, enjoyed everything, and underwent the strangest agitation. It was not until now, when the bright faces of his former self and Dick were turned from them, that he remembered the Ghost, and became conscious that it was looking full upon him, while the light upon its head burnt very clear."

He was a different man until he was captured by the belief that "there is nothing on which it is so hard as poverty; and there is nothing it professes to condemn with such severity as the pursuit of wealth!"

CHARACTER: FUTURE SELF

Strengths and Weaknesses: Knowing that the purpose of these ghostly visits is to do him good, Scrooge hopes to live to be another man from what he has been.

Present/Past/Future Relationships

One school of thought presumes that there are four "attachment styles" that become the building blocks for every relationship. In essence, the attachment a person has with his primary caregiver after birth sets the tone for all associations that follow. Needless to say, few fictional characters fall into the ideal category of "secure" (the best-case scenario) and usually only villains are on the opposite extreme with "avoidant" (the worst). The two styles in the middle (dubbed insecure-resistant and disorganized-disoriented attachments) display a range of attributes more likely for a balanced character, and these are rife with potential internal and external conflicts, goals and motivations, as well as personality traits, strengths and weaknesses, and of course relationships. As David Corbett says in his book *The Art of Character: Creating Memorable Characters for Fiction, Film, and TV*: "Character is not created in isolation or repose; it's forged through interaction with others and the world."

Connections are vital to characters, and I'd venture a guess that there's not a human being on the earth who hasn't been affected—past, present, and future—and *greatly* influenced by his relationships. Our relationships influence every aspect of our being. If a person doesn't have parents (beyond the biological imperative), that situation has a huge impact on who he is and how he interacts with the world. If he does have parents and they are (or were) awful, the association will have profound ramifications on every aspect of his life. Good parents bring about their own powerful significance.

This is true for all relationships in every stage of life. Those we love, those we're *in love* with, those we hate, tolerate, revere, appreciate, regret, are haunted by … all of these relationships make us into the people we were, are, and will be. They also have a direct bearing on decisions we make, as well as places we settle in at any given time. Think of *Great Expectations* and the orphan Pip's multitude of relationships that definitely play a part in making him the person he is, was, and becomes: Joe and his wife, Miss Havisham, Estella, Magwitch. The list could go on, but the point should be clear. Our relationships greatly influence us at all points in our lives, and our characters' relationships will do the same.

Sketch the most important relationships for your characters so you can see who has shaped them and in what ways from past to present. In terms of future relationships, give readers "buds"—as in elements that flourish and grow—to keep them looking forward, both dreading the worst and hoping for the best. In our earlier example from *Island of the Blue Dolphins*, the hunters create tragedy when Karana's father, the chief, is killed. The new chief decides the tribe must leave the island, and he goes off to prepare the way for them. When he returns with a ship and the tribe gets on board, Karana realizes that her young brother isn't with her and, after the ship sets sail, she sees Ramo on the beach, having gone back for his spear. Karana sees herself as a mother to her brother, so leaving him isn't an option for her. She makes a pivotal choice about all her relationships (with her older sister, her tribe, and those that might have been in the New World they set sail for) when she jumps from the ship and returns to her brother, knowing that the two of them will have to survive alone on the island, unless a ship comes back for them.

Our examples of relationships for P/P/F Dimensions are:

"DARK PLACES"

CHARACTER: PRESENT SELF

Relationships:

> **Parents:** Still live in his hometown, though Jason has settled in the big city nearby.
>
> **Other important family:** None.
>
> **Friends:** His partner on the police force, Sharon. He was well respected during his years in the Marines, and he and the other soldiers in his platoon still keep in touch, but infrequently.
>
> **Romantic interests:** Sharon.
>
> **Enemies:** Many—the bad guys associated with those he's put in jail.

CHARACTER: PAST SELF

Relationships:

> **Parents:** His parents never understood him, were constantly asking why he didn't try out for sports, try to be popular, try to make friends, try to do something with his life beyond blending into the wallpaper and attempting to disappear.
>
> **Other important family:** None.
>
> **Friends:** None until he joined the Marines.
>
> **Romantic interests:** None.
>
> **Enemies:** Everyone around him, seemingly by default of the weakling he was.

CHARACTER: FUTURE SELF

Relationships:

> **Parents:** His relationship with his parents is strained and sporadic, but cordial.
>
> **Other important family:** None.
>
> **Friends:** Sharon, military friends, and—mildly—other cops and colleagues on the police force.
>
> **Romantic interests:** Sharon.
>
> **Enemies:** His captor.

A CHRISTMAS CAROL

CHARACTER: PRESENT SELF
Relationships:

Parents: Presumed dead.

Other important family: Fred, his nephew; his sister, Fanny, deceased.

Friends: Marley, his business partner, dead for seven years. Scrooge was Marley's "sole executor, his sole administrator, his sole assign, his sole residuary legatee, his sole friend, and sole mourner. And even Scrooge was not so dreadfully cut up by the sad event, but that he was an excellent man of business on the very day of the funeral, and solemnised it with an undoubted bargain."

Romantic interests: Hints of (by his dismissal of Fred's own marriage) an arrangement that ended badly.

Enemies: Mankind! "Nobody ever stopped him in the street to say, with gladsome looks, 'My dear Scrooge, how are you? When will you come to see me?' No beggars implored him to bestow a trifle, no children asked him what it was o'clock, no man or woman ever once in all his life inquired the way to such and such a place, of Scrooge. Even the blind men's dogs appeared to know him; and when they saw him coming on, would tug their owners into doorways and up courts; and then would wag their tails as though they said, 'No eye at all is better than an evil eye, dark master!'"

CHARACTER: PAST SELF
Relationships:

Parents: According to his sister "Fan," Father "is so much kinder than he used to be, that home's like Heaven!"

Other important family: Fanny, his sister.

Friends: Various fond recollections of schoolmates; Fezziwig, his employer, and Dick Wilkins, who was also an intern and "much attracted" to Scrooge.

Romantic interests: Belle, a "fair young girl in a mourning-dress: in whose eyes there were sparkling tears" from a presumed betrothal made when she and Scrooge were children; "made when we were both poor and content to be so." **Enemies:** Presumably his father, before his change of heart that brought Scrooge home.

CHARACTER: FUTURE SELF
Relationships:
    Parents: Presumed dead.
    Other important family: Fred and his wife.
    Friends: None, though his nephew pities him and his clerk is unfailingly kind.
    Romantic interests: None.
    Enemies: The world is his enemy—even the dog who led the blind—because all he's allowed it to see of himself is his lack of kindness, pity, and sympathy for his fellow human beings. Bob's wife and children, in particular, see Scrooge as the Ogre. "The mention of his name cast a dark shadow on the party, which was not dispelled for full five minutes."

Present/Past/Future Skill Set

Each of your main characters will need a particular skill set (whether it stems from career, education, hobbies, interests, or a combination of all these) that's shaped specifically for the story and for this particular character. On most character worksheets, at least one section is devoted to occupational skills. Few go in-depth concerning education, hobbies, and interests, even though these equally define us as individuals. Such talents and interests are especially important in a work of fiction, when what the characters do is pivotal to their personalities, their strengths and weaknesses, their internal and external conflicts, their goals and motivations, as well as the settings they find themselves in.

To build the form of multilayered dimensions we've been talking about, the skill set the character is equipped with should be directly related to who this person is, what she needs to do, the plots in the story, and even the settings. In the best-case scenario, skills will connect cohesively to all these in some way. Best-selling author Sandra Brown has aptly said something to the effect that if the hero's a firefighter, then the heroine had better be an arsonist. That's how essential the characters' skill sets are to the story elements.

In *The Great Gatsby*, Jay Gatsby is a fabulously wealthy man living in a sprawling mansion; he's famous in West Egg for the lavish parties he throws. While there are a slew of rumors about where he comes from, what he does, and how he made his fortune, no one actually knows. It becomes clear to the main character, Nick Carraway, that Gatsby is heavily involved in organized crime. (The really interesting part of this is that Gatsby, fatally idealistic, believes himself to be a noble and honorable hero instead of what he really is—a deluded, selfish gangster who's hopelessly and unrealistically romantic in his pursuit of recapturing the love he shared with Nick's cousin Daisy a lifetime ago.) If Gatsby really were noble and honorable, as he believes himself to be, this book would fall apart. The great tragedy in this story is a direct result of how Gatsby's rationale for his life of crime and his immoral relationship with an old flame, who's now married and has a child, blinded him to reality and led to a monumental downfall. Anything else other than the questionable career and the predilections of this particular character may not have worked for the story. They were clearly carefully chosen for Gatsby.

In general, you want characters who are good at *something*, even if they don't yet know that they are. Specifically you want them to be exceptional in at least one area to make them memorable to readers. In his book *The Kick-Ass Writer*, Chuck Wendig says, "Sherlock isn't a mediocre detective. ... Sherlock is an amazing detective, and a terrible human. ... Characters can be good at things but they can't be too good—you need balance. If they're the best at something, they should also be the worst at something. Conflict lives here; the space between Sherlock being the best detective and the worst human is so taut with tension the potential story might snap and take out someone's eye."

Some of your character's areas of expertise could and should be deliberately selected career skills, but most will go far deeper than that. For instance, in the fourth book of my Incognito Series, *Dead Drop*, the heroine has had an experience of losing the man she loved to a covert government organization. In the present, she's an FBI agent, and she's spent years fruitlessly searching for this man. When the same organization approaches her son for recruitment, her experiences and skill set kick in, providing her with everything necessary to prevent the same tragedy from happening again. These same experiences and her skill set may also help her now or in the future find the man she still loves.

In another instance, the heroine, a nurse, in my inspirational gothic romance, *The Bloodmoon Curse*, miscarries several times, which devastates her. When she's asked to care for three orphaned children, she's led by all-too-fresh past conflicts, the goal to end suffering for these children (present dimension), and the motivation of also finding the means to heal her own pain in the process (future dimension).

If your character doesn't have a nine-to-five job per se, that fact says something about her character as well. In *A Dangerous Man*, Marilyn Pappano presents a hero who's a retired Army master sergeant. The skills Rory Hawkes learned in the military figure profoundly in the plot of the novel. If Pappano had made him, say, a restaurant owner or even an accountant, the plot would have fallen apart or gone in a direction that simply wouldn't have been anywhere near as effective. Occupation fuses with the character, plot, and setting in this story, and nothing else would have fit quite as well.

In a story that has more than one main character (like a hero and heroine in a romance novel), the other lead should also have an occupation that creates the same level of cohesion. Pappano's heroine in *A Dangerous Man* is a lawyer in a corrupt small town. Her father, the district attorney, tried to fight the corruption and was killed in the process. You can see the level of cohesion in all this, since a small-town lawyer would have little chance of going up against a corrupt system on her own. But her motivation is obvious. And with the backing of a retired master sergeant, she's got a shot at winning.

For a character to succeed, you must set the stage from the beginning so your main character can believably use what's in his bag of skills to rescue, escape, defeat, and fight (in whatever way makes sense in your story). Don't try to pull a fast one by expecting the reader to believe, for instance, that a man who can barely get out of bed in the morning and who's afraid of his own shadow can suddenly knock down walls and take on an armed man with nothing more than a rubber band and a rock. Remember, when David fought Goliath, he'd already killed a lion with his bare hands and had God on his side.

A couple of other things to consider with skill-set construction: Different jobs allow characters to look at the world in a variety of ways through the unique filter of a career. A garbage collector comes from a different world than a soldier, as does a stripper or an accountant. Use this to create dimensionality. A character's job should show the inner character. If a wife takes a second job to please her husband because he's a gambler and a drunk who wastes their money, this says something about her. If someone's in a dead-end job, is there a motivation for wanting something more? Or the opposite may be true: Does a dead-end job show that the character has no aspirations for more?

Your character's skill set doesn't have to make her predictable. In real life, you can find lawyers who are unsurprisingly ruthless and greedy, but also ones who genuinely want to see justice prevail. You can just as easily find doctors and nurses who go the extra mile and those who don't really care about patients. Even stereotypical archetypes usually have families who love them. Just remember, fiction isn't always like reality. To be cohesive doesn't mean you can't break the mold, so long as all the elements work together.

A character's skill set is something honed and developed throughout a lifetime. Show the origins and the present-day usage, and give the reader something to look forward to in seeing what your character's skills could be used for in the future of the story.

Examples of the skill-set dimensions of self follow:

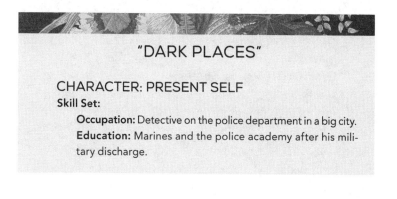

"DARK PLACES"

CHARACTER: PRESENT SELF
Skill Set:
    Occupation: Detective on the police department in a big city.
    Education: Marines and the police academy after his military discharge.

Hobbies: Weight lifting and wood whittling—two things that Sharon comments that he does with a single-minded vengeance that adds to the menace of his exterior.
Interests: Mentors children who were victims of violent crimes.

CHARACTER: PAST SELF
Skill Set:

Occupation: School (he was an average student who usually had his nose buried in a mystery or spy novel).

Education: High school, college, honorable discharge from the Marines.

Hobbies: Wood whittling, something he learned when he attended Boy Scout meetings for about a year, a group he really enjoyed and that gave him as close to a sense of belonging as he'd ever had—until his father decided the organization was inferior to playing a sport.

Interests: Reading suspense stories in which a hero saves victims preyed upon by bullies.

CHARACTER: FUTURE SELF
Skill Set:

Occupation: Same as Present.

Education: Same as Present.

Hobbies: Returning to the Boy Scouts as a leader and mentor.

Interests: Children ... this time his own with Sharon, and being a better father than his own was to him.

A CHRISTMAS CAROL

CHARACTER: PRESENT SELF
Skill Set:

Occupation: Owner of a "counting house" known as Scrooge and Marley, even after Marley passed. "Sometimes people new to the business called Scrooge *Scrooge*, and

sometimes Marley, but he answered to both names. It was all the same to him."
Education: Interned with Fezziwig.
Hobbies: Gain.
Interests: More gain.

CHARACTER: PAST SELF
Skill Set:
Occupation: Apprentice to Fezziwig.
Education: Boy's school.
Hobbies: Reading.
Interests: Life!

CHARACTER: FUTURE SELF
Skill Set:
Occupation: Owner of a counting house.
Education: Of the ghostly kind.
Hobbies: Giving to the poor and destitute.
Interests: Using his wealth to help others less fortunate than himself.

Characters need to be three-dimensional. There's no denying that who we are at every stage in our life has an impact on us. The present was influenced by the past and both will determine the future. Create purpose for characters through these stages on your character sketches to build in three-dimensionality. Use the P/P/F Self to analyze the *how* and *why* aspects in terms of shaping the individual throughout the character's life. These sketches aren't simply a setting down of facts. Dig deeper: What events, situations, people, and places caused this character to be who she is, to think and act, to react and *inter*act the way she did, the way she does currently, and the way she will in the future?

BUILD YOUR THREE-DIMENSIONAL MUSCLES HOMEWORK

Go back to some of your favorite stories and, chapter by chapter, see if you can identify (on something similar to the followingchart template) present, past, and future dimensions of a character. Remember, *present* is the here and now, the current time of the story; *past* is backstory that directly impacts what happens in the here and now; and *future* is that hint of hope and/or dread about where the character is and might be going, and where she may or may not end up.

CHAPTER/ SCENE #	PRESENT DIMENSION	PAST DIMENSION	FUTURE DIMENSION

Appendix B contains exercises from published books to help you get into the three-dimensional mind-set.

. . .

Without each of your character dimensions clearly defined before you start writing your story, your characters may end up two-dimensional at best—they'll have shape without form or depth. How can you imbue your characters with direction, motion, focus, vivid color, texture, harmony, and variety in which change is attainable and value becomes concrete? Only through multifaceted dimensions. In the ideal scenario, you'll know your characters so well before you begin writing that they're just waiting for you to root them deeply into each scene, every situation, and all settings. In the next chapter, we'll learn how to create three-dimensional plots.

THREE-DIMENSIONAL PLOTS

"Let's face it, characters are the bedrock of your fiction. Plot is just a series of actions that happen in a sequence, and without someone to either perpetrate or suffer the consequences of those actions, you have no one for your reader to root for, or wish bad things on."

—ICY SEDGWICK, "HE WAS A MAN OF GOOD CHARACTER"

In every story, the writer has to meet a basic challenge in order to create a successful book. This challenge almost always follows this course (where you see the arrow, substitute the words *leads to*):

CHARACTER → EVENT → CONFLICT → BACKSTORY →

GOALS → MOTIVATION → CHOICE → RESOLUTION

I love how Debra Dixon puts this challenge in its simplest form in *GMC: Goal, Motivation & Conflict*:

- Who = character
- What = goal
- Why = motivation
- Why not = conflict

She goes on to say that "a character wants a goal *because* he is motivated, *but* he faces conflict."

Plots need to have P/P/F Dimensions included for each major character, and naturally they need to have a deliberate and definitive purpose in the story. So a simple plot sketch worksheet that covers the most crucial aspects would include the following:

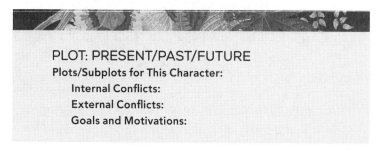

PLOT: PRESENT/PAST/FUTURE
Plots/Subplots for This Character:
Internal Conflicts:
External Conflicts:
Goals and Motivations:

Defining plots in the three-dimensional sketches allows you, the author, to thoroughly know the main characters' conflicts. Remember, the difference in three-dimensional writing is that you'll have a separate sketch for each main character that includes her present, past, and future self. To do that, take the basic sketch above and duplicate it three times across a landscaped page with three columns, labeling the sketches: "Present Self," "Past Self," and "Future Self." You should end up with something that looks like this:

CHARACTER: PRESENT SELF	CHARACTER: PAST SELF	CHARACTER: FUTURE SELF
Name:	*Name:*	*Name:*
Plots/Subplots for this Character:	*Plots/Subplots for this Character:*	*Plots/Subplots for this Character:*
Internal Conflicts:	Internal Conflicts:	Internal Conflicts:
External Conflicts:	External Conflicts:	External Conflicts:
Goals and Motivations:	Goals and Motivations:	Goals and Motivations:

You'll find a blank worksheet in Appendix A for your own use.

Life is conflict, and fiction needs to be even more so. Without conflict, you don't have a story. I like how Chuck Wendig describes this in *The Kick-Ass Writer*: "A plot grows within the story you're telling. … An artificial plot is something you have to wrestle into place, a structure you have to bend and mutilate and duct tape to get it to work. It is external. It is artifice. You want a plot that is internal and organic."

In real life, conflicts generally don't show up one day and go away the next, and they shouldn't in the world of fiction either. Each conflict has a beginning, middle, and an end, and the evolution of that conflict has to be believable, as well as emotional (i.e., worth caring about for the reader). In a story, the range of conflicts includes internal and external, and the goals and motivations that go along with them. These are your plot; you need each of these elements to be well-rounded in all dimensions of self. Goals and motivations must constantly evolve (*not* radically, because characters shouldn't be chameleons, but refined in depth, intensity, and scope) throughout the dimensional stages to fit escalating internal and external conflicts. If each goal and motivation in your story is cohesive, you'll see an unbreakable marriage between them and the conflicts that go along with them when you do the P/P/F Dimension sketches for each main character.

Internal and external conflicts and goals and motivations need to be sketched for past and present dimensions of each major character, because what's happening in the present will show its origins in the past. Think about the future dimension as predictions or premonitions that cause suspense, tension, dread, and longing.

Present/Past/Future Internal Conflicts

Internal conflicts are emotional problems brought on by *external* conflicts, which make a character reluctant to achieve a goal because of roadblocks. They keep her from learning a life lesson and making the choice to act. In fiction, external character conflicts are the reason plot conflicts can't be resolved. Simply put, the character can't reach her goal until she faces the conflict. (Sounds a bit like not getting dessert until the vegetables are eaten, and this is pretty accurate.) The audience must be able to identify with the internal and external conflicts the character faces to be involved in and to care about the outcome. Character growth throughout the story is key to a satisfactory resolution.

The first spark of the story in your mind will usually suggest the character's conflicts, and many times the conflict is based on someone or something threatening what the character cares about passionately. A loved one is in jeopardy, or something the character wants, needs, or desires is at risk of being lost. Questions you might ask to get to the heart of your character's conflicts:

- What are your core principles and values?
- What will you risk your life for?
- Why would you put yourself in danger for this?

These questions will help define your internal and external conflicts. It's your job as the writer to give the character incentives (specifically, goals and motivations, which we'll cover) to not give up until everyone's safe and she has what she's fighting for.

Generally there's an immediate internal conflict that's revealed or hinted at in the opening scenes. This is the beginning of layers of internal conflict. MJ Bush, writing coach, editor, and fantasy novelist on the WritinGeekery blog calls the next level the "root desire," and she suggests that you ask your character five times to tell you what her root desire is, digging deeper each time. Once you get to the core, she advises you to bury it again, because if the reader can see it right away, it'll sound more like you're preaching rather than telling a story. The root goal is something that gets revealed slowly throughout the course of the book. The conflicting desire is, of course, the external one—the obstacle that prevents your character from reaching her root desire or goal in the story.

In S.E. Hinton's classic story *Tex*, the fifteen-year-old hero loves his horse more than anything in the world. But when his seventeen-year-old brother Mason (who's been standing in as father and caretaker) sells the horses to pay bills and put food on the table, Tex's world is turned upside down. His horse gave him a sense of purpose, validity, sanity.

The horse made him happy. Though Tex understands intellectually that his brother had no other choice, he can't accept this. His internal conflict in losing what meant most to him is overwhelmed by the external conflict of his sold horse, and he reacts violently, desiring what he lost. But losing his horse is only his surface internal conflict. His root desire is the father who's all but abandoned them.

Clearly defined conflicts are ones that won't hit your reader over the head or frustrate him. If you don't quite understand the conflicts in your story, your instinct will be to compensate by bombarding the story with unfocused ideas. The reader won't find it any easier to sort through them and identify the true conflict. Loosely defined conflicts usually lead to the reader putting down a book and never picking it up again.

Too many conflicts can easily overwhelm the reader. The same is true if you're unrelenting in driving these conflicts home. I absolutely adore J. Madison Davis's take on this in *Novelist's Essential Guide to Creating Plot*:

> Even the greatest excitement and most spectacular events can become wearying if they are relentless. I remember hearing one disgruntled moviegoer whisper to his wife sometime around the third hour of *Titanic*, "When is this dang boat gonna sink, fer pity's sake?" The writer who has one unremittingly, relentlessly exciting scene following another can wear the reader out. Too much shouting makes us deaf, and shouting even louder after that will not be heard because of the deafness.

Too many conflicts (especially at the beginning and end of a novel) and failing to allow the reader to take a break between action sequences equate to shrill shouting that can deafen the reader. If you want an example of this, try reading Dan Brown's Robert Langdon Series. The action is absolutely relentless. By the halfway mark, I'm usually so exhausted I can barely continue reading. Characters need downtime, as much as readers do, to prevent overload.

Internal conflicts need to be sketched for past and present dimensions for each major character, because what's happening in the present will show its origins in the past. Obviously, it's vital to engage the readers' interest from the very beginning by including the means for him to anticipate (with hope and/or dread) what will happen in the future with these internal conflicts. Think about the future dimension of internal conflicts as premonitions that cause trepidation and longing.

Here are the examples of internal conflicts for P/P/F Dimensions:

"DARK PLACES"

CHARACTER: PRESENT SELF
Plots/Subplots for This Character:
Internal Conflicts: Jason has never truly gotten over what happened to him as a child when he was kidnapped. He struggles with the mental, verbal, and physical abuses he endured before he was rescued. He's afraid to trust anyone, to let himself be weak or vulnerable or unguarded. His relationship with Sharon, his partner and on-and-off romantic interest, is a huge internal conflict for him. He knows he's the problem. Whenever they got too close in the past, he pulled away. Sharon alone continues to believe in him, want him, and—despite how many times he's hurt her by withdrawing—refuses to give up on him.

CHARACTER: PAST SELF
Plots/Subplots for This Character:
Internal Conflicts: All his life, Jason was a victim of cruelty and, in some ways, he couldn't help wondering if this led to his kidnapping. Hunters preyed on the weakest in the herd, which was how Jason felt. The one person he felt he could trust was the janitor at his school. The man seemed to understand him and see him as the opposite of a weakling. The janitor befriended Jason and became like a father to him, telling him that the other kids were the ones who were worthless, not him. This janitor was also a Boy Scout leader; he didn't have children of his own, let alone a wife. The janitor quit his job at the school by the time authorities rescued Jason, a situation that left Jason feeling even more alone in the world than before.

CHARACTER: FUTURE SELF
Plots/Subplots for This Character:

Internal Conflicts: Jason knows that the way he treats everyone either like an enemy to be overcome or a victim to be rescued has led him to a lifetime of loneliness and sadness. He has to learn how to trust others and to realize that vulnerability isn't always a sign of weakness.

A CHRISTMAS CAROL

CHARACTER: PRESENT SELF
Plots/Subplots for This Character:

Internal Conflicts: When his nephew invites him to Christmas dinner, Scrooge asks him why he married. Fred promptly says that he fell in love. Scrooge growls "as if that were the only one thing in the world more ridiculous than a merry Christmas" and dismisses him. But Fred says Scrooge never visited him before he got married—why should his marriage be his reason for not visiting now? Scrooge dismisses him once more out of hand.

CHARACTER: PAST SELF
Plots/Subplots for This Character:

Internal Conflicts: Standing with the Ghost of the Past, Scrooge sees himself at the boys school he attended at Christmas time, a solitary child, neglected by his friends and left behind by all. He sees himself as he was: "a lonely boy ... reading near a feeble fire; and Scrooge sat down upon a form, and wept to see his poor forgotten self as he used to be." All he sees of the past "fell upon the heart of Scrooge with a softening influence, and gave a freer passage to his tears."

In his second memory of Christmas Past, Scrooge was alone again. He wasn't reading now, but walking up and down despairingly. Then Fanny runs in and tells him he's coming home forever, and he can barely be restrained from running out with her.

In the next memory, Scrooge sees himself as a "man in the prime of his life." But the girl, his fiancée Belle, sees something more—Ebenezer "fears the world too much." The golden idol of wealth cheers and comforts him. All his other hopes have merged into the hope of being beyond the chance of its sordid reproach. Nobler aspirations have fallen off one by one, until the master-passion, Gain, is all that engrosses him. This has changed his feelings for all else. Without his former "contract" with her, she knows he wouldn't seek her out nor "choose a dowerless girl—you who, in your very confidence with her, weigh everything by Gain: or, choosing her, if for a moment you were false enough to your one guiding principle to do so, do I not know that your repentance and regret would surely follow?" This memory of her releasing him from their engagement is torture for Scrooge now, in the presence of the spirit. He is aware that he's the one who made the choice to let his fiancée go, as "an unprofitable dream" he woke from in relief.

CHARACTER: FUTURE SELF
Plots/Subplots for This Character:

Internal Conflicts: Hearing the Ghost of Christmas Present say Tiny Tim probably won't survive, Scrooge is overcome with penitence and grief, especially when the Spirit reminds him of his own words when he says, "If he be like to die, he had better do it, and decrease the surplus population."

Present/Past/Future External Conflicts

External conflict (plot) is the central tangible or outer problem that a character must face and solve. The character wants to either restore her lost stability or grasp her root desire by thwarting the external conflict, and this produces her desire to act. However, a character's internal conflicts will create an agonizing tug-of-war with the external plot conflicts. She has to make tough choices that come down to whether or not she should face, act on, and solve the problem.

Stephenie Meyer's postapocalyptic novel, *The Host*, is about Melanie Stryder, who resists an invading alien life that forces human beings to become hosts by taking over the bodies and consciousness of each person. Melanie's invader soon realizes that Melanie hasn't relinquished possession of her mind, despite giving up her physical body. Though the invader's task is to discover the whereabouts of the remaining human resistance, this soul (called "Wanderer") instead finds itself sharing in Melanie's undiminished longings for her lost love, who may still be alive and waiting for her. Both Melanie and Wanderer struggle inside one body with their internal and external conflicts of being who and what they are.

Your audience should be able to relate to both the internal and external conflicts a character faces. This ensures the reader is involved enough to care about the outcome of the story. Plot conflicts work with character conflicts. You can't have one without the other, and they become more intense and focused the longer the characters struggle. Stakes are raised, choices are limited, and failure and loss are inevitable; these are the future dimensions that we need to sketch in order to create the hope/dread responses in readers.

Internal conflicts are different from external, but they're related causally and they depend on each other. Therefore, they need to be cohesive and multifaceted. Internal conflicts are all about characters, and external conflicts are all about plot. But keep this in mind: Both internal and external plots belong to the main character. After all, if both didn't affect her in some profound way, they wouldn't be conflicts for her, and therefore wouldn't even be part of her story. That's why it's so important to do a P/P/F Dimension sketch for each of your major characters in the prescribed areas on your plot sketch. David Corbett says in *The Art of Character: Creating Memorable Characters for Fiction, Film and TV*, "Characterization requires a constant back-and-forth between the exterior events of the story and the inner life of the character." If your character's internal and external conflicts are at odds, your story will be going in two different directions, which will disengage even the hardiest of readers. In stories that work on a cohesive level, internal and external conflicts travel on parallel tracks, merging and colliding in a fiery explosion throughout the course of a book.

Think of the two conflicts this way: Everyone has a hot button—cruelty to animals, cancer, child abuse. You fill in the blank with yours. But not everyone has the strength of passion for your particular hot button. We usually put our passion into something that has touched us deeply in our lives. If your mother died of cancer, you'll want to see that particular disease cured. It's your hot button. This doesn't mean you don't sympathize and care deeply about other causes, even if you're not quite as passionate about them as you are about the ones that affect you most. What it does mean is that if something critical happens in the area of your passion, you're probably going to step up to the plate and fight for what you believe in.

You're telling a story about your particular characters, and they have hot buttons, too. Since it's their story, their hot buttons will naturally be their conflicts. All of these conflicts must parallel, intersect, and collide for a story to be truly cohesive. So, though the external plot conflicts may stem from an outside force or situation, they nevertheless belong to the main character as much as her internal problems do. Like I said, if she didn't care deeply about the external plot, it wouldn't be her story.

Let's use an example of this from the action/adventure movie *Die Hard 2: Die Harder*. The rough and gruff main character, John McClane (played by Bruce Willis), is a cop at the airport on Christmas. He's off duty, but begins to sense trouble is afoot in what seems like the busiest place on earth—and things look like they could get worse before the day is over. The airport cops don't share his sane uneasiness. They've got their own worries to handle. Though McClane is very reluctant to get involved, his integrity won't allow him to stand by idly. He checks out his hunch, figuring he'll let the airport police handle anything that he discovers is amiss.

His gut instinct is dead-on. Terrorists take over the airport. This shouldn't be his problem, but it becomes so because (1) the airport cops refuse to do their jobs, as they're too busy with other tasks; and (2) these terrorists have pushed McClane's hot button. A year before, on Christmas, McClane single-handedly took down a band of terrorists at the Nakatomi building, where his wife worked. Terrorists, particularly those who threaten his wife, are undoubtedly McClane's hot button, his external plot conflict.

Enter his cohesive internal (and three-dimensional) character conflict—his wife is currently on one of the planes circling overhead, unable to land, and rapidly running out of fuel because of the terrorist attack paralyzing the airport. Not only have these terrorists hit John's hot button, they've made it very personal, and there's no way he can sit back and let security handle it. This is *his* problem. If that plane runs out of fuel, the passengers will plummet to their deaths. The problem with landing is that the terrorists still have control of the airport, and they've closed down all the runways, except the one they need for their own getaway. There are no lighted landing strips, so any landing is dangerous because it'll be done blindly. Without a choice, the pilot in his wife's plane announces to the tower he's making an emergency landing and, of course, McClane hears it. If he doesn't act this instant, his wife will die, and the terrorists will escape. The cone has closed to the point that he has almost no room to maneuver. The suspense is nearly more than the viewer can bear. (But he loves it!) All of McClane's goals and motivations (which are so cohesive, we can't talk about internal and external conflicts for this character without including them) come down to stopping the terrorists. This action, in turn, provides his wife's plane with the lighted strip needed to land. In this example, you can really see the differences between internal and external conflicts, but you see how they relate, connect, and collide. You can also see all three dimensions of self.

Let's go over the sometimes-subtle distinction between character (internal) and plot (external) conflicts with some examples from bestselling books.

In all of the Harry Potter books, young wizard Harry constantly battles his internal conflict. His parents are dead and he's been forced to live with his detestable and magic-hating aunt, uncle, and cousin. That's a simplification, of course, of a complex situation. The external plot conflict is Harry coming to terms with his inadvertent relationship to Voldemort, who killed his parents, and how his contact with this evil person affects him inside and out. The external plot conflict is evident in every book. You see how the internal and external conflicts differ—one's outside, one's inside—how they parallel, intersect, and collide, and how you can't really have one without the other.

In *Dances with Wolves*, Lieutenant John Dunbar nearly loses his life in the war, and his sense of purpose and self-worth wavers, although his sense of adventure and duty are intact. Feeling like he doesn't belong where he is, he ventures into dangerous Indian country, where he finds his purpose and his self-worth, and he comes to learn that he belongs to and loves the new culture he finds. These encompass his internal and external conflicts. Plot and character conflicts in this story center around the Indians he encounters, which both threaten him physically and heal his soul, showing him both the ugly and honorable sides of his fellow white men.

External conflicts should be sketched for present and past dimensions of each major character, since we can't understand why a character reacts to an external conflict until we've traced the path of her internal conflicts all the way back to the beginning, rooting and untangling the two dimensions. The external conflicts of the future dimension provide a tense tug-of-war between dread for the worst and the hope for the best, engaging readers throughout the evolving story.

The examples of external conflicts for P/P/F Dimensions follow:

"DARK PLACES"

CHARACTER: PRESENT SELF
Plots/Subplots for This Character:
External Conflicts: Jason's mother calls him and tells him the devastating news that another eight-year-old boy has been kidnapped in the town where he grew up. The circumstances are so similar to Jason's own kidnapping that he immediately goes on high alert.

CHARACTER: PAST SELF
Plots/Subplots for This Character:

External Conflicts: Jason was rescued from his kidnapping as a child only after the damage had been done. He endured mental and physical abuse at the hands of his kidnapper, who was always masked and always spoke in a whisper—and whom he's never been able to identify. The police in his hometown never discovered the identity of his kidnapper.

CHARACTER: FUTURE SELF
Plots/Subplots for This Character:

External Conflicts: When Jason returns to his hometown to aid the police in the search for the missing boy, he opens the cold case file on his own kidnapping. The similarities lead him to investigate the janitor he'd assumed was his friend when he was a child. The same man once again worked at the school the missing boy attended. He'd quit his job weeks ago, citing the reason for his departure as needing to care for an ailing loved one in another city. This was the same reason he cited for quitting his job twenty years ago. Jason realizes he has very little time to find this boy. If they don't find him soon, the damage will be done.

A CHRISTMAS CAROL

CHARACTER: PRESENT SELF
Plots/Subplots for This Character:

External Conflicts: Scrooge claims he can be cross because: "... I live in such a world of fools as this. ... Out upon merry Christmas! What's Christmas time to you but a time for paying bills without money; a time for finding yourself a year older, but not an hour richer; a time for balancing your books and having every item in 'em through a round dozen of months presented dead against you? If I could work my will, every idiot who goes about with 'Merry Christmas' on his lips, should be boiled with his own pudding, and buried with a stake of holly through his heart. He should!"

Scrooge questions how his clerk—who makes fifteen shillings a week—with a wife and family, can talk about a merry Christmas.

CHARACTER: PAST SELF
Plots/Subplots for This Character:

External Conflicts: In Scrooge's first memory, all the other boys at the school have gone home for the jolly holidays, except Scrooge. His father isn't a kind man, but in this second memory of Scrooge's boyhood Christmas, his sister Fanny says their father "… spoke so gently to me one dear night when I was going to bed, that I was not afraid to ask him once more if you might come home; and he said, Yes, you should; and sent me in a coach to bring you. And you're to be a man and are never to come back here; but first, we're to be together all the Christmas long, and have the merriest time in all the world."

CHARACTER: FUTURE SELF
Plots/Subplots for This Character:

External Conflicts: The ghost forces Scrooge to see his clerk's life: his impoverished, hardworking family, and his young, crippled son. "They were not a handsome family; they were not well dressed; their shoes were far from being waterproof; their clothes were scanty; and Peter might have known, and very likely did, the inside of a pawnbroker's. But, they were happy, grateful, pleased with one another, and contented with the time; and when they faded, and looked happier yet in the bright sprinklings of the Spirit's torch at parting, Scrooge had his eye upon them, and especially on Tiny Tim, until the last." Scrooge dreads an end of life in which "to lay in the dark empty house, with not a man, a woman, or a child, to say that he was kind to me in this or that."

Present/Past/Future Goals and Motivations
In *Creating Characters: How to Build Story People*, Dwight V. Swain talks about giving the main character drive, which basically entails

devising something for her to care about. You need to fit her with suitable goals—always keeping in mind the direction you want her to go in—threaten that goal, and establish reasons for her to continue fighting against the threat on the road to reaching her goal. Goals are what the character wants, needs, or desires above all else. Motivation is what gives her drive and purpose to achieve those goals. Goals must be urgent and/or monumental enough to motivate the character to go through hardship and self-sacrifice. But the surface inducement that most people will claim—wanting to do the right thing—isn't strong enough in fiction. Go deeper. Your character can't simply react to conflict; she must act in the face of it. What exactly does she stand to gain if she does something? What will she lose if she doesn't do it? Keep in mind that whatever the external conflict is in your story, it's not simply a container that holds your character—like a potted plant—until she can escape it. The external conflict is the foundation of your story goal/theme, and it's through this "ground" that the roots of her internal conflicts and goals and motivations will branch out and bloom.

Focused on the goal, the character is pushed toward the external conflict by believable, emotional, and compelling motivations that won't let her quit before she reaches the goal. Her anxiety doubles because she cares deeply about the outcome. The intensity of her anxiety pressures her to make choices and changes, thereby creating worry and anticipation (future dimensions) in the reader.

In Susan Hill's classic ghost story, *The Woman in Black*, solicitor Arthur Kipps is sent by his firm to the small town of Crythin Gifford to settle the affairs of the late Alice Drablow. While at the funeral, he sees a woman dressed in black that the children silently watch. Over the next few days, while completely cut off from the mainland at high tide, Kipps goes over the deceased woman's papers at Eel Marsh House. During this time, Kipps discovers the truth: Drablow bore a child out of wedlock and was forced to give him up to her sister. An attempt to abscond with her son led to him drowning in the marshes while his mother looked on helplessly. After her death, she returned to haunt Eel Marsh House and the town of Crythin Gifford. According to local legend, a sighting of the Woman in Black presages the death of a child. Kipps repeatedly sees the malevolent ghost and begins to fear for his fiancée and their future.

Remember, goals and motivations are constantly evolving (*not* changing necessarily, but refining in depth, intensity, and scope) to fit character and plot conflicts. Your character's goals and motivations will certainly adapt throughout the course of a story, since she's modifying or reshaping her actions based on the course the conflicts are dictating.

Let's look, for instance, at Frodo Baggins's evolving goals and motivations in *The Lord of the Rings*. From the beginning, his goal is to destroy the One Ring of power, passed reluctantly down to him by his Uncle Bilbo. He's fully aware of how the Ring will destroy everything he knows and loves if it falls back into its evil master's hands—this is his motivation for acting against the external conflict. Sauron is amassing an army to destroy Middle-earth, and the Ring is the weapon that will ensure his success. Frodo's goal—to get the Ring to Mount Doom so he can cast it into the fires where it was made and destroy it once and for all—remains firm throughout the plot. In the end, the evil of the Ring makes him seem to change his mind, but readers know that if the Ring hadn't ensnared and poisoned him so deeply, he would never have changed his altruistic course. Along the way, his goals become more focused. He begins his journey in the company of the Fellowship, but after a time he realizes the task belongs to him and he must carry the Ring to Mount Doom on his own, with the aid of his loyal friend Samwise Gamgee. When he becomes aware that he doesn't know how to get inside Sauron's lair (where Mount Doom resides), he accepts the help of the fickle creature Gollum, who's as obsessed with the Ring as Frodo is becoming—pointing toward the fear that Frodo may not finish his quest.

These are all expansions of Frodo's original goals. Same with his motivation: Frodo accepts the mission because of what's at stake—those he loves, Middle-earth and, most especially, his beloved Shire. His love motivates him to make the choice to do what seems impossible. The depth and scope of his motivation sharpens when he meets his former companion's brother, Faramir, and again recognizes the oppressive weight of all that's at stake if he doesn't succeed. It changes again when he acknowledges that the irreversible damage done to Gollum stems from the evil hold of the Ring and that the Ring is changing him, as long as it's in his possession. It sharpens yet again when he sees the size of the army Sauron is amassing. And when his best friend seemingly betrays him. Again, all of these are offshoots from his original goal and motivation. You can see present, past, and future dimensions in all of these changing goals, and additionally, you can see that the beginning of the story resonates in the end. No, Frodo doesn't get a happily ever after (Sam gets that instead), yet his story resolution fits perfectly with what we've learned. It's logical, even though it's a twist on what the reader is led to believe is the best-case-scenario ending.

Characters succeed because they rise above their fears, and this requires goals and motivations that are cohesive with the character's personality and the particular skill set you've equipped her with for this task. Also keep in mind that if your conflicts go in a straight line, with no offshoots to complicate them and no failures when the hero makes an effort to solve her problems, your reader will grow bored with the story and less intrigued by the character. You'll rouse more emotion and interest if the intensity of conflicts continues to rise on a causal course. As a story progresses, you'll revisit each main character's internal and external conflicts, as well as the goals and motivations, to show the refined growth and development of characters.

Goals and motivations should be sketched for present and past dimensions for each major character since readers can't understand what compels a character toward certain choices until they've traced the path of her conflicts all the way back to the beginning. Additionally, remember the need for future dimension goals and motivations. You want your reader to be nail-bitingly anxious and resolutely hopeful about the characters' state of mind, choices, and actions as the story unfolds scene by scene.

Not sure if your internal and external conflicts and goals and motivations for each P/P/F Dimension of character are strong and cohesive enough? You can find a cohesion checklist in Appendix A that you can use to evaluate the strength of these elements.

Just as characters do, goals and motivations change, since the conflicts characters face have an impact and change them in a variety of ways. Create purpose for conflicts in the same way you do character traits to build in three-dimensionality. From the standpoint of plot, you're looking at conflicts the characters currently face, have faced, and may have to face in the future. Analyze through P/P/F the *how* and *why* aspects in terms of shaping the individual's conflicts and goals and motivations throughout a lifespan.

Example of goals and motivations for P/P/F Dimensions follow:

"DARK PLACES"

CHARACTER: PRESENT SELF

Plots/Subplots for This Character:

Goals and Motivations: Jason is motivated to find the missing boy before he's harmed. His kidnapper spent the first half of his captivity trying to befriend him—but Jason had refused to capitulate. The abuse started after that. So there's a chance he can rescue this boy before he's physically harmed.

Additionally, just before Jason heard this news and rushed back to his hometown, he'd made the decision to take a chance on trusting Sharon, not to run away when she got too close to him—close enough to hurt him. He's willing to take that risk. He tells Sharon that he wants to have a normal relationship with her, not simply as detective partners, but a romantic relationship.

CHARACTER: PAST SELF

Plots/Subplots for This Character:

Goals and Motivations: Jason's experiences and relationships from his childhood are the reasons he's more and more withdrawn. After his kidnapping, he was beyond reach, infused with the willpower to make himself strong, impenetrable, invulnerable, unreachable from all harm—and, unwittingly, all human contact.

CHARACTER: FUTURE SELF

Plots/Subplots for This Character:

    Goals and Motivations: With the past rearing its head so menacingly, Jason finds himself withdrawing from Sharon again when his focus becomes all about finding this missing boy and bringing the captor—the boy's and his own—to justice. Even when he doesn't want to withdraw from her, he struggles against his basic human desire and feelings for her, afraid of being hurt once he lets down his guard.

A CHRISTMAS CAROL

CHARACTER: PRESENT SELF

Plots/Subplots for This Character:

    Goals and Motivations: "What did Scrooge care! The very thing he liked was to edge his way along the crowded paths of life, warning all human sympathy to keep its distance ..." Scrooge claims to wish to be left alone. He doesn't make himself merry at Christmas and can't afford to make idle people merry. What happens to the poor and destitute is not his business. He believes his only responsibility is to himself and his work. His own business occupies him constantly.

CHARACTER: PAST SELF

Plots/Subplots for This Character:

    Goals and Motivations: As a boy, Scrooge longed for home, and not simply during the holidays. The Ghost of Christmas Past recalls Fanny's delicacy, her large heart ... and her child, Fred, whom Scrooge has spurned so recently.

    When Scrooge recalls fondly his former employer, he wishes to live up to the high praise he and Dick Wilkins bestowed on Fezziwig well into Christmas night: To "have the power to render us happy or unhappy; to make our service light or burdensome; a pleasure or a toil. Say that his power lies in words and looks; in things so slight and insignificant that it is impossible to add and count 'em up: What then? The happiness he gives is quite as great as if it cost a fortune." This praise isn't something his clerk, Bob, could truthfully bestow upon him.

CHARACTER: FUTURE SELF
Plots/Subplots for This Character:
   Goals and Motivations: With the first spirit, Scrooge "went forth last night on compulsion, and I learnt a lesson which is working now." With the second ghost, he's prepared for a change of heart; that "if you have aught to teach me, let me profit by it." By the last ghost, he has conceded that "I know your purpose is to do me good, and as I hope to live to be another man from what I was."

Plots need to be three-dimensional. There's no denying that the conflicts we face at every stage in our lives have an impact on us, who we are, what we do and don't do, and what we might do in the future. Create *purpose* for plots through these elements on the character sketch (and others if you want to go even more in-depth) to build in three-dimensionality. Analyze through P/P/F Self the *how* and *why* aspects in terms of shaping the plot that your characters deal with. These sketches aren't just a setting down of facts. Dig deeper: What events, situations, people, and places caused this character to be, to think and act, react and *inter*act the way she did, the way she does currently, and the way she will do so in the future?

BUILD YOUR THREE-DIMENSIONAL MUSCLES HOMEWORK:

Go through some of your favorite stories chapter by chapter and see if you can identify (on something similar to the chart template below) present, past, and future dimensions of plot.

   Remember, *present* is the here and now, the current time of the story; *past* is backstory that directly impacts what happens in the here and now; and *future* is that hint of hope and/or dread about where the character is and might be going, and where she may or may not end up.

CHAPTER/ SCENE #	PRESENT DIMENSION	PAST DIMENSION	FUTURE DIMENSION

Check out Appendix B for exercises you can use to practice.

. . .

Without each of these dimensions clearly defined before you start writing your story, your plots may end up two-dimensional—again, they'll have shape without form and depth. Plots, like characters, need to have direction, motion, focus, vivid color, texture, harmony, and variety in which change is attainable and value becomes concrete. With your plot elements sketched out three-dimensionally, you'll know what conflicts have caused your characters to act the way they have and why they feel the way they do in any situation, and you'll be able to deeply root these aspects into each scene you write. In the next chapter, we'll learn how to create three-dimensional settings.

THREE-DIMENSIONAL SETTINGS

"Setting can create the world of your story, show characterization, add conflict, slow or speed up your pacing, add or decrease tension, relate a character's backstory, thread in emotion, and more ... Setting can add so much to your story world or it can add nothing."
—MARY BUCKHAM, *A WRITER'S GUIDE TO ACTIVE SETTING: HOW TO ENHANCE YOUR FICTION WITH MORE DESCRIPTIVE, DYNAMIC SETTINGS*

As James Scott Bell says in *Plot & Structure*, "Plots need characters, and characters need plots." I would add that both characters and plots need settings, too. The first spark of a story will generally present the groundwork for your book, whether your approach is in the form of characters, plots, or settings. Ideally, it will be a combination of all three.

In her book *Story Structure Architect: A Writer's Guide to Building Dramatic Situations and Compelling Characters*, Victoria Lynn Schmidt, Ph.D., speaks about individual plot, setting, or character-driven approaches using the example of a tornado storyline. When you approach the storyline from a plot-driven point of view, if a tornado suddenly descends upon the town, the characters have no means to stop it. They brace themselves and react to what's happening. "They don't cause the tornado—the tornado causes them to react to it." When you approach a story in a character-driven manner, even if a tornado comes through the town, characters are given the time to decide what to do. The focus of the story is on the characters' decisions, and that's what moves the story in different directions. The characters have options and they make choices that affect the outcome in a character-driven story. In a setting-dominated story, the focus is almost always on the location, as seen through the eyes of the people who populate it. The focus is on the town—the setting—devastated by the tornado. A combination of all three is necessary, but different writers come at a basic scenario like this in their own unique ways. Writers who are more setting oriented will focus on the town, past, present, and future; writers who are more character oriented will focus on the individual townspeople; and writers who are plot oriented will focus on the action of the tornado. As long as each has all three elements, anything goes in terms of the slant.

Characters must blend naturally into the setting, just as plot must become an organic part of your character and setting. If a story doesn't work, it could very well be because your character, plot, and setting elements aren't melding naturally. Your setting is a basis for building your story—it enhances the characters, conflicts, and suspense, and provides a place for all three to flourish.

SETTING DIMENSIONS: THREE-DIMENSIONAL SETTING SKETCHES

The settings your main characters are in, have been in, and will be in must be fully fleshed out with P/P/F Dimensions. Make sure your settings don't have limited purpose in a story; make them vital. A simple setting sketch worksheet that covers the most crucial aspects will include the following:

SETTINGS: PRESENT/PAST/FUTURE
Important Settings for This Character:

Defining settings on a three-dimensional sketch allows you to thoroughly know main characters and their worlds. Remember the difference in three-dimensional writing is that you'll have a separate sketch for each main character that includes her present, past, and future self. So take the basic sketch and duplicate it three times across a landscaped page with three columns, labeling the sketches: "Present Self," "Past Self," and "Future Self." You should end up with something that looks like this:

PRESENT DIMENSION	PAST DIMENSION	FUTURE DIMENSION
Name:	Name:	Name:
Important Settings for this Character:	Important Settings for this Character:	Important Settings for this Character:

You'll find a blank worksheet in Appendix A for your use, but feel free to find other, more in-depth setting sketch worksheets elsewhere if you feel you need more. Let's break out each section as we did before with character and plot sketches.

The Here and Now

Remember Mary Buckham's words from the beginning of this chapter: *The setting of a story can add so much to the overall composition … or it can add absolutely nothing.* The importance of creating a setting that is cohesive with character and plot can be illustrated by imagining different settings for classic novels. What if *Moby-Dick*, instead of being set at sea, had been set in a lighthouse? Captain Ahab (a man who's never been on anything bigger than a sailboat) goes around town boasting about how he'll get the whale. Much of *Moby-Dick*'s classic appeal would be lost if it'd been set on land instead of the sea. If *The Amityville Horror* had taken place in a department store, the horror would have fizzled. If Harry Potter had gone to a local public school (or St. Brutus's Secure Center for Incurably Criminal Boys, as Dudley's Aunt Marge suggested) instead of the magical boarding school Hogwarts, the series would have been radically altered.

While many stories have settings that suit the character and plot, I'm sure you can come up with dozens where the author could have spent more time making the setting extraordinary—so the reader actually wants to visit it again in another book—instead of simply getting the job done. Writers need to weave pieces of the character and plot details into setting. Good setting descriptions *should* convey characteristics and plot elements—otherwise these descriptions serve as general information without a strong, cohesive purpose. Describe the setting in a way that not only fits your characters and plot, but also supercharges your whole story. What does the setting reveal about the character's personality? What means the most to her in the setting? How will this setting create the stage for conflict and suspense? How can you make it so real your reader will believe the place actually exists?

In Adam Nevill's horror novel, *The Ritual*, four old University friends set off into the Scandinavian wilderness of the Arctic Circle. The setting in this book is vivid, with descriptions that are almost tangible, twisting the trees into imaginary (or maybe not so imaginary) monsters surrounding them on all sides, closing in on and terrifying them at each turn. The setting also reflects the dawning disparity and gaping differences, the impossible distance, between these men—once as close as brothers, now no longer friends. During this trial, they also confront *themselves*, who they really are in the face of evil. The setting descriptions reflect these ever-darkening, dense, and impenetrable realizations that mirror internal conflicts.

> Through their discomforts Dom and Phil were missing everything of interest: the sudden strip marshes, the faces in the rock formations, the perfect lakes, the awesome Måskoskårså valley grooved into the earth during the Ice Age, the golden eagle circling above it, and the views of a landscape it was impossible to believe existed in Europe …
>
> During the late afternoon and into the early evening, when they were too tired to do anything but stagger about and swear at the things that poked and scratched their faces, the forest had become so dense it was impossible to move in any single direction for more than a few metres. So they had moved backwards and forwards, to circle the

larger obstacles, like the giant prehistoric trunks that had crashed down years before and been consumed by slippery lichen, and they had zigzagged to all points of the compass to avoid the endless wooden spears of branches, and the snares of the small roots and thorny bushes, that now filled every space between the trees. The upper branches ratcheted up their misery by funneling down upon them the deafening fall of rain in the world above, creating an incessant barrage of cold droplets the size of marbles ...

... the terrific sound of strong fresh wood being snapped still rang through his ears. A trace of an echo, like the hollow sound made by a stone bouncing off tree trunks, seemed to pass away, deep into the forest. What could possibly have broken a tree like that? Somewhere inside there, not too far back, he could also see the pale sappy fibres and spikes breaking from the bark of a thick limb. Ripped from a blackened trunk like an arm from a torso ...

Readers should never feel that the characters in the story are actors crossing a stage with the setting. The people that populate your world are residents, even if only for the duration of the story. Why set the story here—here and nowhere else? If you can't answer that question, your setting isn't pertinent to the story, and that's no good. Nevill chose his location carefully: An out-of-the-way area of the world that had never truly been explored to its farthest reaches. The dark, wet, miserable setting mirrors the characters' internal conflicts and emotions perfectly. This story had to take place here and nowhere else to make it fully come to life. Characters and plots flourish in this setting.

Settings may provide the backdrop for events to unfold, but they do much more than that by creating the context of each scene. Settings can suggest emotion of any kind; they can suggest conflicts, personality, memories, goals, and motivations, you name it. The connotations are endless. What does the setting reveal about the character's state of mind, preferences, desires? How can this setting be used to establish the foundation for conflict and suspense? Setting can reveal time, place, and culture. Objects, artifacts, symbols, landmarks in an area or in the surroundings that the character inhabits or visits can reveal all of these things by effectively showing instead of telling. Consider that the weather in your setting affects everything else in a scene, whether the POV character goes outside, stays inside, how she dresses, moves, travels, and feels.

In *The Ruins* by Scott Smith, two young couples are on a vacation in Mexico where they make friends with fellow tourists. When the brother of one of those tourists disappears, the group ventures into the jungle to look for him. What starts as a day trip spirals into a nightmare when they find a hill marking the site of ancient ruins covered in vines and surrounded by bare earth. Men from a nearby Mayan village appear and surround the entire hill. These men are obviously afraid of the deadly vines and have salted the earth around the hill to prevent their spread. Anyone who strays too close to this place will become infected with the spores and so the Mayans initially attempt to force them to steer clear but when they get too close—close enough to become infected—they force the day-trippers to ascend the hill to prevent further spread. The vines are alive, evil, and they infest every living thing … leading to death.

> Amy was silent. She didn't want to go, of course, was terrified of the idea, of dropping into the earth, into the darkness. She hadn't even wanted to come here—that was what she wanted to say to Jeff. If it had been up to her, they never would've left the beach in the first place. And then, when they'd discovered the hidden path, she'd tried to warn him, hadn't she? She'd tried to tell him that they shouldn't take it, and he'd refused to listen. This was all his fault, then, wasn't it? So shouldn't he be the one to descend into that hole? But even as she was asking herself these questions, Amy was remembering what had happened at the base of the hill, how she'd retreated across the clearing, peering through her camera's viewfinder, her foot slipping into the tangle of vines. If she hadn't done that, maybe the Mayans wouldn't have forced them up the hill. They wouldn't be here now—Pablo wouldn't be lying at the bottom of the shaft with a broken back; Eric's shoe wouldn't be full of blood. They'd be walking somewhere miles from this place, every step carrying them farther away, and the tiny black flies and the blisters forming on their feet were things perfectly worthy of complaint …

This passage from the book is rife with characterization and plot (including conflicts and goals and motivations), with P/P/F Dimensions, and setting descriptions that convey the menace of the place the group is in through a very unfortunate series of ill-informed, poorly chosen, devastating events.

Also note that even if your setting is real and one that's widely known, your unique view of the place turns it into *your* story world every single time, as if the place is something new, special, and exciting, unexplored by anyone but you and your characters … and now readers.

Just as writers have to get to know their characters and plots before they start the story, they should get to know their settings. The only settings that matter in a story are the ones the characters come in contact with; these have purpose in progressing character and plot. Whether or not your story people love their setting, they should know and/or discover it on the pages in a natural, believable way. Make the setting come alive in the reader's mind by using all five senses. Make him want to visit and revisit it. Make settings so memorable that they exist in the reader's mind long after the story has finished. In *Description & Setting*, Ron Rozelle says, "Settings provide bases of operations for everything that happens in your story or novel and, as importantly, they—along with the characters that will do things in there—provide you with a means to actually tell a story, rather than simply report information." In fiction, settings should be less about objective reality (impersonal) and all about subjective experience (highly personal).

An example of present setting dimensions follows:

"DARK PLACES"

CHARACTER: PRESENT SELF

Important Settings for This Character: Contemporary setting. Jason lives in a big city, where there are few trees, and it's always loud and noisy no matter what time of day it is. He doesn't know his neighbors and, beyond simple appearances, they don't know him. His apartment is a wide-open studio with a single large room, huge windows, and definitely no curtains to block the light. He can't abide darkness—and he even leaves all the lights on when he goes out so he doesn't have to come home to darkness at the end of each day. He's taken the doors off the closets. The hallways leading to his apartment are extremely well lit. Sharon's apartment is too dark and closed in for him to be there comfortably, so when they get together it's always at his place.

A CHRISTMAS CAROL

CHARACTER: PRESENT SELF

Important Settings for This Character: His counting-house in "cold, bleak, biting weather: foggy withal where he could hear the people in the court outside, go wheezing up and down, beating their hands upon their breasts, and stamping their feet upon the pavement stones to warm them. The city clocks had only just gone three, but it was quite dark already—it had not been light all day—and candles were flaring in the windows of the neighbouring offices, like ruddy smears upon the palpable brown air. The fog came pouring in at every chink and keyhole, and was so dense without, that although the court was of the narrowest, the houses opposite were mere phantoms. To see the dingy cloud come drooping down, obscuring everything, one might have thought that Nature lived hard by, and was brewing on a large scale."

The There and Then

Present characters react to setting in both subtle and vivid ways (using all five of their senses), and therefore act differently in these various places. *Memory* of setting also has a poignant impact that can be even more powerful to characters. Where a character came from will reveal endless things about that person—personality, strengths and weaknesses, relationships, conflicts, and certainly goals and motivations. Is the character's current setting vastly different or similar to her past setting(s)? What internal conflicts and motivations can be drawn to describe the setting more tangibly as a result? Are there ways in which the current setting has been influenced by something that happened in the past? Maybe a character moved to the suburbs because something violent happened to him as a child in an urban setting. Does the character own or know about something that draws her back to her origins? What associations can be made between the past dimension of character and plot to deepen the present and past story setting(s)?

In *The Woman in Black*, Hill starts the story with a lot of atmospheric setting descriptions that are enhanced with weather descriptions. These vividly hint at the POV character's mood and frame of mind during specific weather conditions—the mention of a ghost story makes him reflect on the one he lived through in his past. Hill goes on to take the settings and infuse them with interesting, heart-stopping descriptions that aren't merely blocks of information but evocative memories, past events, and tangible sensations.

> The door of the room from which the noise came, the door which had been securely locked, so that I had not been able to break it down, the door to which there could not be a key—that door was now standing open. Wide open.
>
> Beyond it lay a room, in complete darkness, save for the first yard or two immediately at the entrance, where the dim light from the bulb on the landing outside fell onto some shining, brown floor-covering. Within, I could hear both the noise—louder now because the door was open—and the sound of the dog, pattering anxiously about and sniffing and snuffling as she went.
>
> I do not know how long I stood there in fear and trembling and in dreadful bewilderment. I lost all sense of time and ordinary reality. Through my head went a tumbling confusion of half-thoughts and emotions, visions of specters and of real fleshy intruders, ideas of murder and violence, and all manner of odd, distorted fears. And, all the time, the door stood wide open and the rocking continued. Rocking. Yes, I came to, because I had realized at last what the noise within the room was—or, at least, what it reminded me of closely. It was the sound of the wooden runner of my nurse's rocking chair, when she had sat beside me every night while I went to sleep, as a small child, rocking, rocking …

This kind of writing brings extremely well-defined pictures to mind. The whole book (and *all* of Susan Hill's stories) is filled with setting descriptions that make locations as vivid, memorable, ever evolving, and evoking as any character.

Drawing on where a character came from fleshes her out with additional layers that produce realism and lifelike qualities. For example, in *Beowulf*, Hrothgar's great mead hall, Heorot, is a place that symbolizes their achievements, victories, rewards, and comforts. It's also the place that the monster Grendel invades, vividly striking at the very heart of all that matters to these people. In the end, Beowulf liberates the hall from the monsters and gives them back their home. (You can really see all dimensions of present, past, and future in this particular setting just from this paragraph, can't you?) In contrast, the cave Grendel and his mother live shows the exact opposite of the Hrothgar hall—it's dark, forbidding, a place to hide, to seethe, a place for evil outcasts.

Here are the examples of past setting dimensions:

"DARK PLACES"

CHARACTER: PAST SELF

Important Settings for This Character: Jason grew up in a small, quiet, and peaceful town where nearly everyone knew everyone. Sports were all-important to the people he knew. Everyone was obsessed with their favorite teams in particular seasons, decorating their houses with fan memorabilia, wearing merchandise, and gathering on game days. Popular kids were involved in as many team sports as possible. This small town had lots of dense, lush forests and Jason enjoyed spending time walking in them—places where it seemed he was completely alone with no one to badger, bully, or belittle him. During his captivity, he was held captive in a claustrophobically small, dark room without windows or lights; so he never saw his captor (who wore a mask) and the man only spoke in a very low whisper so Jason couldn't identify him by his voice.

A CHRISTMAS CAROL

CHARACTER: PAST SELF

Important Settings for This Character: Scrooge's school as a boy: a long, bare, melancholy room. In his second Christmas memory, "the room became a little darker and more dirty. The panels shrunk, the windows cracked; fragments of plaster fell out of the ceiling, and the naked laths were shown."

The counting house where Scrooge interned: "The busy thoroughfares of a city, where shadowy passengers passed and repassed; where shadowy carts and coaches battled for the way, and all the strife and tumult of a real city were. It was made plain enough, by the dressing of the shops, that here too it was Christmas time again; but it was evening, and the streets were lighted up." Inside "there was nothing they wouldn't have cleared away, or couldn't have cleared away, with old Fezziwig looking on. It was done in a minute. Every movable was packed off, as if it were dismissed from public life for evermore; the floor was swept and watered, the lamps were trimmed, fuel was heaped upon the fire; and the warehouse was as snug, and warm, and dry, and bright a ball-room, as you would desire to see upon a winter's night. In came a fiddler with a music-book, and went up to the lofty desk, and made an orchestra of it, and tuned like fifty stomach-aches. ... When everybody had retired but the two 'prentices, they did the same to them; and thus the cheerful voices died away, and the lads were left to their beds; which were under a counter in the back-shop."

The Where and When

Hands down, the future dimension of setting gets left out the most because there's a tendency to think there's a time-traveling experience to Some Other Place that happens when the character's story resolution is reached. Instead, think in terms of where the character could conceivably end up, scene by scene, based on what you're believably establishing and unfolding as you tell your story.

If you don't give characters fully fleshed out situations, conflicts, and, yes, settings for the future, you've essentially left the reader with nothing to hope for or look forward to. To show future dimension of self is a way of allowing readers something to either anticipate and/or dread in terms of where the character and story are going. They project possibilities, expectations, apprehensions, and anxiety about what might happen in the future at each stage in the storytelling. The future dimension both anchors and deepens the context, because the reader needs to be aware, scene by scene, where this story is and may be going, in what direction events are unfolding, and where it may or may not conclude.

In the case of James Dashner's *The Maze Runner*, the main character, Thomas, wakes up in a setting ("the Glade") with almost total memory loss about who he is and why he's there. It's filled with future dimensions. He's surrounded with other boys, none of whom remember anything either. In a short time after arriving through the lift that brings them food and supplies, Thomas can't help but notice the towering stone walls that surround the Glade. There is no way out of this place … no way except maybe through what's inside the walls—an ever-changing maze. Obviously the walls and the maze itself aren't there for aesthetic appeal alone. There's a definitive purpose to the settings in this book, in all P/P/F Dimensions:

> They reached the huge split that led outside to more stone pathways. Thomas gaped, his mind emptying of thought as he saw it all firsthand.
>
> "This is called the East Door," Chuck said, as if proudly revealing a piece of art he'd created.
>
> Thomas barely heard him, shocked by how much bigger it was up close. At least twenty feet across, the break in the wall went all the way to the top, far above. The edges that bordered the vast opening were smooth, except for one odd, repeating pattern on both sides.
>
> On the left side of the East Door, deep holes several inches in diameter and spaced a foot apart were bored into the rock, beginning near the ground and continuing all the way up.
>
> On the right side of the East Door, foot-long rods jutted out from the wall edge, also several inches in diameter, in the same pattern as

the holes facing them on the other side. The purpose was obvious. "Are you kidding?" Thomas asked, the dread slamming back into his gut. "You weren't playing with me? The walls really move?"

"What else would I have meant?"

Thomas had a hard time wrapping his mind around the possibility. "I don't know. I figured there was a door that swung shut or a little mini-wall that slid out of the big one. How could these walls move? They're huge, and they look like they've been standing here for a thousand years." And the idea of those walls closing and trapping him inside this place they called the Glade was downright terrifying.

Chuck threw his arms up, clearly frustrated. "I don't know, they just move. Makes one heck of a grinding noise. Same thing happens out in the Maze—those walls shift every night, too."

Thomas, his attention suddenly snapped up by a new detail, turned to face the younger boy. "What did you just say?"

"Huh?"

"You just called it a maze—you said, 'same thing happens out in the maze.'"

Chuck's face reddened. "I'm done with you. I'm done." He walked back toward the tree they'd just left.

Thomas ignored him, more interested than ever in the outside of the Glade. A maze? In front of him, through the East Door, he could make out passages leading to the left, to the right, and straight ahead. And the walls of the corridors were similar to those that surrounded the Glade, the ground made of the same massive stone blocks as in the courtyard. The ivy seemed even thicker out there. In the distance, more breaks in the walls led to other paths, and farther down, maybe a hundred yards or so away, the straight passage came to a dead end. "Looks like a maze," Thomas whispered, almost laughing to himself. As if things couldn't have gotten any stranger. They'd wiped his memory and put him inside a gigantic maze. It was all so crazy it really did seem funny.

His heart skipped a beat when a boy unexpectedly appeared around a corner up ahead, entering the main passage from one of the offshoots to the right, running toward him and the Glade. Covered in sweat, his face red, clothes sticking to his body, the boy didn't slow, hardly glancing at Thomas as he went past. He headed straight

BRING YOUR FICTION TO LIFE

for the squat concrete building located near the Box. Thomas turned as he passed, his eyes riveted to the exhausted runner, unsure why this new development surprised him so much. Why wouldn't people go out and search the maze? Then he realized others were entering through the remaining three Glade openings, all of them running and looking as ragged as the guy who'd just whisked by him. There couldn't be much good about the maze if these guys came back looking so weary and worn …

Focused on your setting, what's the worst-case scenario if the character doesn't end up where she's striving to go? What's the best? Make the reader go through all the emotions of anxiety and hope as you project, scene by scene, both the worst and best place for the character to arrive at by the end of the book. In a more focused sense, each scene should project forward to keep the reader fully engaged.

In another example, this one also taken from *The Ruins*, you can feel this main character's internal and external conflicts so clearly. His current goals and motivations are sketchy, the result of past and present events that are terrifyingly limited and point to death in every single direction. The limbo inside his mind as he traverses the landscape (the massive tangle of vines forming the hill) of the present seems to point to a future in which he'll never escape alive:

> The rain had already saturated the clearing, transforming its soil into a deep, viscous mud that clung heavily to his feet. Jeff thought of his earlier attempt to flee, that first night, when he'd tried to sneak down through the vines, how the tendrils had cried out, alerting the Mayans to his approach, and he wondered why the plant was remaining so quiet now, so motionless. Surely it must've sensed what he was intending. It was possible, of course, that this silence betrayed how negligible Jeff's chances were, that the vine could perceive the Mayans standing guard even through the darkness, the mist, the rain, that it knew he'd never make it—he'd either be turned back or killed. At some remove within himself, Jeff could even grasp what this portended, could recognize that the logical course, the sensible one, would be to surrender now, to retreat up the hill to safety.
>
> Yet he kept walking.

Thirty strides, and then he stopped. He stood there peering toward the jungle. All he could hear was the rain slapping down into the mud. The wind tugged at the mist, stirring it deceptively. Jeff kept pulling shapes from the darkness, first to his left, then to his right. Every cell in his body seemed to be warning him to turn back while he still could, and it baffled him why this should be so. Here, after all, was the moment he'd been yearning for, was it not? This was escape; this was salvation. How could he possibly renounce it?

Here's an example of future setting dimensions:

"DARK PLACES"

CHARACTER: FUTURE SELF

Important Settings for This Character: Jason imagines living in a big house that can be filled with natural and artificial light, set in a wide-open area where his kids can roam for miles without danger. He dreams of his own heart being just as wide open, filled with light and no fear of risk, where love is safe and vulnerability is strength.

A CHRISTMAS CAROL

CHARACTER: FUTURE SELF

Important Settings for This Character: "They scarcely seemed to enter the city; for the city rather seemed to spring up about them, and encompass them of its own act." In the heart of the city, merchants hurried up and down and conversed in groups, looking at their watches, and trifled thoughtfully with their great gold seals.

"They left the busy scene, and went into an obscure part of the town, where Scrooge had never penetrated before, although he recognised its situation, and its bad repute. The ways were foul and narrow; the shops and houses wretched; the people half-naked, drunken, slipshod, ugly. Alleys and archways, like so many cesspools, disgorged their offences of smell, and dirt, and life, upon the straggling streets; and the whole quarter reeked with crime, with filth, and misery.

"Far in this den of infamous resort, there was a low-browed, beetling shop, below a pent-house roof, where iron, old rags, bottles, bones, and greasy offal, were bought. Upon the floor within, were piled up heaps of rusty keys, nails, chains, hinges, files, scales, weights, and refuse iron of all kinds. Secrets that few would like to scrutinise were bred and hidden in mountains of unseemly rags, masses of corrupted fat, and sepulchres of bones." ...

"Scrooge hastened to the window of his office, and looked in. It was an office still, but not his. The furniture was not the same, and the figure in the chair was not himself."...

"A churchyard. Here, then; the wretched man whose name he had now to learn, lay underneath the ground. It was a worthy place. Walled in by houses; overrun by grass and weeds, the growth of vegetation's death, not life; choked up with too much burying; fat with repleted appetite. A worthy place!"

In the same way characters and plots have to be three-dimensional, so too do settings for all major characters. The environments we're in at every stage in our life have an impact on us for bad or good or somewhere in between. Create *purpose* for settings in the same way you do characters and plots. From the standpoint of setting, you're looking at where the characters are, were, and where they might end up. At the same time, you're analyzing through setting the *how* and *why* of where the character is, was, and will be in terms of shaping the individual throughout a lifespan.

THE THREE-DIMENSIONAL CHARACTER, PLOT, AND SETTING SKETCH WORKSHEET

We've now completed the character, plot, and setting portions of the three-dimensional worksheet (Appendix A has a blank sheet for your use). To ensure you're getting the maximum amount of "dimension" out of each P/P/F sketch, go back over the sections numerous times to flesh out all you can as much as possible. If you see blank spaces anywhere on the worksheet, you can (and should) do more work there. Sparse areas are invitations to dig deeper. If you haven't already, put these three dimensions side by side so you can compare the developments between the dimensions to ensure cohesive, deep, and logical progressions without gaps.

As we said earlier, not everything you end up putting in your three-dimensional sketches will make it into your story. There's good cause for not overloading a book with the sheer weight of each main characters' three-dimensional self, but the writer's comprehensive knowledge of his characters, plots, and settings will be well worth the work put in, because the story will be thoroughly fleshed out.

Without each of these dimensions clearly defined before you start writing your story, your settings won't be as realistic to the reader as the place he's sitting with your book in his hands. Just as we said for characters and plot, settings *can* have direction, motion, focus, vivid color, texture, harmony, and variety in which change is attainable and value becomes concrete. Focus on all aspects of dimension to achieve this in your settings. In the ideal story, you'll know your settings so well before you begin the multilayered task of bringing the book to life, the groundwork for three-dimensional writing will be laid out and waiting for you to write each scene with deep roots.

BUILD YOUR THREE-DIMENSIONAL MUSCLES HOMEWORK

Go back to some of your favorite stories and, chapter by chapter, see if you can identify (on something similar to the following chart template) present, past, and future dimensions of setting. Remember, present is the here and now, the current time of the story; past is backstory that *directly impacts* what happens in the here and now; and future is that hint of hope/dread about the place the character is, was, and may end up—what are the best and worst options?

CHAPTER/ SCENE #	PRESENT DIMENSION	PAST DIMENSION	FUTURE DIMENSION

If you need help getting started, exercises from published novels can be found in Appendix B.

. . .

Once we begin a project with the necessary preparation of crafting three-dimensional characters, plots, and settings, we're left with the hands-on process of translating these dimensional foundations into opening and resolving scenes, along with the all-important bridge scenes between. In the next chapter, we'll examine the step-by-step technique of crafting multidimensional scenes.

4

ANATOMY OF A THREE-DIMENSIONAL SCENE

"A scene is the basic building block of a piece of fiction, one that portrays characters in action, moving the story forward by their behaviors, words, and thoughts. The essential elements present in almost every scene are action, conflict, images, and dialogue—all unified by a singular dominant purpose."

—JAMES V. SMITH, JR., *FICTION WRITER'S BRAINSTORMER*

All that came before this point was the "primer" layer in getting ready to write a three-dimensional story. These primers were meant to benefit you, the writer, and provide the potential to get to *this* very place: Fully developing each and every scene of your book. To understand what we need to include in each, this chapter explores the kinds of scenes each story requires.

THREE TYPES OF SCENES

The most basic way for an "engineer of story" to visualize the scenes that make up his book and the function of each of those scenes is with the generalization that there are three types of scenes:

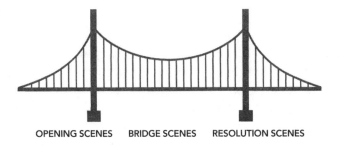

OPENING SCENES   BRIDGE SCENES   RESOLUTION SCENES

Opening and resolution scenes are the crucial support structures that bridge scenes are built between. Each must be well constructed with purpose, strong enough to carry the loads required of them. Put succinctly, as Nancy Kress does in *Beginnings, Middles, & Ends*, "What you write in the beginning of your story is intimately connected with the middle, which in turn gives birth to the end." Crafting effective opening and resolution scenes is a complex subject that an entire book on its own could cover. We'll go over them briefly, individually, focusing on the ways they differ from bridge scenes and specific methods for nailing them. However, the basic techniques used in writing these types of scenes, which we'll detail in-depth in the bridge scene section, is essentially the same.

Opening Scenes

Opening scenes introduce characters, plots, and settings, and where the story is going. Writers can take more time unpacking opening scenes than they can anywhere else in the story. The first and last scenes are almost always the ones authors can write with ease in a fully fleshed out way. They already have an "introduction" in their heads (i.e., the spark that inspired the story for them in the first place. And remember what we said in the Introduction: If you don't have a story ripe enough to carry you through the beginning stages of the project, create a story folder to hold all your ideas—more about this in chapter six—and brainstorm on it longer, growing the idea over a solid period of time until it's ready to be worked on). Nancy Kress calls this "the honeymoon": when the author is still in love with whatever gave him the story idea in the first place. With the spark driving him forward, he can frequently write one scene after the other, maybe skipping directly over the bridge scenes after the opening is established, pushing out the resolution scenes that he may also see clearly, until the initial idea is expended.

Compared to the books that were written a hundred years ago, authors are given fewer and fewer words to "get to the point" these days. Whenever I think of a classic that would have been written almost beyond recognition for today's readers, I think of *The War of the Worlds* by H.G. Wells, published in 1898. Here's an explosively exciting theme— the earth being invaded by hostile aliens—that couldn't have started with a more boring introduction (the author, like many authors in that time period, falls into so many aspects of passive writing instead of actively writing a thrilling tale), as witnessed below:

> No one would have believed in the last years of the nineteenth century that this world was being watched keenly and closely by intelligences greater than man's and yet as mortal as his own; that as men busied themselves about their various concerns they were scrutinised and studied, perhaps almost as narrowly as a man with a microscope might scrutinise the transient creatures that swarm and multiply in a drop of water. With infinite complacency men went to and fro over this globe about their little affairs, serene in their assurance of their empire over matter. It is possible that the infusoria under the microscope do the same. No one gave a thought to the older worlds of space as sources of human danger, or thought of them only to dismiss the idea of life upon them as impossible or improbable. It is curious to recall some of the mental habits of those departed days. At most terrestrial men fancied there might be other men upon Mars, perhaps inferior to themselves and ready to welcome a missionary enterprise. Yet across the gulf of space, minds that are to our minds as ours are to those of the beasts that perish, intellects vast and cool and unsympathetic, regarded this earth with envious eyes, and slowly and surely drew their plans against us. And early in the twentieth century came the great disillusionment.

If this book were written today, we would have seen whipsawing action at this invasion—mountains crumbling, buildings crashing down around screaming citizens running for their lives in the growing chaos of the attack, fire lighting the sky. ... But times, and fiction, were different then. And, as unbelievable as it is now, when this story was adapted for a radio broadcast in 1938, it utterly terrified its listeners, who thought the events were real. Can you even imagine?

There's no denying that the first page—specifically the initial 250 words—is your story's make-or-break stage. To give you a startling visual, the paragraph from *The War of the Worlds* above is just under 250 words (it has 231). You can see how frightfully small of an opportunity you have. In these 250 make-or-break words, your reader (whether an editor at a publishing house, literary agent, bookstore browser, the library try-it-before-you-buy-it patron, or the optimistic soul who buys his books by the crate and has a massive home library because he wants to devour life-altering written words that he can go back to over and over again in his lifetime) makes the decision whether to turn the page or to close the book and never open it again. The wisest author advice I've ever heard about writing a killer opening is to assume that the reader is in a terrible mood when he opens your book and, for that reason, you can't let yourself believe you have until page two to win him over. *Engage immediately.* Doing anything else is at your peril.

There are several distinctive methods for starting a story. Many books have started with each of these types, sometimes effectively, sometimes not so much. Below each type of opening, I include a variety of titles of published novels that use the same type of opener, but be aware that some of the examples could fit into more than one type of opener. Because including a full scene for each of the examples would be overwhelming in this book (and not really the point of *Bring Your Fiction to Life*), I've listed titles that you can research on your own either by trying to find excerpts online or checking out the books from your local library. While I have opinions on which ones are most effective, I won't comment. I'll simply leave it for you to evaluate whether you think each case works and/or whether another type of opener would have been stronger.

1) Stolen Prologue

In this opener, the climax scene is pulled out of the middle/end of the book and put at the front as a prologue. A stolen prologue opening can also be an intriguing "future of the present" summary (not word for word, and maybe not told in the nail-biting way it will be shown later) that reveals something that happens much later in the book, in the present. This scenario is intended to give the reader a taste of the biggest, most exciting sequence in the story. Movie producers use this ploy a lot to get a film started with a bang.

Just to be clear, a prologue *per se* isn't what's in question here. It's the "stolen" aspect we're focused on. A strategy like this can work very well, hooking the reader into your story to find out what it all means and/or how it came about. It can also easily become old and contrived. Some authors and readers even consider it cheating, especially if it's not done in a compelling way, or if, once the reader actually gets to that point in the book, the drama of the prologue becomes repetitive instead of compelling.

One reason writers may use this kind of opening scene is because the actual beginning of the story is boring and/or slow (and perhaps they want the editor or agent receiving this submission, the one who will probably read only the first chapter, to read the exciting middle/end of the book instead of the actual snail beginning). If you've set up this kind of opener in your book, ask yourself about your purpose in using it and whether you've done it for a legitimate reason that makes the book stronger. If the sole reason is because the "real" beginning is shaky, you might want to rethink using this as a starting point and pep up the true opener so it does the work it needs to. If the stolen prologue actually works and serves the purpose, go with it.

Examples:

- *Twilight*, Book 1: Twilight Saga by Stephenie Meyer
- *The Bloodmoon Curse*, Book 1: Bloodmoon Cove Spirits Series by Karen Wiesner
- *The Club Dumas* by Arturo Pérez-Reverte
- *LogOut* by J.L. Hansen
- *The Harrowing* by Alexandra Sokoloff
- *Wuthering Heights* by Emily Brontë

2) Information Galore

In this type of introduction, the reader is given a ton of information that sets the premise of the story that follows. This can be written in a variety of ways—in the style of a prologue or synopsis, as a report of some kind, as a military dossier, in the style of a newspaper article, etc. Any of these can have a "true story" conveyance or be tailored to the fictional story about to be told.

Michael Crichton is one author who often started his books with these types of introductions, and he made this method work in whatever way he happened to present the information. For example, in *Jurassic Park*, he opens with a highly scientific and logical introduction detailing the field of biotechnology and genetic engineering in the late twentieth century and how a fictional company, InGen, instigated some sort of "incident" that led the company to file for Chapter 11 bankruptcy in order to protect its interests. This incident is the basis of the book. Crichton's introduction effectively lays the groundwork for instilling a sense of real life into readers before the story truly begins with the fictional incident unfolding from that point on.

There can be very good reasons for using this kind of opener. If the information is actually based on true-life events, but may not fit into the story per se, that doesn't mean it's not important to convey anyway. If it's not based on actual events, then maybe the underlying structure of the information presents a scientific, historical, or some other basis that lends authenticity to the story to follow; hence, the necessity of using this "info galore" delivery system to lay down the premise. This is another situation where asking yourself, "If I take this out altogether, does it damage the credibility of my story?" may be the deciding factor about whether it should be presented this way or cut.

Examples:

- *Eldest*, Book 2: Inheritance Cycle by Christopher Paolini
- *Eaters of the Dead* by Michael Crichton
- "In the Walls of Eryx," a short story by H.P. Lovecraft
- *Riptide* by Douglas Preston and Lincoln Child
- *The Time Machine* by H.G. Wells
- *Jurassic Park* by Michael Crichton

3) Backstory-Dramatized Flashback, Dream, or Flash-Forward

This type of story opening injects a prologue or first chapter with a flashback that takes a pivotal event or memory from a character's past and establishes where the story problem originated, slamming us into the heart of the drama. Another prospect is including a flash-*forward*—an event that happens in the future of the story about to be told. This event is inserted as a prologue. By using this method, you end up with a highly dramatized "real-time" (written as if it's happening in the present, though the reader will find out following the prologue that the scene was actually something pulled from later in the book). A scenario like either of these options potentially supercharges the story, placing the reader into the midst of something emotionally powerful or that has the highest impact or action-packed situation of the book.

In his article "Where to Begin? When, Where and How to Write a Prologue," Lital Talmor talks about the defining moment in the protagonist's past, which must be told to the reader in order for him to understand the character. Talmor goes on to say, "Think how cold and alien Batman would be if we hadn't first seen young Bruce standing bewildered over the bodies of his parents." Giving the reader insight into a character's motivating internal conflicts, stemming from an external conflict, with a flashback, dream, or flash-forward can harness instant intrigue.

Examples:

- *Where the Red Fern Grows* by Wilson Rawls
- *No Greater Loss* by Diane Craver
- *Beneath the Shadows* by Sara Foster
- *Private London* by James Patterson and Mark Pearson
- *Running with the Demon*, Book 1: The Word & The Void Series by Terry Brooks
- *The Historian* by Elizabeth Kostova

4) Change She Is A-Comin'

This type of opening establishes the main character's world *as it is*. The beginning is a normal, ordinary, average-day viewpoint just before "the inciting incident" descends and tears everything apart. Depending on the genre of your story and whether the opening is done right, this method can be intriguing. If your character loves her life as is, this is probably the world she wants to get back to before she was so rudely interrupted by the external conflict. This can really resonate at the end of the book, because the reader will remember the world before so vividly.

This kind of opener can also be slow, indulgent, leisurely ... and sometimes incredibly boring, if there's not enough interest to grip the reader's imagination. As you're writing your "change is coming" opening, if you feel you're struggling to get into the story, your readers probably will, too.

Examples:

- *Divergent*, Book 1: Divergent Trilogy by Veronica Roth
- *Craving a Hero*, Book 3: St. John Sibling Series by Barbara Raffin
- *The Ruins* by Scott Smith
- *Mrs. McGinty's Dead* by Agatha Christie
- *The Physick Book of Deliverance Dane* by Katherine Howe
- *Girl with a Pearl Earring* by Tracy Chevalier

5) Here's Johnny

I can't remember where I heard this quote, but a writer said, "Don't waste time—begin the story at the last possible moment." While this always makes me laugh, because the two images presented are contradictory, that's what this method is all about. Get to the point with your opening, yes, but start where something crazy and exciting is happening. Whatever conflict or inciting incident catapults your story should be present from the first sentence and, from there, bust up everything the main character knows and loves; nothing will ever be the same.

By jumping into the action of the current story at the precise moment and time of the inciting incident, the writer doesn't have a lot of time to establish the facts of character, plot, and setting. This method requires a great deal of master-storytelling acrobatics to get everything that needs to be included in the opener precisely when and where the story (and the reader) needs them to be. Note (because you may wonder in seeking out some of the examples I've included), this can be written as a prologue of any kind.

While not every story is so action packed that a T-Rex razes a swatch of destruction in the main character's path as it sweeps through the area, the intensity of this kind of conflict-laden opener is ideal for every story, regardless of genre. In context of your story's tone, you have to work hard to suck the reader in with a skillfully developed punch of action that gives the who-what-where-when-why succinctly, effectively, and instantly so the pages fly by and the real world goes all but unnoticed by the reader.

Examples:

- *The Maze Runner*, Book 1: Maze Runner Series by James Dashner
- *A Familiar Evil* by Anne Patrick
- *Dark Rising*, Book 2: Alex Hunter Series by Greig Beck
- *The Da Vinci Code*, Book 1: Robert Langdon Series by Dan Brown
- *Magic Kingdom for Sale—Sold!*, Book 1: Magic Kingdom of Landover Series by Terry Brooks
- *The Intrigue at Highbury (Or, Emma's Match)*, Book 5: A Mr. & Mrs. Darcy Mystery by Carrie Bebris

Tips for Sharp Opening Scenes:

- Carefully consider and craft your hook—the opening line of your book. This pivotal sentence should either contain or suggest the end of your story. That first line should resonate throughout the book, parallel and/or reflect the resolution, and maybe even tie into the final sentence. Additionally, the first scene of your book sets the tone for the entire book, always, and establishes a premise for more of the same. If you're writing an edge-of-the-seat, nail-biting adventure, then a leisurely, coming-of-age opening can only lead to disorienting disappointment. This isn't to say that a slow beginning that hints at more action later isn't perfectly acceptable (e.g., *Divergent* by Veronica Roth). But that hint toward impacting action is crucial to ensuring reader acceptance and satisfaction. Your first sentences should intrigue or raise curiosity about the story throughout the opening scenes. James Scott Bell advises asking yourself, "Who cares?" and "What's the purpose?" to ensure validity and clarify the reason for each scene even existing. Progression is vital from one scene to the next. If something is actually happening, the reader will be patient for more, with a sense of anticipation rather than frustration.

- Unless executed extremely well, scenery and climate openings that are highly descriptive may actually distance the reader instead of engage her. Remember what we said earlier about how even the most breathtaking setting is barren without the character to give it context and purpose? Keep that in mind with any portion of your opening scenes that begins with setting "establishing shots," which in movie language are the first shots of any new scene, are the ones that show the audience where the action will take place.

- Be wary about opening on a scene littered with several characters. Too many characters confuse instead of hook readers. Three characters should be the maximum in your first scene. (I would also advise limiting the number of characters in *any* scene in your book. It's too easy to lose the main character in a party of others.) Judiciously choose the starring characters and the vital roles they'll play in your scenes.

- There is such a thing as too much action in the opening scenes. If the reader can't orient himself to what's going on, who it's happening to, and/or why it's important, he'll throw himself off the spinning globe or just plain close his eyes. If you want to see a shockingly visual disorientation of this kind in an opening scene, try watching *Quantum of Solace*, Daniel Craig's second time out as James Bond. I felt physically dizzy, and a little nauseous, during the first fifteen minutes or so of the opening action in which the viewers are taken on the most neck-breaking, gorge-rising car chase of their lives. (You may have noticed that we've included the trinity of story elements in the last three tips: character, plot, and setting. You need to include each equally in your opening scenes without going overboard on any one in order to create the right balance. Not easy, but practice and revision will help you hone this skill.)

- Use the opening scenes to get into the main characters' heads and hearts while simultaneously dragging the reader into the immediate problems. If the reader doesn't have a strong desire to invest emotionally in the characters from the very first scenes, he won't care what happens next, let alone how everything is resolved.

- Your story beginning promises a certain ending. Follow through on the expectations established from the first page of the book (which isn't to say you can't have a surprise twist at the end—more on that in the next section). Author Randy Susan Meyers says, "I believe the writer has a covenant with [readers]. You provide the best possible stories—they will bring you into their heart[s]. And, come the day you separate, the moment it's time to say goodbye, do you want to break their heart[s]? Or do you want them to sigh, close the book with regret that it's over, and think how they can't wait for your next novel?" You want your readers to be completely satisfied with each and every book you write, not only so they'll reread each, but also so they'll put you on their must-buy list and tell all their friends about you.

You'll find a blank worksheet for crafting your opening scene in Appendix A. The only thing different about this particular worksheet than the ones that follow is the first part, the "Opening Setup." Here you'll establish the "when" of the story from the viewpoint of a reader who knows absolutely nothing thus far. Everything we've talked about in this section concerning methods and tips for introducing characters, plots, and settings comes into play in the setup opening you'll have in your own story.

Resolution Scenes

The first and last scenes are almost always the ones authors may write with ease, in a fully fleshed out way. The spark that inspired the story for him sometimes comes built in with the ending already formed. In

J.K. Rowling's case, the Harry Potter story simply dropped into her head on a four-hour train ride. Before publication of the final book in the Harry Potter Series, when asked by a reporter, Rowling stated she couldn't change the ending even if she wanted to. "These books have been plotted for such a long time, and for six books now, that they're all leading a certain direction." She has said that the last chapter of the book was written "in something like 1990" (it was published in 2007), as part of her earliest work on the series. Rowling has also said that "early on I knew I wanted Harry to believe he was walking toward his death, but would survive."

Your opening scenes always introduce an "implicit promise" (as Nancy Kress calls it) to the reader. If you don't deliver what you've promised within your first scene by the time your story ends, you've stolen time, money, and even reader emotions, all with a careless shrug of purposeful neglect. Kress says, "The ending dramatizes the triumph of some of the forces developed in the middle, which, in turn, were set in motion by the characters and conflict introduced in the beginning." Your ending requires that the reader be given what's needed to feel satisfied that that implicit promise made at the beginning has been fulfilled.

To that end, there are a handful of rules that govern the end of a story, and these are all but written in stone by authors and writing instructors. I'll include a list of published novels with killer endings (by no means a definitive list) at the end of this section.

1) The Leading Lady (or Man) Leads

The main character leads the action and saves the day. She's not in a supporting role, nor can she be rescued when the going gets tough. She can't fall backwards into success. This is her story, her time to be a superhero, her moment in the spotlight. Never allow resolutions to stem from symbolism, events, or other people; she must solve her own problems. Failing to do so is sometimes referred to as "coincidence resolution." While you can have a plot that begins this way, the coincidence must fade to be replaced with very clear choices, purpose, and action. Something similar to the coincidence resolution is the *deus ex machina*—"god from a machine"–ending. This device introduces a resolution brought about by something outside the story, something cataclysmic or even supernatural that's not cohesive—basically, anything illogical introduced at the end of the story to resolve a central conflict. You can't wrap up a story with an act of nature, something symbolic that parallels a character's conflict but isn't actually part of it, or in a stranger-to-the-rescue type of event—it won't be believable or fair to the reader, who's spent the entire novel waiting to see your character reach the goals of self-fulfillment and success.

That triumph also has to be hard-won. She'll probably have a face full of bruises and a heart of pain that will haunt her until the day she dies, but those scars are also ones she can wear proudly. In *Writing Fantasy Heroes: Powerful Advice from the Pros (Rogue Blades Presents)*, we learn, "Great heroes have flaws. If a hero is perfect, invulnerable, then he is free of challenge and also free of honor. What is effortless is not honorable; difficulty wins glory and brings the hero to life." Don't take the true victory away from your main character by letting anyone or anything else do the work for her.

2) There's No Place Like Home (But I Still Love Visiting Oz!)

The main character has to change based on the story experience. She can't be the same person she was when she started. She can't settle back into her same life, though she may return to the place she started. She's changed—her core self has altered in a way that changes all her perceptions. What the character has gone through has produced a life-changing effect on her, and the way she views the world has been transformed. In resolution, this character may find contentment and/or balance in her life, but never the same groove she was in previously. Most readers hope that the change will lead to a "happily-ever-after," but it doesn't have to, if something just short or extreme fits better.

Also remember that this change can't be evidenced only by word of mouth—the reader must be able to see the change in a way that shows that the character is actively a changed person. If you want a bold example of this, remember that Ebenezer Scrooge didn't simply think about how different he felt the morning after his encounters with the ghosts. When he realized he had a second chance to be a good person, he ran around his frigidly cold bedroom in his nightdress, dancing. He bought the prized turkey for Bob Cratchit, raised Bob's salary, and assisted him in caring for his family—ultimately becoming a second father to Bob's son Tiny Tim. Scrooge donated to the poor. He built a relationship with his nephew. The changed man is joyfully leaping off the last pages of the story, and the reader doesn't doubt for a second that it'll stick. Not all stories need such a dramatic moment of change, of course. The end of your story may be much more subtle, but you must allow the reader to at least see a glimpse of this change.

In fiction, true change and growth should come from strength within, just as it does in real life. How radical that evolution is will depend on many factors; but without character growth there's absolutely no reason for the story to have been told in the first place.

3) Finish What You Started

How your story ends is essentially a reward to your reader for taking the journey with you. James Scott Bell says, "You want to leave your readers with a last page that makes the ending more than satisfying. You want it to be memorable, to stay with readers after the book is closed. ... Your audience will judge your book largely by the feeling that they have most recently, namely, *the end*. Leave a lasting impression and you will build a readership."

That said, a happy ending is never promised or required. On her website, Australian-American author Justine Larbalestier talks about one such book that didn't have a happy ending: "I recently read *House of Mirth* by Edith Wharton for the first time and I was gutted. Unlike, most US-*ians*, who've at least some inkling of what to expect from a Wharton book, I had zero expectations or, rather, zero correct expectations. So, I went into the *House of Mirth* blind, like a lamb to the slaughter. Let me tell you: There was NO mirth. It was the bleakest most horrible ending imaginable. And the awfulness started about halfway through the book, which is when I first started weeping. But it kept getting worse. And worse and even worse. Until it had the worst ending of all time and I was crying so hard, snot was pouring out of my nose. ... Have I mentioned that it's a wonderful book? That Wharton is a brilliant writer?"

While you want your readers to leave satisfied, in no way, shape, or form are you promising at any point that a *happily-ever-after* is in the offing. There's a difference between a satisfying ending and the happy ending. K.M. Weiland, writer and mentor, assures, "Readers won't hate you for writing a sad story (although, granted, not all of them will be ready or willing to stomach it). In fact, if you execute it properly, you have the opportunity to leave an impression they'll carry with them all through their lives." Some genres do have certain requirements about happy endings, such as romances and most children's books, but not all writers have this obligation. Author E.A. Hill even adds two more things authors don't "owe" by telling their stories: "They don't owe annihilation of all evil. They don't owe restoration for every injustice faced by their characters."

4) The Lazy or Esoteric Bowing Out Before "The End"

Frank R. Stockton leaves it up to the reader to decide which came out of the door—the lady or the tiger—at the end of his novel, *The Lady, or the Tiger?* This is the inspiration behind what writers dub a "Lady and the Tiger" ending. While some love this kind of ending, a few would call this type of resolution a cop-out.

All loose ends must be tied up adequately in your story—preferably without rehashing every step in dragged-out, tedious detail. I personally believe these kinds of unfinished stories are written for the sole purpose of making the author and/or select readers feel superior about knowing something other, lesser minds don't and can't grasp. Not providing satisfactory resolutions violates the contract between the writer and the reader, forcing the reader to do without an effective tie-up of some or all story threads. I also suspect the authors did this because they simply *wanted* to leave the resolution of the story arc mysterious and unanswered. They either didn't have a good resolution planned, or they wanted to contain the mystery indefinitely. For example, we never did get a straight answer about what really happened to Mulder's sister in *X-Files*—not in nine seasons nor a couple movies (nor did I get the definitive answer in the miniseries that aired in January 2016).

If the author is never going to answer a nagging question, why invest anything, especially time and passion, in the story? Leaving a story thread dangling isn't something an author can do without making readers furious, perhaps enough to refuse to read your books for life. They'll feel cheated, and rightly so. Don't underestimate the damage a vengeful reader can do to your career. (Have you read Stephen King's *Misery*, where the writer's number one fan kidnaps him and keeps him captive at her home until he—properly, by her standards—rewrites the ending of the series he's famous for?) To write a story is to promise the closure and/or resolution of unanswered questions.

The author is vital in creating three-dimensional characters because the story people you create will have *your* unique spin, *your* originality, a tiny sliver of *your* essence, and those characters can't exist without *you*. In the same way, the end of your story doesn't and can't exist without you—*your* individual viewpoint. So don't cheat your reader by being lazy and avoiding the provision of an actual ending complete with answers to all burning questions.

5) The Perfect Payoff

In *Plot & Structure*, James Scott Bell says, "… almost all great jokes are built on a structure of three—the setup, the body, and the payoff." Stories are no different with the beginning, middle, and end. Specifically, all story endings must be logical, with a sense of inevitability. Everything's been leading up to your closer, regardless of red herrings, artful concealments, and delaying tactics. But is the ending warranted and utterly logical? Does it fit what you've been promising the reader from the beginning as the payoff for coming along for the ride? Endings should always require a "the only way it could end" declaration, but that doesn't mean they can't (and shouldn't) be surprising, too (see the "Tips for Resolution Scenes" section for incorporating endings with a cool shocker). There's a big difference between a twist (where the reader is stunned, speechless, gratefully overjoyed) and a trick (where the reader feels cheated, the victim of a bait and switch, unforgivably incensed).

Steven Pressman says in his article "Setups and Payoffs," "If the payoff is really good, we realize, in the end, that there was no surprise at all. What had seemed to be a turn of fate proves to be inevitable and, as we realize it, we receive the gift of insight. We should have seen it coming!"

Maybe you can't please everyone with your story ending, but you should at the very least satisfy them with a coherent conclusion. In Victoria Grossack's Crafting Fabulous Fiction column, her article "The End" states, "Those who are perpetually disgruntled may at least concede that the end suits the story."

Tips for Resolution Scenes:

- In the back of your mind, at every point in the storytelling, should be the fact that the end of your story is where you're going. You're continuously building toward the wrap-up. Your direction is crucial because, as we said about openings, your story beginning should resonate throughout the rest of the book. It should match up with the resolution and may even tie into the final sentence. The end grounds and justifies the whole of the story.
- A twist can turn a predictable (sometimes even inevitable) ending into one that slaps the smug smile right off the reader's face, and this is the one situation where the reader would be thrilled about it. Adding twists to your stories makes for an exciting read, because the author effectively leads the reader to believe one thing (that *also* makes perfectly logical and cohesive sense) while completely turning the tables at the last minute. Putting a twist into your story is a surefire way to make a suspenseful story into a nail-biting one. Ask yourself, *What's the most shocking thing I could have happen? What is the reader absolutely not expecting?* For a twist to be believable, it must be set up from the very beginning. Resolutions need to fit perfectly with every angle this twist presents. Think about the book (and the movie, which is just as good) *Presumed Innocent*, by Scott Turow. If you haven't read or watched this before, I encourage you to do it at your earliest opportunity. The twist at the end utterly haunted me for years afterward. The truth was there before

my eyes the whole time, yet I never saw it, and it punched me in the stomach brutally when it came. A twist is so breathtaking because it comes out of nowhere (despite the fact that the reader will have to concede that all the evidence was there from the start), and it satisfies the reader more than a predictable, inevitable outcome ever can. *Always* look for the unexpected twist ending in your stories because it'll make your closing so memorable. In some cases, the twist may be the very thing the reader wanted to happen but didn't dare let himself hope for.

- Most story endings are inevitable, as I just pointed out; however, if you're not certain how your story should end, consider writing alternate endings and presenting them to your critique partners or beta readers. While the final choice about how you end your story is your own, at the very least, other possible scenarios may narrow your focus on the heart and theme of your story and how it should tie up.

- Should you have an epilogue (not necessarily "the end" so much as "at the end")? Epilogues usually amount to resolution details beyond the ending. Answering this question depends a lot on genre and necessity, and there are some very good reasons to have one … along with some reasons to avoid it. In a romance novel, there's no question that there has to be a happily-ever-after scene following the climax (forgive the pun). If your story requires some kind of settling of details to ensure reader satisfaction, then it absolutely needs to be there. If the epilogue is required to open the door for another book in the series, don't hesitate to include it. But an epilogue that "hovers like a bad hangover" or sounds like you're "writing another novel," as Edward C. Patterson so eloquently describes, may not be worth including. Is there a point to the main character sitting in the sun and contemplating all she's been through? There's also some question whether parlor mysteries require an obligatory, ten-minute denouement. Many readers like to see the genius unraveled in this way. But how enjoyable is the unveiling? Additionally, did you spin out a grueling, four-hundred-page saga only to offer an anticlimactic, two-paragraph resolution? What fits the story? Is there anything left to say? In many cases, it's better to go out with a bang than a *will-it-ever-end?* drone.

- It's the *final*, not always the *first*, impression that will bear lasting judgment. Your story endings should always be memorable, if not earth shattering. The reader should feel that every minute of his time in your world—putting off, giving up, or altogether missing other things—was well spent. Make the reader exit with a sense of wonder. Give him a passionate desire to reread the book in the future.

- While it's been said the opening sentence can make or break the book, the ending is what makes or breaks *the author*. When you write the ending of your book, your main concern must always be for the reader and his level of satisfaction: *Was the journey I'm asking a reader to take worth the time and money he invested in it?* No author would want a reader to finish his book by saying, "It was good, but I didn't like the way it ended." That sentiment turns what was originally a potential fan into someone who avoids your work at all cost because you let him down. As David Villalva says, the end of your story isn't just the turning point of the story—it's the turning point between you and your audience. "This key milestone is where you reward audiences in dramatic fashion for sticking around. It's where your audience decides whether or not they'll commit to your next story. Have you ever finished a story and immediately sought out everything else put out by its creator?" If that's not your ultimate goal as an author, I don't know what is.

A Short List of Books with (Arguably) Killer Resolutions
(in no particular order):

- *The Lord of the Rings* by J.R.R. Tolkien
- *Jane Eyre* by Charlotte Brontë
- *Imposter* by Philip K. Dick
- *The Fall of the House of Usher* by Edgar Allan Poe

- *Gone with the Wind* by Margaret Mitchell
- *The Great Gatsby* by F. Scott Fitzgerald
- *A Tale of Two Cities* by Charles Dickens
- *It* by Stephen King
- *To Kill a Mockingbird* by Harper Lee
- *Charlotte's Web* by E.B. White
- *The Wonderful Wizard of Oz* by L. Frank Baum
- *I Am Legend* by Richard Matheson
- *Frankenstein* by Mary Shelley
- *Les Misérables* by Victor Hugo
- *Emma* by Jane Austen

In Appendix A, you'll find a blank worksheet for crafting your resolution scene. The only thing different about this particular worksheet than the ones that come before is the last part, the "Tie-Ups and Resolutions." Here you'll resolve all conflicts from the viewpoint of a reader who expects you to keep the promise you made when you started the story. Everything we've talked about in this section concerning rules and payoffs in resolution comes into play in the ending you'll have in your own story.

Bridge Scenes

In his novel *Spidersilk*, Akutra-Ramses Atenosis Cea includes this line: "The painted picture ... seemed eerily real as if there actually was a way to step through it into the wild jungle. ..." Isn't this a beautiful picture of how compelling words can draw readers into a story? However, the work of writing a scene so vividly that readers actually feel like they're inside it is no easy task. The last thing a writer wants is readers looking at his story from afar, or worse, a "fast travel" moment where readers are unceremoniously dumped in the center of a dark, bleak island that has no bridge or boat on any side and no roadmap to tell them where they are, how they got there, why they've been dropped there so rudely, or what happens now. At first, this might be exciting, but when the reader becomes aware he's trapped with nowhere to go because the basic grasp of scene setup hasn't been created, disappointment and surrender are inevitable.

Essentially, the difference between opening and bridge scenes can be described in this "fast-travel" way. Those of you who play video games will understand what "fast travel" is. In older games, there was no way—or only limited means—of doing this. Every single time you visited a destination, you had to find it again—essentially, whatever you went through to get to that place the first time, you had to go through each and every time you wanted to go to that location. It required the same travel every time. Needless to say, playing a game like this can become very tedious. (For a mind-boggling crash course in this, play *The Elder Scrolls: Morrowind*, in which the only means of fast travel are a few intervention spells and the propylon chambers, provided you'd collected all the indexes.) In modern games, developers have invented a mode of fast travel, in which, once an area of the overall game map has been discovered, the character is allowed to travel back to that location in the future without the hassle he went through the first time. This is a lot like what needs to happen in a book. New locations must be discovered (detailed and described in-depth) at the opening of a story or when they're first introduced, but familiar locations don't require such an elaborate setup after the initial visit.

Hands down, the middle bridge scenes are the trickiest to develop because the majority of your story unfolds within them, and that has to happen with ideal pacing. Every bridge scene should show a realistic, vivid picture of the story landscape *within the first few paragraphs* and *as succinctly as possible* such that the reader can step into it right alongside the main character and feel informed and eager for the next plot development. Until the scene is established sufficiently, the reader can't enter, let alone be transported, there without unfortunate repercussions.

Each bridge scene has to meet three basic requirements:

1. **ESTABLISH THE THREE-DIMENSIONAL CHARACTERS** (especially the POV character) you worked so hard to develop.

2. **ADVANCE THE PLOT.** In his book *How to Write Dazzling Dialogue: The Fastest Way to Improve Any Manuscript*, James Scott Bell says, "Be clear on every character's agenda in a scene, and the agendas in conflict. Before you write, take just a moment to jot down what each character in the scene wants, even if (as Kurt Vonnegut once said) it is only a glass of water."

   If the scene doesn't have a clear purpose in progressing the story, it needs to be questioned. Nancy Kress says of middle scenes, "Like Dante [in writing *The Inferno*], [the writer] becomes overwhelmed. Things look dense, savage, and harsh. Paths disappear. Guidelines don't seem to offer enough guidance." Having three dimensions of character, plot, and setting are crucial to advancing a story through the middle scenes.

3. **CONSTRUCT THE SETTING.** Readers must be led through the story world step by step with information that first anchors, then orients, and finally allows them to move forward with a sense of anticipation. Scenes can't really function without time and place being indicated early (and concisely) enough so your reader doesn't become lost, looking to establish where he is, was, and where he's going.

Ensuring that all of these requirements are accomplished in each scene in a creative, non-info-dump way isn't for the faint of heart, and might demand a lot of revision. But the harder readers have to work to orient themselves, the easier it becomes to set down the book, possibly for good.

The three basics to scene setup we established aren't all that's needed. The secret to writing three-dimensional bridge scenes is that all must set *up* before they can set *out* to tell their crucial piece of the story. In real life, a bridge has two sides and both must be firmly anchored to something tangible to successfully function. But your goal isn't simply to get your characters from Point A to Point B. Scenes have to connect, join, fuse, and be secured in such an intrinsic way that they flow from start to finish, one to the next, in a natural progression. The secret to providing scenes that anchor and orient readers, and lead them with purpose throughout your story landscape, always with a whisper of what's to come, is twofold:

1. **CONNECT THE BRIDGE FROM ONE SCENE TO THE NEXT SEAM-LESSLY.** You can use this method for all the scenes in your book, because the technique is the same from one to the next. The only difference is that in the very first scene of the book (the opening scene), you're starting from the viewpoint of the reader knowing *nothing* about what came before—hence the need for more room and clever acts of brevity that introduce the story elements of character, plot, and setting. Opening scenes are not the place to write long, boring, overwhelming details and explanations for every character, place and scenario, but, in the beginning when you're telling your story, you are introducing brand new characters, settings and situations. Therefore, it will take more time and words to establish all of these to clearly illuminate the reader's path forward without strewing the path with obstacles or hurdles that do nothing but block the way. You want to include just enough to set up and establish characters, settings and situations. Opening scenes allow us more space to do that because you're starting from the very beginning, and these initial chapters need to show readers the five W's (who, what, where, when, why). I remember reading the opening chapters of a story for a critique partner once, and I was literally dumped in the middle of the woods and watching from shadows as this man skulked around a house—a house which I was never told was his own. I was also never told that the person inside the house was an illegal squatter. I couldn't find the point of anything, kept getting lost and frustrated as the scenes played out around me without any explanation. Knowing those few crucial details would have made everything else come into sharp focus, but the author had been erroneously told that she shouldn't give away basic details like that at the beginning of a scene because it would kill the action. I don't deny that there was high action, but none of it made the slightest bit of sense without basic context. There's nothing worse than dropping a reader in the middle of nowhere in the dark of night and he isn't given enough details to

figure out where he is, what's going on, and who this character running ahead of him in the darkness is. In the same way that the first step in using a microscope is to focus the lens, we need to provide the focus for characters, settings and plots in our opening scenes.

2. **EXTEND THE BRIDGE INTO THE NEXT SCENE.** What you're doing here is foreshadowing future events (the future dimension we discussed earlier). Victoria Lynn Schmidt describes this as "making the reader wonder what could possibly happen next, without making [him] incredulous after it happens." Obviously, extending the bridge toward the next scene won't be done in the opening paragraphs but closer to the end of the scene. As we said about an opening scene, the difference with resolution scenes is that they should tie up all the story threads while leaving a satisfactory sense of finality, rather than making the reader question what happens next.

Doing these two things is something that takes a lot of practice to master, since you don't want an opening with a recap like "Last time in our story …" let alone a transitional punch in the face from recap to the current story, such as: "And that brings us to the present …" Nor do you want to leave your reader hanging, wondering if your story is actually going anywhere. The reader needs to dread/hope about future events, or he won't care to keep reading. Unfortunately, there is no magical formula that translates the five W's into wonderfully written prose, since you definitely don't want each scene to be set up exactly like the last. As Chuck Wendig eloquently describes in *The Kick-Ass Writer*: "Sometimes a scene needs something that completely changes the landscape of the story. Every scene can't have a bunker-buster plot moment … but sometimes you'll get the sense in a scene that it's time to take a sharp right turn—shatter the guardrail, leap off the highway, and drive off into an entirely unexpected direction. Don't fear this. Allow the scene to execute in a surprising way."

Preparation (and a blank worksheet, included in Appendix A) should do the trick of ensuring we get all of this sketched out early so, when it comes time to write and revise the story, we produce prose with an efficiency of words that's creative and innovate in transporting informed, eager readers into full-fledged dimensionality of story. The worksheet you'll find in Appendix A is presented across three pages to differentiate between opening, bridge and resolution scenes.

A simple three-dimensional scene worksheet that covers the most crucial aspects would include the following:

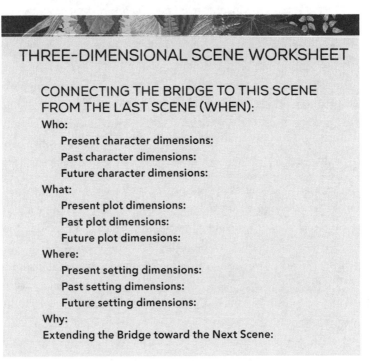

THREE-DIMENSIONAL SCENE WORKSHEET

CONNECTING THE BRIDGE TO THIS SCENE FROM THE LAST SCENE (WHEN):

Who:
    Present character dimensions:
    Past character dimensions:
    Future character dimensions:

What:
    Present plot dimensions:
    Past plot dimensions:
    Future plot dimensions:

Where:
    Present setting dimensions:
    Past setting dimensions:
    Future setting dimensions:

Why:

Extending the Bridge toward the Next Scene:

A note about the dimensions listed on the worksheet: While I've inserted the P/P/F character, plot, and setting dimensions in specific places on the worksheet that make the most sense, there's absolutely no need for you to relegate them to those spaces. If you find they fit better elsewhere on the worksheet for each scene in your book, feel free to mix them up. You'll see a section for *present* dimensions under all three of the *who, what,* and *where* sections, but remember that this worksheet is for your own use. If there's some overlap and your P/P/F Dimensions spill into the other sections of the worksheet, that's perfectly fine. The point in including them here, and in your own projects, is to make sure you include something for each dimension of character, plot, and setting. You don't need to be concerned if any of the dimensions end up in totally different parts of the worksheet than where they're laid out in the template. As long as you include something for each dimension, it doesn't matter where it ultimately ends up. Also, not everything on the worksheet will make it into your written draft(s) of the book. You're including it so you have the big picture of core elements of story in all dimensions.

You may be asking yourself, *Do I really need to have a present, past, and future dimension in every scene?* The answer is yes. The only real issue here is *how much* each scene needs of each. Every scene will have different requirements because, as we said, the last thing you want is every scene to be just like the last one. The worksheet is laid out in a way that ensures three-dimensionality.

Your present dimension is the current situation. What's happening in the now? This may encompass most of the five W's. The past dimension will reach back to what happened before the prevalent story, drawing out character, plot, and setting developments and revelations to enhance the present. Again, any section of the worksheet could cover this, and how much of each worksheet you use will be different for every scene. Don't worry about overlap or filling in too much. In tagging your future dimension, you're looking ahead to lead the reader to dread/hope for what might happen. All areas of the worksheet may have future dimensions included, but especially the "Extending the Bridge toward the Next Scene" section— obviously, the whole point of that section is looking ahead. While some scenes won't have huge amounts of one or more of these dimensions, your scenes should have at least a hint of each. Give yourself the full picture, and make sure you don't neglect the reader's necessary dread/hope response from one scene to the next. Without it, he won't be immersed in your story.

Another point that you might be wondering about at this juncture is when to fill out this worksheet. I'm a big believer that every single story should be outlined before it's written. That's my modus operandi every single time, and it's not something I would ever want to grow out of because it's the only way to be sure I have a solid story before I ever write a word. Chapter six will go over the "ideal" scenario of writing in stages for completing a book, but that is very much the acme. New writers or those who aren't willing to work with an outline in any form can still use the three-dimensional writing method, which is why I put that content near the end of this book instead of at the beginning. Chapter six is specifically geared toward career and/or highly disciplined, professional writers who want a great deal of structure and discipline in their approach to writing. Beginning authors may find it easier to fill out this worksheet after they've started or finished writing their books and want to figure out if they're on the right track with their dimensions. For an author who prefers to begin with some kind of a roadmap, filling the worksheet out for each scene in the book *before* he starts writing will allow him to build in three-dimensionality well in advance of committing the story to a first draft that ultimately isn't strong enough.

Let's break out each section of this worksheet to facilitate examination. Since we've already gone over opening and resolution scenes, our focus here will be on bridge scenes. The blank Three-Dimensional Scene Worksheet in Appendix A has three pages. Page 1 is for the "opener" and Page 3 is for "resolution" scenes. The middle worksheet covers bridge scenes, and you'll be able to carry the information you'll learn here into the set-up and resolution scene sections of the worksheet. Remember, you need one separate "middle" worksheet for each scene of your book between the opening and closing scenes. So, if you're writing a novel, you may need twenty-five or more worksheets, depending on your finished number of scenes.

In our discussion of the sections on this worksheet, I'll include the "Dark Places" examples that we started in previous chapters. This will be most similar to your own worksheets after you've filled them out. I've also included the more detailed examples for each section from *A Christmas Carol*. Since many of these elements in that book aren't written in any kind of order within the actual story, I've speculated based on assumptions made from the actual text in my examples, as well as arranged the elements in the best way to make sense of them.

Connecting the Bridge to this Scene from the Last (When)

In previous chapters, we've established that modern novels may have more than one or two main characters in addition to many, many other supporting characters, all of whom have individual POV scenes throughout the course of the story. Because of this, it's even more important to anchor the reader with the basic setup that orients him from one scene to the next.

Establish the "when" in this section by alluding to what's happened previously (hopefully, without being annoyingly repetitive or long-winded—though that only matters in story drafts, not on the work-sheets), and get the reader up to speed for what's about to happen in this scene. For bridge scenes, it's vitally important that you give a definable sense of how much time has passed since this particular POV character's last scene. I remember reading a scene in an unpublished novel once in which I was given no information about how long it'd been since the previous scene took place. When I later (I no longer cared to know, I was so frustrated with the story) found out that it'd been *months* since the previous scene, I was jolted out of the story. How much time has passed since the last scene needs to be stated upfront, either succinctly, or written in such a way that the amount of time that's passed is assumed within the first few paragraphs of the scene.

Our example to connect this scene from the last:

"DARK PLACES"

Connecting the Bridge to this Scene from the Last: The night before, Jason made the monumental decision to ask Sharon, his partner on the police department as well as his on-again, off-again love interest, to take another chance on him. He's planned the whole evening, he's nervous, probably acting like a skittish cat expecting a dog to appear any second. But somehow Sharon ignores that when he asks her in the coffee area of the police department, and she agrees to have dinner at his apartment after work.

A CHRISTMAS CAROL

Connecting the Bridge to this Scene from the Last: "When Scrooge awoke, it was so dark, that looking out of bed, he could scarcely distinguish the transparent window from the opaque walls of his chamber. He was endeavouring to pierce the darkness with his ferret eyes, when the chimes of a neighbouring church struck the four quarters. So he listened for the hour. To his great astonishment the heavy bell went on from six to seven, and from seven to eight, and regularly up to twelve; then stopped. Twelve! It was past two when he went to bed. The clock was wrong. An icicle must have got into the works. Twelve!"

Who

You should have only one main character per scene and this is the only character you can get inside the head of for this scene. Does anyone really want to hear me get on my soapbox (again) about the evils of head hopping? I didn't think so. In this section, include the POV character's name, along with the names of other story characters in the scene for the second section. In this orientation, only concern yourself with characters that play a vital role in the scene.

"DARK PLACES"

Who: Jason Delaney

    Present character dimensions: He tells Sharon that he wants to have a normal relationship with her, not simply as detective partners, but romantically. His mother calls to tell him an eight-year-old boy has been kidnapped in his hometown, and he knows there may be a connection to his own kidnapping, since the scenario is similar and his captor was never identified or caught. He can't allow another child to go through what he did.

    Past character dimensions: As an eight-year-old child, Jason was kidnapped and held captive in the woods for a period of ten days until he was rescued. This horrible event is what led him to vow to become strong, never become a victim again, and to do everything in his power to help other kids who go through this. His past set him on his career path. He started in the Marines right out of high school and excelled, but ultimately chose to go into law enforcement after his discharge.

Future character dimensions: Jason's mother calls him, and he's just asked Sharon to give him another try, so he tries to get his mom off the phone … and then she tells him the devastating news that another eight-year-old boy has been kidnapped in his hometown. He has to act. Nothing else is as important.

Additional character in scene: Sharon.

A CHRISTMAS CAROL

Who: "Scrooge went to bed again, and thought, and thought, and thought it over and over and over, and could make nothing of it. The more he thought, the more perplexed he was; and the more he endeavoured not to think, the more he thought." [*present plot dimensions*]

"Marley's Ghost bothered him exceedingly. Every time he resolved within himself, after mature inquiry, that it was all a dream, his mind flew back again, like a strong spring released, to its first position, and presented the same problem to be worked all through, 'Was it a dream or not?'" [*past plot dimensions*]

"Scrooge lay in this state until the chime had gone three quarters more, when he remembered, on a sudden, that the Ghost had warned him of a visitation when the bell tolled one. He resolved to lie awake until the hour was passed; and, considering that he could no more go to sleep than go to Heaven, this was perhaps the wisest resolution in his power." [*future plot dimensions*]

Additional characters in scene: Ghost of Christmas Past.

What

Establish what the main character and supporting characters are doing physically, mentally, or in any other manner at the time the scene opens. This section could easily be confused with the "Why?" section, and there's no reason that should disturb you, since the worksheet is for your own use. The fact is that *what* and *why* are two sides of the same coin. Don't worry about overlap, or if they aren't clearly defined, so long as you have something in each section to guide you. Also don't worry if any of your dimensions end up in different areas of the worksheet than they've been relegated. The point is that each dimension is given a place. Where it ends up ultimately doesn't matter.

"DARK PLACES"

What: Jason hangs up and all thoughts about getting back together with Sharon are gone. She asks him what's wrong.

Present plot dimensions: Jason tells her a boy has been kidnapped in his hometown.

Past plot dimensions: While Jason was rescued from his kidnapping as a child, this didn't happen until the damage had been done. He endured mental and physical abuse at the hands of his kidnapper, who was always masked, speaking in a whisper—and whom he's never been able to identify and the police in his hometown were unable to identify.

Future plot dimensions: Jason is motivated to find the missing boy before he's harmed. His kidnapper spent the first half of his captivity trying to befriend him—but Jason had refused to capitulate. The abuse had started after that. So there's a chance he can rescue this boy before he's physically harmed.

A CHRISTMAS CAROL

What: Scrooge lay in a stunned state until a ghostly hand drew the curtains of his bed aside. Starting up into a half-recumbent attitude, he found himself face to face with the unearthly visitor of "a child's proportions." "From the crown of its head there sprung a bright clear jet of light, by which all this was visible; and which was doubtless the occasion of its using, in its duller moments, a great extinguisher for a cap, which it now held under its arm." [*present plot dimensions*] Scrooge asks him to put on the cap and the spirit responds: "Would you so soon put out, with worldly hands, the light I give? Is it not enough that you are one of those whose passions made this cap, and force me through whole trains of years to wear it low upon my brow!" [*past plot dimensions*] The ghost announces he's there for Scrooge's welfare, his reclamation. [*future plot dimensions*]

Where

Where are the main character and other characters in the scene? In this section, establish location(s) in a broad sense (the world, the country, the city and state) as well as specifically (character's house, the room in the house, etc.). Include short details about P/P/F Dimensions, but don't concern yourself if they end up in the sections provided for it or somewhere else on the worksheet for that scene. Ultimately, you may not use everything in the actual scenes you write from this, but at the very least you'll have the big picture.

Note that the following may feel like repeated information from the previous chapter. However, analyzing the settings of these examples is necessary to get a clear, complete picture for P/P/F Dimensions.

"DARK PLACES"

Where: Jason's apartment.

Present plot dimensions: Contemporary setting. Jason lives in a big city, where there are few trees, and it's always loud and noisy no matter what time of day. He doesn't know his neighbors and they don't know him beyond appearances. His apartment is a wide-open studio with a single, large room, huge windows, and definitely no curtains to block out the light.

He can't abide darkness—and he even leaves all the lights on when he goes out so he doesn't have to come home to darkness at the end of each day. He's taken all the doors off the closets. The hallways leading to his apartment are extremely well-lit. Sharon's apartment is too dark and closed-in for him to be there comfortably, so, when they get together, it's always at his place.

Past plot dimensions: Jason grew up in a small, quiet, and peaceful town where nearly everyone knew everyone. Sports were all important to the people he knew: everyone was obsessed with their favorite teams in particular seasons, decorating their houses with fan memorabilia, wearing merchandise, and gathering on game days. Popular kids were all involved in as many team sports as possible. This small town had lots of dense, lush forests and Jason enjoyed spending time walking in them—places where it seemed he was completely alone with no one to badger, bully or belittle him. During his captivity, he was held captive in a claustrophobically small, dark room without windows or lights, so he never saw his captor (who wore a mask) and the man only spoke in a very low whisper so Jason couldn't have identified him by his voice even if he wanted to.

Future plot dimensions: While coming to his decision to ask Sharon to take him back, Jason imagined living in a big house that can be filled with natural and artificial light, set in a wide-open area where his kids can roam for miles without danger. He dreamed of his own heart being just as wide-open, filled with light and no fear of risk, where love is safe and vulnerability is strength.

A CHRISTMAS CAROL

Where: The spirit transports him to "an open country road, with fields on either hand. The city had entirely vanished. Not a vestige of it was to be seen. The darkness and the mist had vanished with it, [*present plot dimensions*] for it was a clear, cold, winter day, with snow upon the ground." This is the place where Scrooge was bred and born. [*past plot dimensions*] He's "conscious of a thousand odours floating in the air, each one connected with a thousand thoughts, and hopes, and joys, and cares long, long, forgotten!" Scrooge trembles and a tear escapes. [*present plot dimensions*] Scrooge "recognising every gate, and post, and tree they pass; until a little market-town appeared in the distance, with its bridge, its church, and winding river. Some shaggy ponies now were seen trotting towards them with boys upon their backs, who called to other boys in country gigs and carts, driven by farmers. All these boys were in great spirits, and shouted to each other, until the broad fields were so full of merry music, that the crisp air laughed to hear it!" [*present plot dimensions*]

"I wish," Scrooge muttered, putting his hand in his pocket, and looking about him, after drying his eyes with his cuff: "but it's too late now."

"What is the matter?" asked the Spirit.

"Nothing," said Scrooge. "Nothing. There was a boy singing a Christmas Carol at my door last night. I should like to have given him something: that's all." [*subtle allusion to future "change" in character and plot dimensions*]

Why

What's going on in this scene that relates to the overall unfolding of story? Like I said above, this section may easily be confused with the "What?" section. Overlap only proves that your story is organic and cohesive. That said, make sure you answer these questions as you work scene by scene: *What's the point, purpose, or drive of the scene? What story progression will be revealed here? How can you reach into this character's past to flesh her out in a way that's pertinent to what's happening now? What whispers of future situations can be included here?*

"DARK PLACES"

Why: Jason starts packing. While Sharon doesn't try to stop him from going, she does ask to go along, and when he asks why, she reminds him that he just said he wanted to get back together. Is he reneging so quickly? Jason is reminded how sure he was that he wanted to try again to have a normal relationship with Sharon, the one person on the earth who actually knows him and says she loves him—and he believes her. Somehow the past came rushing back with his mother's news, and he finds himself faltering.

A CHRISTMAS CAROL

Why: The Ghost of Scrooge's past returns him to people and places he knows and remembers from his youth: His childhood, his sister, his apprenticeship with Fezziwig, the memory of the broken betrothal when he was "at the prime of his life" because his love of money replaced his love for his fiancée Belle. This is followed by a glimpse of her happy life with a husband and children, but no Scrooge.

Extending the Bridge Toward the Next Scene

Clearly, this might and probably will be done closer to the end of each bridge scene. In this section, you want to give the reader some light for the path ahead. What development may he have to dread/look forward to in future scenes? This is the bulk of your future dimension that should be hinted at in every scene.

You may have trouble identifying what this is, so, in addition to our simple and main scenario examples, I've included some examples of this from published novels below.

Here's one that shows how the bridge was extended from chapter one into chapter two from James S.A. Corey's science fiction saga, *Leviathan Wakes*, the first in The Expanse Series (I've tagged the extensions):

> "Send a message to the beacon that we're on our way. And let Ceres know we're going to be late. [*extension*] Holden, where does the Knight stand?"

"No flying in atmosphere until we get some parts [*extension*], but she'll do fine for fifty thousand klicks in vacuum."

"You're sure of that?"

"Naomi said it. That makes it true."

McDowell rose, unfolding to almost two and a quarter meters and thinner than a teenager back on Earth. Between his age and never having lived in a gravity well, the coming burn was likely to be hell on the old man. Holden felt a pang of sympathy that he would never embarrass McDowell by expressing.

"Here's the thing, Jim," McDowell said, his voice quiet enough that only Holden could hear him. "We're required to stop and make an attempt, but we don't have to go out of our way, if you see what I mean."

"We'll already have stopped," Holden said, and McDowell patted at the air with his wide, spidery hands. One of the many Belter gestures that had evolved to be visible when wearing an environment suit.

"I can't avoid that," he said. "But if you see anything out there that seems off, don't play hero again. Just pack up the toys and come home." [*extension*]

"And leave it for the next ship that comes through?" [*extension*]

"And keep yourself safe," [*extension*] McDowell said. "Order. Understood?"

"Understood," Holden said. As the shipwide comm system clicked to life and McDowell began explaining the situation to the crew, Holden imagined he could hear a chorus of groans coming up through the decks. He went over to Rebecca.

"Okay," he said, "what have we got on the broken ship?"

"Light freighter. Martian registry. Shows Eros as home port. Calls itself Scopuli ..."

Another example (with the extensions tagged) of how the bridge was extended from one chapter to the next from the first novel in Joseph Delaney's Last Apprentice Series, *Revenge of the Witch*:

"Well, you'd better start by learning how to manage a boggart," the Spook said, shaking his head sadly. [*extension*]

"That was your other big mistake. A whole Sunday off every week? That's far too generous! Anyway, what should we do about that?" he asked, gesturing towards a thin plume of smoke that was still just visible to the south-east.

I shrugged. "I suppose it'll be all over by now," I said. "There were a lot of angry villagers and they were talking about stoning."

"All over with? Don't you believe it, lad. A witch like Lizzie has a sense of smell better than any hunting dog. She can sniff out things before they happen and would've been gone long before anyone got near. No, she'll have fled back to Pendle, where most of the brood live. We should follow now, but I've been on the road for days and I'm too weary and sore and need to gather my strength. But we can't leave Lizzie free for too long or she'll start to work her mischief again. I'll have to go after her before the end of the week and you'll be coming with me. It won't be easy but you might as well get used to the idea." [*extension*]

When you're working through the exercises in Appendix B, you may wonder what could possibly be called a "future dimension" in the scene offered for you to analyze with *Tyrannosaur Canyon*. This scene might be similar to many you'll see as you get into the three-dimensional-writing mindset. Remember, the future dimension is all about subtle hints (although it *could* be blatant—there's no magical formula or definitive right and wrong here) of what's to come, whether referring to character, plot, or setting. So in the last section of the excerpt for *Tyrannosaur Canyon*, the future dimension could easily be: "If he really pushed his horse, he could make Abiquiú in two hours." You might find more for this dimension than that, of course, but that is one example.

"DARK PLACES"

Extending the Bridge Toward the Next Scene: Jason doesn't think twice: He plans to return to his hometown to aid the police in the search for the missing boy. But his mind is also wondering if this connects to his own kidnapping. He wants to open the cold case file and see if there are any similarities between the two. Sharon wants an answer though: Does he want to get back together? He finally answers: Yes. And she tells him to prove it.

Let her go along with him, let her help him. Let her be the moral support he'll need during this time.

A CHRISTMAS CAROL

Extending the Bridge Toward the Next Scene: Scrooge can't bear to see his past played out in this way and begs to be removed from the scene. When the spirit struggles with him, Scrooge thrusts the cap down over its head to extinguish the light. Scrooge finds himself back in his bed. But Marley said three ghosts would haunt him ...

You can include as much as you want in each section on this worksheet—whatever helps you most when outlining, writing, and revising your scenes—knowing that this doesn't have to be your best prose. Eventually, however, what aspects of this make it into your actual writing need to be revised so each scene fulfills all the requirements we've been going over and will continue to go over.

Keep in mind that your "orienting" set-up doesn't have to, nor should it necessarily, be inserted as a single, first paragraph. Just make sure within the first few paragraphs that the reader has what he needs to figure out the basics of the scene. While you're writing or revising, cast a critical eye to make sure you don't overload the opening paragraphs with introspection (interior character monologue), description, or backstory. A variety of aspects (including all of these things along with dialogue, action, narrative, etc.) are needed to flesh out a scene, and each requires its own, most likely *differing*, size, space, and time for development. Work the anchoring, orienting information throughout the first few paragraphs of the scene in an organic, appropriate way so all your scenes have variety, and avoid repetition or a "template" feel.

In the same vein, your extension into the next scenes shouldn't be done in one bulk, final paragraph at the end. Hints of what's to come should be dropped in at various stages in a scene, and there's no magic formula for how and where to include them. Experiment—even if that means temporarily forcing them to fit in the scene the way you'd shove a book under a table leg until you have the time and tools to repair it properly.

If you have trouble doing this with your own work, specifically adding past and future dimension to your scenes, take a look at the examples provided throughout this book and try out the exercises in the appendix so you can see how this plays out in published stories. Getting in the three-dimensional mindset and using these techniques will get easier with practice. Seeing it in the books you love to read is also helpful.

In the bonus, online material associated with this book, you'll find a breakdown of all the three-dimensional worksheets filled out, thus far, from my novel *Bound Spirits*. You'll also find an excerpt from the book—the second chapter—so you can see how all three dimensions were developed within the fully fleshed out story.

BUILD YOUR THREE-DIMENSIONAL MUSCLES HOMEWORK

Go back to some of your favorite stories and, chapter by chapter, see if you can fill out a Three-Dimensional Scene Worksheet (included below, or in Appendix A) for each. Pay special attention to how each scene opens—how it anchors, then orients, and finally allows the reader to move forward with a sense of anticipation. Look at how the author of a book connects scenes one to the next and finally to the last, how he presented the 5 W's scene by scene, and how he extended beyond each scene to give you something to dread and hope for. Notice how he ties up his resolution scene(s), and how effectively the end resonates with the beginning. Do you feel you got the payoff you were expecting? Why or why not? Try to see the present, past and future dimensions of character, plot, and setting in every scene.

THREE-DIMENSIONAL SCENE WORKSHEET

CONNECTING THE BRIDGE TO THIS SCENE FROM THE LAST SCENE (WHEN):

Who:

    Present character dimensions:

    Past character dimensions:

    Future character dimensions:

What:

    Present plot dimensions:

    Past plot dimensions:

    Future plot dimensions:

Where:

    Present setting dimensions:

    Past setting dimensions:

    Future setting dimensions:

Why:

Extending the Bridge toward the Next Scene:

. . .

Having come into a project with the necessary preparation for crafting three-dimensional characters, plots, and settings, we've established the hands-on process of translating these dimensional foundations into opening and resolution scenes along with those all-important bridge scenes inbetween. In the next chapter, we'll examine a couple additional methods for ensuring three-dimensionality in your stories.

5

ADDITIONAL TECHNIQUES FOR THREE-DIMENSIONALITY

"It is not just a question of blowing up a building or shooting a prime minister. Such bourgeois horseplay is not contemplated. Our operation must be delicate, refined and aimed at the heart. ..."

—IAN FLEMING, *FROM RUSSIA WITH LOVE*

In this chapter, we'll discuss the construction of back cover blurbs that mirror our P/P/F Dimensions, as well as a special technique that ensures three-dimensionality through the use of a P/P/F Dimension Development Chart. Although, as we said in the Introduction, this book assumes you'll be using the method described throughout for a brand-new project, the technique can also be used for projects you've written one or more drafts of that need more work or, ideally, for an outline that includes every single scene in your book. The chart contained in this chapter will help you pinpoint the precise scene where a lack of three-dimensionality could be plaguing your story. We'll also talk a little about how to know whether it's time to start over if a draft of your story isn't working, and how to do that in the most beneficial way. Note that this chapter is intended to enhance, not replace, what was learned in the previous chapters.

THREE-DIMENSIONAL BACK COVER BLURB BREAKDOWN

In the best stories, writers weave present, past, and future dimensions from start to finish in a seamless tapestry. In this way, you'll see the threads of a main character's three dimensions in nearly every back cover blurb you read—in condensed form. A back cover blurb is a breathtaking summary of your entire story, as well as the internal and external conflicts and the goals and motivations of the main character(s). No easy task.

When to write this is completely up to you. While I was writing *Bring Your Fiction to Life*, one of my critique partners was blown away at the prospect of writing the back cover blurb *before* the book was written. It was inconceivable to her that this could even be possible, and it seemed backwards—writing the story was a prerequisite, in her opinion, since she could only be clear about what needed to go on the back cover after she wrote the story. After her comments, I can actually see that this makes a lot of sense. However, I'm on the opposite end of this. From my point of view, I can't imagine *not* starting a project with the back cover blurb. Literally, it's the first thing I do once I have the original idea for a story and I've decided on a title. Though I sometimes have to tweak the blurb once the book is finished, my ideas for the story only become clear to me after I've written the back cover blurb; and it's a rare thing that the blurb is rewritten extensively after the book is finished.

As a general rule, professional, traditionally published writers who submit story proposals that can be accepted by their publishers long in advance of writing the book need to learn how to do this. For newer writers, the easiest way might be to wait until the story is written before attempting a back cover blurb. When you write yours is completely up to you.

What we're focusing on here is including your P/P/F Dimensions in your blurbs, but before we can ensure these dimensions are included in the story summary, we need to learn how to write a blurb. Let's go in-depth on what this is and the specifics on how to construct an effective story summary.

Your blurb should preferably begin with a high concept: one to three tantalizing sentences that effectively encompass your entire story. The *exact* number of sentences isn't written in stone, and the point, of course, is to be brief but utterly intriguing. Here's a simplified explanation of what your high-concept needs to contain:

> A character (*who*) wants (*what*) a goal because she's motivated (*why*), but she faces conflict (*why not*).

Try putting your book into this formula and play around with it until you've got something intriguing. Unfortunately, very few publishers and authors utilize high-concept sentences, and certainly not the way movies do so effectively. Some examples from movies that were released in the recent past:

> A cryptic message from MI6 spy James Bond's past sends him on a trail to uncover a sinister organisation.
>
> —*Spectre*

> During the Cold War, a Brooklyn attorney is tasked with negotiating a prisoner exchange between an American pilot who was shot down over the USSR and a Soviet spy serving a forty-five-year sentence for espionage against the United States.
>
> —*Bridge of Spies*

> Life-changing events cause the relationship of two lifelong friends to be tested as they attempt to deal with the joy and sorrow in their lives.
>
> —*Miss You Already*

> A young Irish immigrant navigates her way through 1950s Brooklyn but soon her new vivacity is disrupted by her past, forcing her to choose between two countries and the lives that exist within. —*Brooklyn*

> Armies of witch hunters battled their unnatural enemy across the globe for centuries, including Kaulder, now the last, cursed with immortality by the Queen Witch he destroyed and must face again when she's resurrected and an epic battle ensues that will determine the survival of the human race.
>
> —*The Last Witch Hunter*

An American businessman and his family settle into their new home in Southeast Asia only to find themselves in the middle of a violent political uprising.

—*No Escape*

A gifted gardener and landscaper is chosen to design the landscaping at the palace of Versailles for Louis XIV, a job that brings with it gender and class barriers, and she must also contend professionally with a controlling royal gardener who begins to fall in love with her.

—*A Little Chaos*

Now, let's talk about the back cover blurb itself. What elements should and shouldn't be included in a back cover blurb? How long should it really be? Here are some tips you should keep in mind while you hone your back cover blurb:

- Ideally, you want to weave all major plot threads into the blurb—as concisely as possible.
- If a character is a *main* character, that's a strong reason to include her; however, it's not necessary in every case, especially if the blurb reads better with the inclusion of only one character. Most secondary characters won't be included because there usually isn't room or necessity.
- Setting might also be included in this sentence, but generally only a hint, usually in the form of a specific location.
- The time period can usually be drawn from the blurb without the need for overt declarations, as you can see in the high-concept movie sentences.
- The genre(s) specific to your story should be apparent. If you have a paranormal romance, both the romance and paranormal aspects should be alluded to in the blurb, even if it's just in the tone. Connect the genre(s) of your story in your mind and evaluate whether each genre is effectively portrayed. In the same vein, the blurb must match the *tone* of the story genre(s). In other words, if it's a romantic comedy, your blurb should portray that aptly—it should be funny, or at least amusing enough to pull a smile from the reader. If it's a

paranormal romance, your blurb should feel eerie, maybe even a little scary. Suspense in any form should induce tightness in your chest as you read the blurb. Looking at the high-concept sentences for movies, I bet you could see the genre in the sentence, as well as the general tone of the film.

- A high-concept sentence, as we've said, is rarely more than one to three sentences total. However, the back cover summary that follows it can be anywhere from one to four paragraphs and still be effective. While shorter is generally better, that's not always the case. If the whole package is short and punchy, it's practically guaranteed to be intriguingly memorable. If you've reduced your blurb to a single-sentence high concept, and a paragraph for the back cover blurb *and made it exciting*, you've really mastered this. But keep in mind that a *too*-short blurb can sometimes be less than dazzling. Instead of being memorable, it can lack details to capture true interest. Play with yours to find the right balance. Sometimes making the last sentence a question can add intrigue. Adding ellipses can also make the reader eager for more. Sometimes highly effective blurbs don't fit into formulas. Don't worry if your first few passes aren't brilliant. Keep honing.

- Quite simply, back cover blurbs should captivate readers. A back cover blurb should make you say "Huh!" or "Wow!" If your blurb doesn't illicit intrigue or the desire to read the book, it's not effective. It's true that while you're in the process of working on the project, you may be the only person reading the blurb you come up with—but don't underestimate the importance of intriguing *yourself*. Your blurbs should illicit enough excitement about writing the story that you'll have a hard time resisting the urge to jump into the writing *immediately*. The point is, if the blurb doesn't make you want to read the story, it's ineffective. The goal is to get readers to pick up the book. Keep refining it until you have that.

- The reason we're discussing back cover blurbs in this book is because writing one can help you zone in on all three dimensions of your story. If your story blurb doesn't include present, past, and future dimensions, is it because one or more of those aspects is missing from your story? The back cover blurb will help you focus on evaluating whether your story has everything it needs. It's extremely important that you include the three dimensions in your back cover blurbs, as well as your books, for all the same reasons we've talked about for the last four chapters. Three-dimensionality brings a story to life; it makes characters, plots, and settings realistic, intriguing, and memorable. If you can't see these within your back cover blurb, there's a chance your story isn't three-dimensional.

Using these tips, we need to come up with one to four paragraphs that define the entire scope of your story. The first step in achieving a three-dimensional blurb is to fill in the blanks of this form for the *main* characters in your story.

who _____ (name of character)

wants to _____(goal to be achieved)

because _____(motivation for acting)

but who faces _____(conflict standing in the way)

I'm using the back cover blurb from *A Christmas Carol* so you can see how this is done, but—and this is a big *but*—I want to stress that this isn't what I consider a well-written back cover blurb—only because it gives away the ending. It works as an example for our purposes because who hasn't read, heard of, or seen a movie version of this story? But when writing your own back cover blurbs *never* give away the ending of the story. I've tagged each of the back cover blurb elements for you within this blurb (note that the high-concept sentence included is condensed from the 2009 Disney animated movie of the book, since the book itself didn't have one):

Ghosts of Past, Present, and Future take miserly Ebenezer Scrooge [name of character] *on a journey in the hope of transforming his bitterness.*

On Christmas Eve, Scrooge is haunted by the ghost of his former business partner Jacob Marley, who warns him that he will be visited by three spirits. [*motivation for acting*] During the night, the ghosts of

Christmas Past, Christmas Present, and Christmas Yet to Come show Scrooge the scenes of his youth, the poverty-stricken Christmas currently being endured by his loyal clerk Bob Cratchit and his crippled son Tiny Tim—and the lonely future that awaits him if he continues in his grasping ways. [*conflict standing in the way*] He awakens on Christmas morning chastened by his nocturnal experiences and resolves to be a better man. [*goal to be achieved*]

You should have noticed that none of these blurb elements are in the same order as the fill-in-the-blanks form. While it's possible the blurb elements could end up in that order, it's rare that they will. Your story is unique, so your blurb needs to fit that originality. The point of the form is to give you a jumping-off point to hone something intriguing. Also, it doesn't matter how many instances of each element crop up in a single blurb (you could have one or more of each), as long as they all appear at least once.

Naturally, this was only the first step in coming up with our three-dimensional back cover blurb. The second step is to ensure that all three dimensions are evident in the blurb. To that end, I've tagged the three dimensions in the prior example below:

> *Ghosts of Past, Present, and Future take miserly Ebenezer Scrooge on a journey in the hope of transforming his bitterness.*
>
> On Christmas Eve, Scrooge is haunted by the ghost of his former business partner Jacob Marley, [*present dimension*] who warns him that he will be visited by three spirits. [*future dimension*] During the night, the ghosts of Christmas Past, Christmas Present, and Christmas Yet to Come show Scrooge the scenes of his youth [*past dimension*], the poverty-stricken Christmas currently being endured by his loyal clerk Bob Cratchit and his crippled son Tiny Tim [*present dimension*]—and the lonely future that awaits him if he continues in his grasping ways. [*future dimension*] He awakens on Christmas morning chastened by his nocturnal experiences [*present dimension*] and resolves to be a better man. [*future dimension*]

As I said in my discussion of back cover blurb forms, it doesn't matter if the three dimensions appear in any order nor does it matter how many instances of each dimension crop up in the blurb, as long as *all three dimensions are included at least once.*

Because I believe example is a powerful teacher, I provide some examples of blurbs (many from my own books, since a large number of mine have high-concept sentences) as well as a few from best-selling novels, in a variety of genres. Keep in mind that it's fine if you would tag some of these a little differently than I have. The point is that all three dimensions appear in each blurb.

Pretty Fly, Book 6: Falcon's Bend Series
(mystery/police procedural)

Will you walk in, pretty fly ... and will you walk out once you're trapped inside the spider's lair? [future dimension]

Shayna Vincent returns home to Falcon's Bend after her romance turns disastrous. [*present dimension*] When she and Gage Keveris became a creative design team at the prestigious Bethany Advertising Agency, she'd had no idea he was married to a career-ambitious woman who traveled more often than she came home. [*past dimension*] Over the last year and half, Shayna found herself falling in love with her partner and friend without a clue what he was hiding. Now that she knows the truth, she can't bear the pain of being near him when they can't be together. [*present and future dimensions*]

While staying with her little brother Danny, a Falcon's Bend Police Department detective, she meets up with an old crush from high school. Shawn Futrell has been widowed twice, [*past dimension*] his third wife is missing, and he's the father of a sixteen-year-old from his first marriage. When Danny finds out his vulnerable sibling has been in contact with Futrell, he tries to put a stop to it by telling her that Shawn's wives' deaths were more than a little suspicious—regardless of whether or not the police have been able to find any evidence to pin on him. [*present dimension*]

But bad boy Shawn is still movie-star gorgeous, and Shayna can't stop recalling how besotted she was with him as an impressionable teenage girl—one Shawn never took seriously back then [*past dimension*] but seems intent on making up for lost time with, now.

[*present and future dimensions*] What pretty fly could resist the invitation of such a seductive spider?

Bounty on the Rebel's Heart, Book 3: Incognito Series
(action-adventure/romantic suspense)

Rebel Porter is a man on the edge. [present dimension] *His wife was killed to silence evidence he uncovered on a dangerously corrupt man of power.* [past dimension] *Now Reb is in hiding,* [present dimension] *and he's as afraid to lose someone else to the bounty on his head as to lose his heart to another woman.* [future dimension]

Corrupt head of Network operations Giles Jameson has gone MIA. [*present imension*] As a boy, he'd been brought in with the choice: join or die. Giles joined, vowing secretly to bring down the Network. Working with an organized crime ring, Giles had killed a senator. The son of that senator was Rebel Porter, who grew up to be an investigative reporter who spent his life searching for Giles and the covert organization he believed he headed. When Reb disclosed his findings on public radio, Giles covered up the breach and silenced Reb by arranging to have his wife killed. [*past dimension*] Now, sixteen years later, Giles has begun his lifelong mission to destroy the Network for good. [*present dimension*]

Network operative Natalie Francis goes undercover, posing as Reb's former lover [*present dimension*]—investigative journalist Adrienna Kelly [*past dimension*]—to find Reb and his evidence against Giles Jameson and the Network. [*present dimension*] Together they uncover a conspiracy that could upset the wrong people and silence both of them for good. And, when Natalie realizes she's fallen for the man she's been protecting, she considers the impossible—escaping the Network. [*future dimension*]

Crooked House, Book 3: Bloodmoon Cove Spirits Series
(paranormal romance)

Some doors, once opened, can never be closed again. ... [future dimension]

Orphan and widow Corinne Zellman is stunned when she receives several urgent letters from a lawyer, telling her she's the only surviving heir of Edward Buchanan, [*present dimension*] a relative of her recently deceased husband. [*past dimension*] Though Corinne ignores the first few summons, too grieved to consider them anything but cruel hoaxes, she takes notice when yet another arrives, [*present dimension*] this time with a family ring identical to the one her husband wore and lost just before he was killed. [*past dimension*] Stuck in a dead-end job and curious about the family [*present dimension*] the love of her life seldom spoke of [*past dimension*], she reluctantly pulls up stakes and heads to Bloodmoon Cove, where the persistent elderly gentleman lives. There, with her best friend Ruby, she finds Crooked House, the family "estate." Crooked House certainly lives up to its disturbing name, as does Edward Buchanan, who is old and pale and disappears so frequently she can almost believe he's nothing more than a ghost. [*present dimension*] It isn't long before Corinne begins to suspect that her new family member had ulterior motives for insisting she come live with him. [*future dimension*] But to believe that is to believe that Rafe Yager, a hardened soldier, [*past dimension*] is entirely correct when he says Crooked House is dangerous. [*present dimension*] The longer she stays, the less chance she'll ever leave again. [*future dimension*]

Ghost hunter Rafe is one of the last descendants of the Mino-Miskwi Native American tribe whose elders disappeared during a ritual at their sacred place at the top of Bloodmoon Mountain. [*past dimension*] Rafe has come home based on a terrifying vision of wide-eyed, wholesome dreamer Cori losing her soul to an evil she doesn't recognize. [*present and future dimensions*] Crooked House is falling and its sinister legacy demands recompense for her husband's death—something that was no accident, as she supposed. Can Rafe save Cori from a sacrifice she never meant to make when she unknowingly came to love a monster? [*future dimension*]

Rose and Thorn, Book 6: Adventures in Amethyst Series
(contemporary romance)

Every rose has its thorn. ... [future dimension]

Reece Childs finally has his rose—Lona Rose, that is, [*present dimension*] a woman from his past and everything he's ever wanted after a lifetime of the kind of transgressions he holds inside the darkest part of him ... and never, ever wants Lona to find out about. [*past dimen-*

sion] He'd been as close as a kiss to having her as his wife, too. [*present dimension*] After a whirlwind courtship, he and Lona flew to Las Vegas to get hitched. Having more than one disastrous divorce already under her belt had shattered Lona's illusions about the institution of marriage and made her superstitious about taking that journey again. So they came back and let everyone in town believe they were married. [*past dimension*] Now their daughter, Honey, is two years old and life seems perfect. [*present dimension*] Reece never anticipated the thorny, black sins from his past to destroy his present and future happiness. [*present, past and future dimensions*]

When Reece came back to Amethyst and fell for Lona Rose, he'd left behind truck driving and everything associated with it. He'd had no clue that Angelina Batista, his "port" in the city he made his most frequent run to, was pregnant. [*past dimension*] She shows up in Amethyst, demanding in no uncertain terms that he be a father to and provider for their son, who's not much older than Honey. Not only has Angelina picked up and left everything else behind to pursue him, but she has medical proof that the boy is his. [*present dimension*]

The world drops out on Lona, who confronts secrets about the man she loves that she could never have imagined in her worst nightmares. She's furious and intent on doing everything to drive this overbearing usurper as far from her happily-ever-after as she can. She's equally unwilling to share her man with someone he never loved, regardless of the intimacy in their uncommitted relationship. [*present and past dimensions*] Yet she soon suspects she's fighting a losing battle because, even to keep her happy, Reece can't turn away from his own son. ... [*future dimension*]

***Retired and on the Rocks*, Book 1: Denim Blues Mysteries**
(inspirational romantic mystery/private detective)

A missing engagement ring leads to murder. ... [future dimension]

It's been a month since Denim McHart hung up his private investigating career after he ended up with a bullet in his leg. [*past dimension*] The injury has forced Den to reevaluate future goals in his career, his love life and his spiritual life. To keep himself busy in early retirement, he's been attempting to restore an antique table and he's officially bored. He can't seem to keep his mind off his investigative partner, [*present dimension*] the lovely and complicated Sylvia Price whom he's had an on-again, off-again romantic relationship with in the past. [*past dimension*] When Sylvia calls him out of the blue, he doesn't waste time getting down to their office. [*present dimension*]

In this past month, Sylvia has been dealing with her own feelings for Den, [*present and past dimensions*] her overwhelming guilt for the pivotal event that happened years ago and caused her mother to be mentally unstable, coinciding with her inability to forgive herself the way she knows the Lord has forgiven her. [*past and future dimensions*]

Before the sparks can fly between Den and Sylvia in the direction he has his heart set, [*future dimension*] she says they've got company. Jilted bride Naomi Deva tells him that her groom—Mayor Thomas Julian—dumped her at the altar. Reluctantly, she admits he'd caught her in a compromising position with the best man only minutes before the ceremony. [*present dimension*] Naomi also reveals the reason why she's sought them: The local police department hasn't been able to turn up the 6.1 carat diamond engagement ring Thomas gave her ... and the groom wants it back. Immediately. [*future dimension*]

Clumsy Girl's Guide to Falling in Love, Book 1: Friendship Heirlooms Series
(inspirational romance/chick-lit)

They were two abnormal peas in an even stranger pod. ... [present, past, and future dimensions]

Zoë Rossdale is the clumsy girl who always has her elbows, feet, eyes, and brass-red hair going in the wrong directions. She floats around in her own world, comfortable there alone, only to be jarred back into the real one when her obliviousness gets her in trouble again. [*present dimension*] After a lifetime of being evaluated critically—first by her own father, and then by everyone around her—and found wanting, [*past dimension*] she's trying to change ... for her own good. She's reaffirmed her commitment to Christ and vowed not to do any of the stupid, possibly illegal, things she'd done for years on the pitiful excuse of surviving. After nearly being fired from the only job she could get to keep her from starving and living on the streets, she's going to school once more and trying to do better for her über-patient boss. [*present and past dimensions*] And she's allowed her best friends to talk her into getting contacts, some new clothes, and a more flattering hairstyle. They tell her she looks beautiful, but she feels more like a dodo bird than ever before [*present dimension*]—until she literally runs into the only man she's ever gone loopy over. [*past dimension*]

Curt Bertoletti has spent years trying to forget the seriously messed-up Zoë and her embarrassing ways. The only person who'd ever approved of the ditzy klutz was his mother, [*present and past dimensions*] and his mother has become relentless in her cause to get him married and settled down. Surely that's what conjured the appearance of Zoë. … [*present dimension*] Zoë, who looks so little like the girl he remembers. [*past dimension*] Even as he vows that he won't stray again—out of weakness or whatever it was that had him stone-gone over her before [*present, past and future dimensions*]—he can't help remembering how well he and Zoë fit together. No other woman had ever gotten that misty look in her eyes when she looked at him—or kissed him like she'd forgotten anyone or anything else existed. No other woman made him so happy, so mad, so sad, and so content. [*past dimension*] Though he's walking stronger in the Lord than he ever has before and he finally knows what he wants in life, [*present dimension*] he's convinced Zoë Rossdale is not it [*future dimension*]—matchmaking mother or no matchmaking mother. [*present dimension*] So why can't he forget her and be done with it? [*future dimension*]

For better or worse, Zoë will always be Zoë—the clumsy girl with her dress tucked into her pantyhose, toilet paper stuck to her shoe and trailing in her wake, the girl whose idea of falling in love is to stand at the edge of the precipice, throw out her arms, and confidently jump into a free fall. If Zoë will always be Zoë, the only question left is, can they both live with that fact? Forever? [*future dimension*]

The Whistler, by John Grisham
(suspense thriller)

We expect our judges to be honest and wise. Their integrity and impartiality are the bedrock of the entire judicial system. We trust them to ensure fair trials, to protect the rights of all litigants, to punish those who do wrong, and to oversee the orderly and efficient flow of justice. [*past dimension*]

But what happens when a judge bends the law or takes a bribe? It's rare, but it happens. [*present dimension*]

Lacy Stoltz is an investigator for the Florida Board on Judicial Conduct. She is a lawyer, not a cop, and it is her job to respond to complaints dealing with judicial misconduct. After nine years with the Board, she knows that most problems are caused by incompetence, not corruption. [*present dimension*]

But a corruption case eventually crosses her desk. A previously disbarred lawyer is back in business with a new identity. He now goes by the name Greg Myers, and he claims to know of a Florida judge who has stolen more money than all other crooked judges combined. And not just crooked judges in Florida. All judges, from all states, and throughout U.S. history. [*past and present dimensions*]

What's the source of the ill-gotten gains? It seems the judge was secretly involved with the construction of a large casino on Native American land. The Coast Mafia financed the casino and is now helping itself to a sizable skim of each month's cash. The judge is getting a cut and looking the other way. It's a sweet deal: Everyone is making money. [*present dimension*]

But now Greg wants to put a stop to it. His only client is a person who knows the truth and wants to blow the whistle and collect millions under Florida law. Greg files a complaint with the Board on Judicial Conduct, and the case is assigned to Lacy Stoltz, who immediately suspects that this one could be dangerous. [*present and future dimensions*]

Dangerous is one thing. Deadly is something else. [*future dimension*]

The Girl on the Train, by Paula Hawkins
(psychological thriller)

Every day the same. ...

Rachel takes the same commuter train every morning and night. Every day she rattles down the track, flashes past a stretch of cozy suburban homes, and stops at the signal that allows her to daily watch the same couple breakfasting on their deck. She's even started to feel like she knows them. Jess and Jason, she calls them. Their life—as she sees it—is perfect. [*past and present dimensions*] Not unlike the life she recently lost. [*past dimension*]

Until today. ... [*present dimension*]

And then she sees something shocking. [*present dimension*] It's only a minute until the train moves on, but it's enough. Now everything's changed. [*future dimension*] Unable to keep it to herself, Rachel goes to the police. But is she really as unreliable as they say? Soon she is deeply entangled not only in the investigation but in the lives of everyone involved. Has she done more harm than good? [*present and future dimensions*]

Library of Souls, Book 3: Miss Peregrine's Peculiar Children Series, by Ransom Riggs
(young adult fantasy)

A boy with extraordinary powers. An army of deadly monsters. [*present dimension*] An epic battle for the future of peculiardom. [*future dimension*]

As the story opens, sixteen-year-old Jacob discovers a powerful new ability, and soon he's diving through history to rescue his peculiar companions from a heavily guarded fortress. Accompanying Jacob on his journey are Emma Bloom, a girl with fire at her fingertips, and Addison MacHenry, a dog with a nose for sniffing out lost children. [*present dimension*]

They'll travel from modern-day London to the labyrinthine alleys of Devil's Acre, the most wretched slum in all of Victorian England. It's a place where the fate of peculiar children everywhere will be decided once and for all. [*future dimension*]

The Daughters of Red Hill Hall, by Kathleen McGurl
(romantic suspense)

When Gemma discovers a pair of ancient dueling pistols encrusted with rubies in the basement of the local museum, she is immediately intrigued. ... [*present dimension*]

On a fateful night in 1838 two sisters were found shot in the cellars of Red Hill Hall. [*past dimension*] And when Gemma begins to delve deeper into their history she begins to realize that the secrets of that night are darker than anyone had ever imagined. [*future dimension*]

As the shocking events of the past begin to unravel, Gemma's own life starts to fall apart. Loyalties are tested and suddenly it seems as if history is repeating itself, as Gemma learns that female friendships can be deadly. ... [*past, present, and future dimensions*]

In these blurbs, you can see P/P/F Dimensions of the story, which carried through into the books themselves. If your blurb doesn't make you see all three dimensions of the story, you may be missing the same within your novel. To help you practice this, read a variety of back cover blurbs from published books and try to pinpoint the P/P/F Dimensions. In Appendix B, I've provided a mix of back cover blurbs from published novels that you can use to trace three-dimensionality. Once you can identify these aspects, writing your own blurbs with three dimensions in mind will become much easier.

EVALUATING YOUR DRAFT WITH A P/P/F DIMENSION DEVELOPMENT CHART

Although this book assumes you'll be using the described methods for a brand-new project, the techniques involved can also be used for projects you've written one or more drafts of that need more work. Additionally, these methods can be used while you're in the outlining stage of your project—and that really is the desired situation, since you should ideally figure out whether you have a solid story *before* committing it to a written draft. The chart we're going to talk about in a moment will help you in whatever stage your book is in by pinpointing the exact scene(s) where a lack of three-dimensionality could be plaguing your story. In the best-case scenario, it may also assure you that you've done a thorough job (if you find you've covered all the three-dimensional bases).

If you've already completed at least one draft of your project, or an outline of it, you've probably made significant progress in developing your characters, plots, and settings, and the three dimensions for each. Your scenes may be all there. However, there will be times when you're not sure if your story has problems or weaknesses, especially underdeveloped dimensions of character, plot, or setting. You may require a bit more help pinpointing issues with three-dimensionality, so you can take steps to eliminate them.

This is where the P/P/F Dimension Development Chart can be used most effectively. If you've already completed the character sketches from the first three chapters, as well as a Three-Dimensional Scene

Worksheet for every single scene in your book, this chart will be simple to fill out. Having the three dimensions of every scene listed side by side on this chart will really help you identify—down to the *exact scene*—where dimensionality may be lacking. You can use this chart at any time in working on a project. For some authors, the chart might only be used when there's trouble. Why do more work than you have to? With a draft or outline of your story already written, you have the basis for evaluating where aspects of your story aren't three-dimensional. You can find a blank chart for your use in Appendix A. If you want to create your own template, set up a chart in your word processing program or across a blank piece of paper so it looks like this:

P/P/F Dimension Development Chart

CHAPTER/ SCENE #	PRESENT DIMENSION	PAST DIMENSION	FUTURE DIMENSION

Let's quickly go over each item listed here.

Chapter/Scene

Filling in this column should be easy. You can include the chapter and/ or scene number. (One chapter may contain many scenes, although some authors write very brief chapters containing only one scene each. Several blank lines, or a series of asterisks, are visual indicators telling the reader that one scene has ended and a new one is beginning.) So something as simple as "Chapter 2, Scene 3" is all that's needed here. But this column should be linear, because you want to pinpoint if you've included P/P/F Dimensions in every single scene.

I will note that in my development chart for *A Christmas Carol* (later in the chapter), I made a deliberate decision to "assume" scenes, though Dickens didn't actually divide them this way. Of a technicality, this short story has five chapters (five total scenes). However, there are definite breaks or transitions or "focuses" within these five scenes. I divided them based on these transitions to fully show the various dimensional developments in each. Some writers and/or stories tend to have long scenes, and that's where a situation like this can easily happen. While long scenes aren't, strictly speaking, wrong, they are inconvenient—especially for our purposes in this book. They also tend to be complicated. There's a lot for the reader to absorb, and though it's stretched over a lengthy scene, he has to keep track of a variety of details to make sure he doesn't get lost in the ongoing developments as he progresses through the story. If the scene is too complicated, he may lose his way. While it was popular to have long scenes when *A Christmas Carol* was published, shorter scenes are in fashion now, and I feel there's good reason. If you want your book to be read swiftly, with pages flying, you can write one scene per chapter and keep those scenes short, with a single theme or purpose. This is an effective way to keep your readers from noticing on a conscious level that they're sitting in the real world with a book in their hands. This accomplishes several things:

- In the most obvious sense, fairly short chapters allow the book to move along swiftly from one chapter to the next. Try reading a James Patterson thriller (and possibly his stories in other genres) if you want to see how this works in an almost shocking way. I won't deny that the brevity in these stories at times compromises dimensionality a little or a lot. However, if you want to see how pages can fly, you'll get that with his stories.
- When chapters are short, there's generally a single focus. In other words, the scene has a singular purpose, a goal to achieve. The complication to the reader is minimal. He absorbs the premise easily and is ready to move on from that point when it's time. In the ideal that an author should continually be striving for, he'll get a hint of "future dimension" that will provide him with the eagerness to keep going.
- Your reader is likely to read more in one sitting, since many will glance ahead to the next chapter when considering whether or not to stop reading for the time being. If the next chapter is short, he'll

be much more inclined to read "just one more" chapter. Frequently, he won't put the book down for *several* more short chapters.

- Short scenes may produce more reviews that are likely to include comments like "page-turner," "nail-biter," and "couldn't put it down." Who doesn't want that?

For example, Tracy Chevalier's *Girl with a Pearl Earring* has no specific chapters or scenes. However, the book is divided into four parts, each based on a year in the life of Griet, the main character. Each scene within those parts is very short—in most cases, no more than a page or two—and scenes are divided with a fancy curlicue rather than numbered sequentially. I read the book in one sitting, in less than seven hours. The short scenes flew, always leaving me panting for more from one to the next. The singular focus was within each of these unspecified scenes, along with a whisper of what was to come.

The only book I've ever read that does the opposite of "short, focused scenes" and yet has the same effect is *The Ruins* by Scott Smith. There are absolutely no chapters and almost nothing to interrupt the flow. When a scene ends, he skips one line and moves directly into the next without actual chapter breaks or even asterisks to break things up. Somehow this makes for a book I read from start to finish in a single sitting whenever I take it off my keeper shelf. I literally cannot put it down once I start it.

POV Character

All you need in this column is the name of the POV character in a particular scene. As I said earlier, most books these days include many main characters, and all have to be three-dimensional—so you have to evaluate the POV characters throughout their dimensions in order to be sure each is multifaceted. If you want, you can do a separate chart for each individual character so you can be sure their progressions all through the story are solid, logical, cohesive, and that the three dimensions are evident for each. If you choose to include all main characters on one chart, specify that character in this column. If your story, like our example *A Christmas Carol*, has only one POV character in every scene, you can forgo including this column altogether on your chart.

Scene Title

In this section of the chart, give your scene a brief title. Specifically, you want something that nails the gist or purpose of that particular scene, since that should give you a solid understanding about whether the scene is absolutely necessary to the story. If you can't come up with an overall scene title, it may mean that you're uncertain of the point of the scene and whether it needs to be included. Evaluate carefully.

Present, Past, and Future Dimensions

The next three columns will get right to the heart of your three-dimensionality … or lack thereof. Go through your story, scene by scene, setting down the three dimensions developed in each scene in as few sentences as you can. Remember, your present dimension is the current situation. What's happening in the now? The past dimension will reach back to what happened before the prevalent story, drawing out character, plot, and setting revelations that illuminate, enhance, or reveal present situations. In tagging your future dimension, you're looking ahead to create dread/eagerness in the reader for what might happen later. While some scenes won't have huge amounts of one or more of these dimensions, your scenes should have at least a hint of each.

Every scene you write must advance the story. Each scene should show definite progress from the one before and offer something new and exciting that propels the characters forward, toward the resolution. Using the P/P/F Dimension Development Chart, you'll be able to see whether each scene develops your characters, plots, and settings three dimensionally, catapulting your story to a tight conclusion. If any area on this worksheet is blank, it's a pretty sure bet that's where your story is lacking depth and dimension.

So you can see how this is done, I worked out the scenes from *A Christmas Carol*. Note that Dickens was playing on the idea of music (a carol) with his title and therefore called his chapters "staves," which is a musical term.

CHAPTER/ SCENE #	SCENE TITLE	PRESENT DIMENSION	PAST DIMENSION	FUTURE DIMENSION
Stave 1, Scene 1	Bah! Humbug to Christmas	Scrooge dismisses his nephew, his clerk, and two charity collectors' attempts to rouse his Christmas spirit. He wants to be left alone to keep Christmas in his own way.	Scrooge scoffs at love (hints at Belle), at his clerk "picking his pocket" when he intends to take Christmas Day off yet collect his pay (hints at Fezziwig), and opening the heart freely to think of people below them as if they really were fellow passengers to the grave (hints at the lonely boy he once was before his beloved sister brought him home).	Scrooge wonders why his nephew married and what reason he has to make merry when he's poor. He questions how his clerk with fifteen shillings a week, and a wife and family, talks about a merry Christmas. He points to prisons and union houses and "a decrease in the surplus population" when it comes to the poor and destitute at this time of year.
Scene 2	Marley's Ghost	Scrooge is visited by his old partner. Marley rebukes him. Mankind is Scrooge's business. The common welfare is his business; charity, mercy, forbearance, and benevolence all are his business. The dealings of his trade were but a drop of water in the comprehensive ocean of his business!	Scrooge has built his life on the very principles Marley did when he was alive: Business. It's enough for a man to understand his own business, and not to interfere with other people's. Scrooge's business occupies him constantly.	Marley warns that —if his course isn't changed— Scrooge will end up like Marley, dragging heavy chains of regret behind him forever as he attempts to do good and instead can do nothing in death the way he might have in life. To that end, three ghosts will haunt him before night's end.

BRING YOUR FICTION TO LIFE

Stave 2, Scene 1	The First of the Three Spirits	The Ghost of Scrooge's Past Christmases comes to show him *what was* (and what made him into the man he is today).	Scrooge is one who has helped make the ghost's cap, forcing him to wear it low, to shut out the light he gives.	The ghost has come for Scrooge's welfare, for his reclamation, if only he takes heed.
Scene 2	Scrooge's "Past Ghost": Boyhood Past	Scrooge spent many lonely Christmases by himself at the boys school he attended.	Scrooge's father had a change of heart and sent his sister Fanny to bring him home to live for good.	Fanny had a huge heart and Scrooge recalls his family with love and sorrow ... and the poignant reminder that Fanny's son Fred is still alive.
Scene 3	Scrooge's "Past Ghost": Young Man in Prime	Scrooge, happy, as an apprentice at Fezziwig's counting house—before the desire for gold took over his whole life.	Scrooge recalls with highest praise his first employer. He had the power to render his workers happy or unhappy; to make their service light or burdensome; a pleasure or a toil.	Scrooge's own clerk is rendered unhappy, his service burdensome, a toil by his power.
Scene 4	Scrooge's "Past Ghost": Young Man in Transition	Scrooge's fiancée Belle sets him free from their betrothal, insisting that he wouldn't be content with her, since his master passion is Gain and she has no wealth of her own.	In a vision, Scrooge is shown a glimpse of himself after Marley's death—through the eyes of Belle's beloved husband. He says Scrooge is "quite alone in the world."	His barren present life resounds into the future. "The very thing he liked was to edge his way along the crowded paths of life, warning all human sympathy to keep its distance."

Stave 3, Scene 1	The Second of the Three Spirits	The Ghost of Christmas Present comes to show Scrooge *what is* (and what he's closed his eyes to for so long).	Scrooge hasn't allowed himself to think beyond his own greed, selfishness, and master passion of Gain since his youth. This is something he's aware of after the first spirit recalled to his mind his past.	Scrooge understands that he has no choice about what he's about to see. He learned a lesson from the previous spirit, and it works within him. He urges the spirit to teach him what he will and let him profit from it.
Scene 2	Scrooge's "Present Ghost": Bob Cratchit's Misfortune	Bob's family is poor, all but destitute from his meager salary. Yet they're full of life and love and graciousness. They celebrate the holiday with joyous gratitude of those who are blessed with riches.	While Bob generously toasts Scrooge as the "Founder of the Feast," his true role is as the ogre to this family.	Bob's youngest son, Tiny Tim, is a cripple. The spirit says, "If these shadows remain unaltered by the Future, none other of my race will find him here. What then? If he be like to die, he had better do it, and decrease the surplus population."
Scene 3	Scrooge's "Present Ghost": Fred's Unwavering Goodness	Fred details his visit with his uncle the day before. He'll have nothing bad to say about Scrooge because his offenses carry their own punishment. Despite how he works night and day to gain wealth, he does no good with it, it's of no use to him anymore, nor does he so much as make himself comfortable.	Although Fred's wife and friends deride him for his loyalty to his uncle, Fred pities Scrooge because he's the one who suffers most for his ill whims, lacking any pleasant companions or moments.	Fred intends to go year after year to wish his uncle a merry Christmas, if for no other reason than for the chance that, at his death, he may leave his clerk a handsome bequeath.

BRING YOUR FICTION TO LIFE

Stave 4, Scene 1	The Last of the Spirits	The Ghost of Christmas Future comes to show Scrooge *what will be* (if he continues on his current course).	Scrooge has been mulling a change of life in his mind, and thought and hoped he saw his newborn resolutions carried out in this.	Scrooge is aware the visit from the Future Spirit has some latent moral for his own improvement, and he resolves to treasure every word he hears, everything he sees, and especially to observe the shadow of himself when it appears with the "expectation that the conduct of his future self would give him the clue he missed and would render the solution of these riddles easy."
Scene 2	Scrooge's "Future Ghost": The Dead Man, Plundered, Ungrieved	The Spirit shows him three men talking about someone who's died, who'll be grieved by no one—his funeral only attended should a lunch be provided, and his wealth left to God only knows. This scene moves to one in which the dead man is plundered, stripped right down to his skin. A family is saved at the man's death.	The verdict pronounced on this dead man by all: "He frightened every one away from him when he was alive, to profit us when he was dead!" No one grieves. In one instance, the fortunes of a struggling family are lightened at the timely death of this man.	Scrooge knows this is the way his own life is going. This unhappy man's end might be his own.

Scene 3	Scrooge's "Future Ghost": Bob Cratchit's Grief	Tiny Tim has died, and his family grieves him.	Tim's family remembers him with great fondness and vow to never forget him.	Scrooge sees the marked contrast in the grief displayed by the death of Tiny Tim and the lack of grief displayed in the case of the plundered man's death.
Scene 4	Scrooge's "Future Ghost": The Dead Man Revealed	When Scrooge asks the spirit who the unloved dead man was, he's taken to a graveyard.	On the stone of a neglected grave is the name Ebenezer Scrooge.	Scrooge himself was the unloved, ungrieved, plundered dead man.
Scene 5	Honoring Christmas All the Year	Scrooge cries that if he is past hope, why bother showing him any of this?	Scrooge is now infinitely aware that "Men's courses will foreshadow certain ends, to which, if persevered in, they must lead." But what was the purpose of what was shown him if not for, "... if the courses be departed from, the ends will change." Scrooge insists, "I am not the man I was. I will not be the man I must have been but for this intercourse."	Scrooge begs the spirits to tell him that he can change the future with an altered life and promises to, "... honour Christmas in my heart, and try to keep it all the year. I will live in the Past, the Present, and the Future. The Spirits of all Three shall strive within me. I will not shut out the lessons that they teach. Oh, tell me I may sponge away the writing on this stone!"

BRING YOUR FICTION TO LIFE

Stave 5, Scene 1	The End of It	Scrooge finds himself in his own room, everything just as it was. And it's Christmas Day. The spirits did it all in one night.	To make up for his lack of goodwill toward his clerk, he sends his family the prize turkey anonymously, donates generously to charity, and enjoys the holiday with his nephew.	Not only does Scrooge raise Bob's salary, he becomes a second father to Tiny Tim. He also becomes as good a friend, as good a master, and as good a man, as the good old city knew, or any other good old city, town, or borough, in the good old world. From that time on, he abstained from interacting with spirits.

Don't give up after your first attempt at creating your own chart. Creating depth requires many substantial layers, and you may become frustrated, but keep going because this kind of thing takes a lot of practice. Success is worth the effort.

You'll find a blank checklist to develop your own P/P/F Dimension Development Chart in Appendix A. If you want to read the entire text of *A Christmas Carol* so you can see how these dimensions were developed within the fully fleshed out story, visit http://www.gutenberg.org/files/46/46-h/46-h.htm.

The bonus, online material associated with this book has the breakdown of my book *Bound Spirits* mapped out with the Three-Dimensional Character, Plot, and Setting Sketch Worksheet, the Three-Dimensional Scene Worksheet for the first part of the book, a Three-Dimensional Back Cover Blurb Breakdown, the P/P/F Dimension Development Chart (again, with just the first part of the book to get you started, though you can find the entire example on my website), as well as an excerpt from the book to see how the three dimensions were brought to life. Appendix B provides exercises that will help you build your three-dimensional muscles. If you can identify (and pull out of each scene) the three dimensions in published examples, you're more likely to see them in your own work.

REWRITING FROM SCRATCH

There are situations where the techniques we've talked about in this book would require more work than starting the book from scratch. This is especially true if, after trying all the methods described, you still aren't sure what's working and what isn't in your story. If you're still having problems, you may also need to take a look at your book's cohesiveness, which we talked about in earlier chapters. In all dimensions, character, plot, and setting must be cohesive and work together in such a way that removing a single element would be impossible, because all three have seamlessly become a part of the story, making it impenetrable and airtight. Characters must blend in naturally with your setting, just as your plot must be an organic part of your character and setting. If your characters, plots, and settings aren't cohesive, every aspect of your story will suffer. If you want to know more about creating cohesive stories, I wrote the book on it. Pick up a copy of *Cohesive Story Building* for an in-depth look at this necessity in crafting. I've included a Cohesion Checklist for your use in Appendix A. Using the checklist, you can pinpoint the areas you might need to rework to produce cohesive characters, situations, and locations.

After trying this, if you're still unsure, it might be time to consider rewriting from scratch. The first step is to make a list of notes of all the problems you think the book has (or might have). Put your notes in a story folder (in the next chapter, we'll talk about creating a story folder for each of your strongest story ideas), and then leave it on the shelf until your mind starts going to work on it again.

Put your works-in-progress on a shelf whenever you feel like you've hit a barricade and can't get through it to the next stage in the project. Take whatever steps are necessary to refresh your creativity. During this break, think about the story in the back of your mind and take notes whenever new possibilities come to you. Ideas on a back burner can do amazing, unanticipated things.

After you've gained some perspective on the work, take out the story folder and start over, preferably outlining the story scene by scene, using solid material from your previous drafts as the basis, concentrating on three-dimensional writing throughout with the worksheets provided. When I first started trying to use an outline before I wrote the book, I didn't find it easy. I used a process I call "outlining and writing in tandem," and that meant outlining as far as I could, scene by scene in the book. When I hit a roadblock, I would start *writing* the book's first scene. Sometimes writing that scene showed me what should happen next in my *outline*. In that case, I returned to outlining the book as far as I could go from there. If I hit a roadblock, I'd write the next scene in the book. I always returned to the outlining, if I could, as soon as I wrote a scene, because the process of writing expanded the idea in my mind and gave me ideas for how to progress the story from the point I was in outlining it. My goal, of course, was to finish outlining the book long before I finished writing it. I don't need to do that anymore, but I did when I first started, and the tandem method worked beautifully.

Outlining and rewriting another full manuscript draft might sound like an immense amount of work, but in actuality, you've already done most of that work. At this point, you can consider all you've done as layers upon layers. You'll be able to use at least some of your previous work in this process. You're better off because, chances are, this process will require much less time and effort to get something cohesive and multilayered.

Don't be discouraged if your own interest in the project periodically wanes. Work through it if you can. Don't give up easily. But if you're not making any progress after a long time, simply set the book aside for whatever interval of time you need—using the strategies we talked about to keep the story on a back burner in your mind. Additionally, try your hand at the exercises provided in Appendix B. These are ways of seeing "how it's done" by professional authors so you can bring the three-dimensional mind-set you've learned back to your own writing.

BUILD YOUR THREE-DIMENSIONAL MUSCLES HOMEWORK

Go back to some of your favorite stories and see if you can identify P/P/F Dimensions within the back cover blurbs. If you're really feeling inspired, try writing back cover blurbs for some of your most developed story ideas that you haven't written yet—making sure you include all three dimensions—and see if you don't find that the story idea you started with expands and clarifies through this process. If you don't end up with a perfect blurb, you'll still probably come up with new ideas for those stories. Practice makes perfect.

. . .

In the next chapter, we'll discuss the crucial need for published, professional authors who want to make a career out of writing to come into every project with a multilayered approach to storytelling.

6

MULTILAYERED STORYTELLING

"The waste of life occasioned by trying to do too many things at once is appalling."

—ORISON MARDEN

Earlier in this book, I talked about how adamant I am about outlining every single story before I write a word of it. That's my modus operandi without fail, and it's not something I would ever want to stop doing because I truly believe it's the only way to be sure I have a solid story before I commit to writing. I don't see the point of writing (and rewriting again and again) a book that may not be strong enough or good enough to sell. I consider that to be writing a book backwards. My goal is to find out if I have a strong story worth writing first—in my world, by creating a scene-by-scene outline, so I'll never have regrets and almost never have to do any of the steps more than once.

In this chapter, we'll go over the "ideal" scenario of writing in stages to complete multiple projects every year. But first, it absolutely needs saying that this is very much "the acme" method of writing. New writers or those who aren't willing to work with an outline in any form can still use the three-dimensional writing methods described in this book, which is why I put this chapter near the end instead of at the beginning. Additionally, newer writers might have trouble "setting projects aside" since getting to work on something else until it's time to start the next stage of a project could spell disaster. Waiting for the muse's inspiration may become the excuse for long-term procrastination. It's harder for some authors to get back into a story once they've left it. So "setting aside" could mean "abandoning" for those writers, and this wouldn't be a good thing for them. This chapter is specifically geared toward career and/or highly disciplined writers who want a great deal of structure in their approach to writing a book and developing a productive writing career. If your goal is to write only a few novels in your lifetime, one per year, or even just one altogether, the approach described in this chapter may be too intense for you, and therefore useless. The rest of this book will have all you need to help you with three-dimensional writing for your project(s).

As I've said, beginning writers may find it easier to fill out the worksheets I've provided to produce three-dimensional layers *after* they've started writing their books, whether they've finished a draft or are somewhere in the middle of it, and want to figure out if they're on the right track with their dimensions. For an author who prefers to begin a project with some kind of a road map, filling out the worksheet for each scene in the book before beginning the writing will allow him to build in three-dimensionality. Writers at any point in their craft can benefit from the three-dimensional writing techniques I've described throughout this manual. For the Type A authors who really want to kick their writing production into high gear, this chapter is for you.

THE IMPORTANCE OF LAYERS IN THREE-DIMENSIONAL WRITING

Professional painters work in layers, preparing and priming the surface to achieve a smooth finish that strengthens, coheres, intensifies, and enhances all that goes on afterward. In a similar way, layers in three-dimensional writing are crucial—and a story lacking all dimensions shows it the same way a puzzle with even one missing piece does. Oh, the disappointment of not seeing it complete after all the hard work has been put in. Three-dimensional layers start with our process of development. Without layering, a story is one-dimensional, unbelievable, boring. But with proper layering, the characters will become so lifelike readers may believe these characters are fully capable of stepping right off the pages into the room.

Layering makes for strength and depth in story building, translating into stronger, deeper, and more emotional characterization; suspenseful, intriguing plots; and vivid, breathtaking settings. That's all the more reason for editors to love you and for readers to come back again and again. Layering has another component that writers should take into account. A multilayered story almost always produces three-dimensionality by virtue of it multilayered construction. The process by which a writer builds three-dimensionality is by *layering* and building up and bringing *together* the strengths of all elements within his story.

As we said in the Introduction, multidimensional writing has three aspects that need to occur to bring about the potential for three-dimensionality. We've already covered the initial two with three-dimensional characters, plots, and settings sketches, and crafting three-dimensional scenes. Another crucial step is multilayered storytelling, and, to achieve this, we need the proper mind-set. Even in the most basic sense, our *approach* to writing a story is crucial in providing the proper layers that ensure three-dimensionality.

My writing reference book *Cohesive Story Building* focuses on writing in stages and story building with these multiple layers. If a story has gone through one draft (without an outline or any kind of blueprint to precede it) and the author revises that, especially without gaining distance by setting the project aside, that story has two layers. Strength and dimensionality will probably be lacking. Unless the writer overhauls the first draft in its totality many, many times (which isn't exactly productive), the story may not have the layers required to achieve three-dimensionality. With the kind of layering realized by working in stages, a story has the potential to become three-dimensional, strong, cohesive, realistic, and richly textured.

Setting the Stages for 3-D Writing with Story Folders

In the Introduction, we talked about working on projects that are ready—ripe for development. Ideally you'll have lots of story ideas for a particular project, vivid characters, exciting plots, and unforgettable settings already in your head, and possibly in the form of free-form notes. At this point, the story is ready to drop into your hands like ripe fruit. While it's possible to finish a book without it being "gravid" with promise before you begin, it'll be infinitely harder to get that unripe story to produce fruit.

Here we'll talk about techniques for getting stories to that impending point, as well as what to do if you have a lot of stories ready to go that are all vying for your attention. I recommend creating *story folders* for every book idea you have, no matter how sparse your ideas are. I especially advise this if you think you might not write the story for years. I've said many times in this book (and all my others) that having a story on the back burner of your mind can do wondrous things.

Writers spin fantasies in their heads, and this is where most of their work is done in conceiving a story. In previous writing reference titles, I've likened the process of writing to brewing coffee in a percolator. The stories inside my head are in a creative coffeepot, brewing away. In the percolating stage of the writing process, stories come to life in large or small spurts. This can amount to a sketch of a character or two, setting description, some vague or definite plotline or action scenes, glimmers of specific relationships, and maybe even a few conversations. Most of it wouldn't make sense to anyone except me. When a story idea is constantly boiling up, it's time to put it into an outline form and puzzle it out. When it's not quite ready, it sits on the back burner, simmering gently. In this way, over the course of years, I can conceivably come up with everything I need to write a story without taking my concentration away from the story that I'm currently puzzling out. I have at least fifty stories inside my head at any given time, brewing away gently until the time comes when they're ready to be written. That's why it's so important to have story folders to hold these ideas; they prevent me from forgetting anything that could become a vital piece of the story puzzle.

Using two-pocket folders, write the title of each book on the front, and then transfer all your notes (including any outlining and writing you've done on the story—anything that you might need or use) into this folder. If you don't currently have physical notes, but the story idea is strong enough, you can create a folder for it, planning to fill it over time. I have a specific folder just for glimmers of ideas. Sometimes a glimmer becomes a full-fledged story that gets its own story folder; so it's useful to keep a folder for any glimmers you may come up with over time.

To show you how important it is to have such a folder, I'll tell you a story culled from experience: I had a dream about a ghost in a specific house multiple times over a period of years. Once I had this dream three times, I realized it was the glimmer of a story. I wrote all the notes I could and put it in my "vague story ideas" folder. Time passed, and I started writing my Bloodmoon Cove Spirits Series, made up of various types of fictional ghost stories. That particular story was on the back burner the whole time, and I figured I might someday incorporate the idea into the series. One night in November 2015, I had another ghost dream that was so vivid I immediately got up and told my husband about it. Then I wrote down all that happened in the dream. That weekend, I remembered my other ghost dream, and I thought I had enough to write back cover blurbs for both of these ideas, fitting the two of them into the Bloodmoon Cove Spirits Series. I sold the stories on the basis of those blurbs. This has happened to me so many times now that I've made it a habit to add even fragments of ideas to my "vague ideas" folder. I never know when they might become full-fledged stories in the future.

You can also make story folders with individual spiral-bound notebooks or computer files, if either of those options works better for you. In this way, whenever you have a thought about this story, you can write notes about it and tuck them into the appropriate place. By the time you're ready to begin working on a particular story, ideally, you'll have a nice stack of "impending story fruit" to pick from.

Again, I can't stress how important it to start each project with a "ripe" idea—one that's ready to go through the initial stages. If you don't have a story folder bursting with ideas, don't take it off the shelf until it's ready to be worked on—unless you have no choice because of an approaching release date. If you start and discover you can't get far—and your deadlines allow it—put it back and work on something that is ready. What you've added will be progress when you are more prepared.

Another reason for creating story folders as soon as you have the first spark of an idea is that, while jumping from project to project may be an effective way to work for some writers, ultimately, it can prevent you from making significant progress with any one project. Most writers can't concentrate on more than one story at a time if they want to move forward steadily. You don't want story ideas to distract you if they're moving at a frantic pace toward fruition while you're working on another project. When you have deadlines—or even if you don't—it's not a good idea to abandon a project you're working on just because something more exciting shows up at an inopportune time. This is natural though—you want it to happen. But if you're trying to make headway with one project when another suddenly commands your attention, you need to find a way to set the new ideas aside and refocus your concentration on your current project. You can do this by writing out notes on the new idea and relegating the idea to its project folder, which you can pick up and review at a more convenient time. Shelving the idea is a quick process, because most of the time the notes you'll write about a growing story at a given time are only enough to fill a sticky note or a single sheet of paper. Occasionally, you may need to take a little more time to purge the abundant ideas from your head so they don't overwhelm you. In that case, find time to write down all the notes that come to you until you're stalled or are temporarily free of it. By shelving the story folder once more, you effectively retain all the ideas, but stall "the harvest" until you have more time to focus on the project. Once you've done this, you can concentrate fully on your current work-in-progress again.

Finally, in creating story folders, you also give yourself the foundation for years of potential writing material. For career authors, this is so critical to your momentum and your ability to deliver well-crafted stories indefinitely. Think of it this way: If you have a publisher who likes your work and regularly accepts whatever you submit, what will happen if you run out of ideas? Your career will stall and, let's be honest, publishers (and readers) are fickle. If you're not making yourself present and active at their publishing house often, they may forget about you. Creating story folders allows you to have many, many ideas in different stages of development over time, and that builds momentum. Since working on stories that are ripe is ideal, having story ideas on the back burner (simmering until the day you're ready to put them into action) is imperative. Your stories written with this process will be better and stronger, especially if you're writing in layers, as you're about to see.

Writing in Stages

Now that you've got a solid way of organizing all your story ideas to ensure you have lots of projects growing over a period of (hopefully) years, let's talk about writing in stages. In the ideal writing situation, a book goes through eleven stages (though the last two are optional, which I'll explain later), including:

- Stage 1: Brainstorming
- Stage 2: Researching
- Stage 3: Outlining
- Stage 4: Setting Aside the Project
- Stage 5: Writing the First Draft
- Stage 6: Setting Aside
- Stage 7: Revising
- Stage 8: Setting Aside
- Stage 9: Editing and Polishing
- Stage 10: Setting Aside
- Stage 11: Final Read-Through

Let's go over each of these, discussing the whys and wherefores for each step. I'll also describe my own writing process so you can see how this all works to ensure the creation of solidly layered stories without becoming so overworked that burnout sets in.

Stage 1: Brainstorming

In *Sometimes the Magic Works*, Terry Brooks says that dreaming (a term referring to the back-and-forth process of brainstorming in the mind) opens the door to creativity and allows the imagination to invent something wonderful. It happens when your mind drifts to a place you've never been—a place you can come back to and tell readers about. This is possibly where writers got such a bad rap from those who see us constantly daydreaming. Little do they realize that, until a writer has brainstormed adequately, he won't have a story to tell.

Constant brainstorming, or brewing, is the most important part of writing an outline or a book. No writing system, technique, or tool will work for you if you're not brainstorming constantly during a project, through all the stages. From the beginning of a project—before you even write a word of it—through the outlining, the writing, and revising, and the final edit and polish, *brainstorm!* It's the second half of the secret to never burning out, never facing writer's block. (Waiting until a story is ripe to begin working on it is the first half.) Start brainstorming days, weeks, months, or even years before you begin working on a story; jot down notes as they come to you and put them into their own folder.

Brainstorming is the very ambition, focus, and joy necessary to planning and completing a project. Both inspiration and productivity flow from this exercise, and brainstorming should never truly stop after you begin writing. Brainstorming is so often what turns an average story into an extraordinarily memorable one. Dreaming about your story infuses you with the inner resources to write with that coveted magical element that turns work into passion. It's also the secret to sitting down to a blank screen or paper and immediately beginning to work without agonizing over where to start. Brainstorming has the amazing side effect of forcing a writer to move from Point A to Point B and to continue on from there. Having given you a few sparks, it helps you to connect the dots to get those elements to fit together, logically and cohesively.

Without adequate brainstorming, a writer has no motivation for fantasizing about every aspect of the story he'll write. The process of writing will be dry, one-dimensional, and he'll likely never make it past chapter three.

By brainstorming days, weeks, months, or even years before beginning tangible work on a story, you create the layers for your story over time; this type of planning also produces cohesion in your work. Brainstorm enough, and when you start the project, it'll be like turning on a movie and writing fast to keep up with everything you see.

In general, I spend at least one to five years brainstorming and jotting down notes (which I put in my story folders) for every book I write. As I said previously, I have about fifty stories in my head at any given time, each one on the back burner, percolating and becoming mature. By the time I'm ready to transform ideas into an outline form, I almost always have a sizable folder filled with notes about anything for the story that came to me over the time it sat brewing. This is ideal, since I'm already motivated when I begin a project.

Stage 2: Researching

Research is a layer of the story, but it's also a form of brainstorming. While you're reading, you're thinking of ways you plan to use the material you're researching. Research will give you the knowledge you need to plan a story. It will also give you story ideas. That's why it's so important to do your research *before* you begin a project—not during, if you can help it. This isn't to say that you won't need to do some follow-up and/or further narrow your research when you realize your outline or first draft has taken a turn you hadn't planned for, or needs more than you've already acquired. Ideally, you'll do your research in between other stages in your various projects. Your research may form the basis for character development, an appropriate setting, and much of the plot, fitting them together naturally. You'll know you've done your research well when you can write about everything in your story intelligently, without questioning anything, and when your research naturally becomes an integral part of the book.

Even for my most complex books (namely, my mystery series and my action/adventure/suspense Incognito Series), I spend only about a week researching. After doing this for so many years, I've found techniques that allow me to do massive amounts of research in a short amount of time—you can find these in my other writing reference titles, *First Draft in 30 Days*, *Cohesive Story Building*, and *Writing the Fiction Series*. Critique partners have commented on the in-depth, complex research I must have done while writing my books. Yes, my days may be very long—sometimes fourteen hours or more—during the researching stage, but I build that research week into my schedule before I start a project so all my research is fresh for the book I'm planning to outline.

Stage 3: Outlining

An outline is essentially any guideline a writer uses to create and assemble a story. Whatever form an author chooses to use, it needs to show the details *behind* the finished product—details that many times are invisible, fitting seamlessly with all the other elements of a story, like tension and mood, but that need to be identified and developed even before writing begins, to ensure three-dimensionality.

While unpublished or newer authors might want to just write without boundaries or prerequisites to teach themselves the process of crafting a solid story, published and career authors often desire more discipline if they're going to create amazing stories every single time. Unfortunately, the idea of a published author writing a story without some sort of plan is acceptable, even encouraged, and prevalent. Don't get me wrong, those authors who have been through the process of writing a book many, many times have an outline regardless of whether it's formally written down or not. Their own experience in the process is guiding them. An author who's written nothing, or only a few books, and works without a plan to get him started may end up with unstable, disjointed stories of the sort that reviewers rip to shreds. Author Terry

Brooks says, "I believe, especially with long fiction, that an outline keeps you organized and focused over the course of the writing. I am not wedded to an outline once it is in place and will change it to suit the progress of the story and to accommodate new and better ideas, but I like having a blueprint to go back to. Also, having an outline forces you to think your story through and work out the kinks and bad spots. I do a lot less editing and rewriting when I take time to do the outline first." I would emphasize what he said about changing an outline to suit the progress of a story. Most writers don't realize just how incredibly *flexible* an outline is in that regard. Let's analyze that deeply.

First things first: A story needs the proper foundation, framework, and internal workings to be strong. Choosing the right elements before the first draft is begun will prevent endless rewrites and one-dimensional stories. The primary goals in producing an outline are as follows:

- To encourage your mind to brainstorm a story from start to finish (in my world, that means a summary of every single scene in the book), providing yourself with a strong, rich layer.
- To allow yourself to see the holes in your story before you start writing the first draft. With a scene-by-scene outline, you have the means to evaluate what still needs work, what needs to be revised and fine-tuned, before you commit it to a full, written draft.
- To help you stay focused when you start to write the book, keeping you from getting sidetracked by small details. Everything you need is right there in one consolidated document. You won't have to go looking for anything and interrupt your progress, because all the hard work of puzzling out your story was completed in the outlining stage.
- How does all this work in the real world? In mine, I always outline a book scene by scene before I write it. I work chronologically until my outline contains every single scene I'll have in the book; it's also okay to write an outline in a nonlinear fashion. Sometimes it helps to know the end of the book before you outline the beginning and/ or middle, so feel free to outline nonchronologically if the story comes to you in that way. Additionally, you may need to utilize a

process I call "outlining and writing in tandem," which basically means outlining as far as you can go, scene by scene, in the book; then writing the first scene, and if you stall, going back to the outline, and switching back and forth between these if you need to, always returning to the outlining and staying with it as long as you can. Use that method if you need to, until you get used to the idea and process of outlining a book before you start writing.

Something I want you to notice is that this isn't simply an outline that you're creating. When I outline, this is unmistakably the first *draft* of my book because it is my book ... just in condensed form. An outline like this is so complete it contains every single one of my character and setting developments, along with plot threads unfurled with the correct pacing and the necessary tension from start to logical finish. Because it's an outline, it doesn't even need to be my best writing.

Once my outline is complete and contains every single scene in the book, I read it over, filling in any gaps or holes, fleshing out the scenes with dialogue, introspection, action, descriptions, whatever. Basically, I *revise* the outline in the same way I would a first draft. Most authors don't and won't spend endless time revising the words and sentence structure in an outline, since they're the only ones who'll see it. And this makes for a lot less obsession over every word and sentence, and puts the revision where it should be in the logical order of writing a book—near the end. Revising one hundred pages of an outline will certainly be much easier than revising four hundred manuscript pages. Incidentally, writing your manuscript based on an outline this complete might almost make you feel guilty, like you're cheating, because the writing process should itself be simple. That's my experience every single time.

Now, before we go any further in proving the flexibility of an outline, let's talk about something that most authors who don't like to use an outline say: They fear using an outline will kill their enthusiasm for writing the book, or that their creativity will be hampered or caged. Nothing could be further from the truth. I've *never* felt stifled by an outline. Just the opposite, in fact. The outline frees me to explore every aspect of a book—without risk. It allows my ideas (and my characters) to come to life on their own and grow. Use your outline to explore *any* angle you want. If new characters crop up, wonderful! Include them. If they're not right for the story, removing them won't take you much time at all. Explore a new story thread—follow it wherever it takes you. If it's a logical thread, keep it. If it's not, delete it. You'll only lose a little time, and your story will be stronger for it. If you realize halfway through or even *all* the way through outlining a book that some of your ideas aren't working, it's a matter of deleting the offensive scenes and starting again in a new direction. This is a change that probably won't take longer than a few days to make in the much shorter outline (instead of the months or even years it might take to identify and correct a full draft of a book created without an outline).

When I was working on the outline for *Until It's Gone*, the fifth book in my Wounded Warriors Series, after a period of about a week I completed drafting up to the final scenes. Then I ran into problems because I was starting to see I had a secondary character playing a major role that didn't fit him, and that my main plot thread wasn't working the way I'd hoped. I spent a good amount of time brainstorming in different directions that would make the story stronger. Ultimately, I had to cut maybe two dozen scenes I'd already outlined—not the major problem it sounds, since everything around these scenes was good.

The next day, I deleted the unworkable scenes from the story file on my computer, keeping a printout of them in case I needed them later. Then I started laying in my new story threads and placing the groundwork for the revised role of that character. By the end of that day, I had the outline back to the same point I'd had it the day before—only now the story worked beautifully. The following day, I continued going over my outline, filling in new ideas that fit the revised portions. The end of the book came together easily because the rest of the story now meshed.

I lost only a day or two by deleting bad ideas and exploring new, stronger ones. If I'd skipped the outline and gone directly to writing the book, I would have spent at least a month (probably a great deal longer) getting three-quarters of a 72,000-word book written and *then* having to delete most of it because it wasn't strong enough. Endless pages would have been scrapped in a revision that would have reshaped most of the book from scratch. Exploring new angles, characters, and concepts while outlining allows you to avoid spending countless hours laboring only to discover your ideas didn't work. That's flexibility of story that can't be denied. A written draft is never so pliable.

Working the kinks out of a story *within the outline* is the ideal productivity, and it's within every writer's grasp. The clearer a writer's vision of the story before writing, the more fleshed out, cohesive, and solid the story will be once it makes it to paper. Remember, your blueprint is just one of *many* layers of your story. If you're jumping directly into the writing, you're missing so many layers that will have to be tacked on awkwardly or laboriously overhauled and reshaped during multiple revisions … revisions that ultimately may not fix the foundational problems your story has.

I talked about creating an outline so complete it actually qualifies as the first draft of your story at length in *First Draft in 30 Days*. If you'd like to see examples of this outlining process, pick up a copy of that book or visit the *First Draft* website at www.firstdraftin30days.com. I've also included a worksheet in Appendix A if you want a template for creating a scene-by-scene outline.

In general, it takes me anywhere from a week to two weeks to outline a book, regardless of eventual size and complexity. I only work on weekdays, and the first week, as I said, I spend mainly researching for the book I'm about to outline—finding, organizing, and incorporating the ideas within the story I'm envisioning in my head. At the end of that first week, I may have half a dozen scenes outlined, because it's a rare thing when I don't have the slightest clue where to start a story. The years stories are on the back burner are usually when I've figured out where a book needs to start. So outlining those scenes along with all my research is the jumping-off point. Additionally, this first week is for setting the time line and straightening out the background for the story. This is especially crucial in a series, since each book has to make sense within the series' framework. I may work very long days while

I'm outlining—eight hours or more, but it's just as likely that I'll cut off early, because I need to let my mind brainstorm in different directions the story should go.

That first week is really the hard part of the process. When I come back to the story after the weekend, I've spent a tremendous amount of time brainstorming (literally, anything and everything else I'm doing, I'm also brainstorming) and feverishly writing notes about upcoming scenes in the story. Almost always, within a day or three of the second week of outlining, the story is coming to me like a massive snowball flying down a mountainside, gaining momentum and picking up everything it can along the way as it roars downwards, all but out of control. I end each of these outlining days by writing freehand notes on upcoming scenes in a notebook as often as the ideas come to me. So the next day, I'm pretty much set up for what I'm going to outline when I sit down at my computer.

Keep in mind, a lot of my stories are part of a series (currently I've authored seventeen series), and, based on previous books, I can usually guess almost exactly how many scenes a book will have before I start outlining it. The process is so instinctive after having written almost 125 stories, I'm not entirely sure how it happens, but I can count on it like clockwork now. Experience has also taught me what size a specific genre will end up for me. My mysteries are always between 75,000 and 120,000 words long when I finish them, taking them through all the stages we're talking about here. A contemporary romance novel (without a suspense angle) will be between 50,000 to 85,000 words.

In extremely rare cases, I don't finish the outline during that second week (knocking off early on Thursday or Friday) and the outlining extends into a third week, but I can't remember the last time that happened. In general, seven to eight days, including research, is my norm for completing an outline based on years of brainstorming. Whatever size the story is—long or short—this is the case. Once the outline is set and solid, and I don't wake up in the middle of the night with niggling areas that need shoring up, I'll set the project aside as long as I possibly can so I'll still meet deadlines. The outline is the foundation

I'll later use to write the book, knowing I won't have to face a sagging middle, deflated tension, a poorly constructed plot thread, weak characterization, or blasé settings, because all these serious problems have been fixed in the outline stage. Starting the following Monday (unless I'm allowing myself a longer break), I move on to another project altogether, one which may be in the same or another stage in the process.

Below is an outline of the first four chapters of my upcoming novel, *Identity*, so that you can see an example of the kind of detail I include:

Identity, A Falcon's Bend Series Short Story
(Falcon's Bend Case Files, Volume III)
By Karen Wiesner and Chris Spindler
Release date: March 2018
Outline
©Karen Wiesner

Timeline: This story takes place between Tuesday, September 25–Saturday, October 6.

Genre: Suspense

Back cover blurb: With his own adopted young son to guide him, Falcon's Bend Police Department Investigator Pete Shasta has been working on a relationship with both of his parents after their traumatizing divorce during his childhood. They're closer than ever before when his father is diagnosed with end-stage cancer. Pete and his brother Jordan know for sure that their younger sister Crystal, whom they'd all lost touch with years ago, should be here with them. When Pete's own investigation into her whereabouts comes up empty, they hire a private detective to find her. Unfortunately, by the time she's located, it's too late. Their father is gone, leaving an immense inheritance for all of them to share. But their sister is no longer the girl any of them remember, proving the hard lessons Pete's been learning of late: that a person's identity changes as they get older and priorities shift for better or worse. But is his sister's homecoming too little, too late … in more ways than one?

Cast of Main Characters:
Pete Shasta (main investigator and Point-of-View {POV} Character)
Lisa Shasta, Pete's wife
Teddy Shasta, Pete & Lisa's two-year-old son
Jordan "Jordie" Shasta, Pete's younger brother
Crystal "Crys" Shasta, Pete and Jordie's older sister
Ted Shasta, Pete's dad
Abby Shasta, Pete's mom

Chapter 1
POV Character: Pete
Date: Tuesday, September 25
Time: Middle of the night

Pete is unable to sleep, because his father is dying of cancer and all he'd wanted in the world was to see his runaway daughter, Crystal, before the end. [*When Crystal was 16, she thought she was pregnant, ran away from home to live with an aunt in Texas.*]

Pete has a memory of something that happened years before, after their parents divorced. Even years before the divorce, Pete's mother was checked out of the family, sleeping around. So when Pete and Jordie were growing up, their sister Crystal was taking care of them. She'd been forced into stepping up and being a mother to Pete and Danny and "a housewife" to their dad. Their dad had just gotten home from work, and Pete and Jordie were supposed to be in bed. Their older sister Crystal always put them to bed, gave them their dinner, their baths, made sure homework was done. Their dad was frequently late home from work (FBPD where he was a detective).

Pete's memory during his childhood: He'd gotten up and heard his sister sobbing (not something she usually did—she was a bulldog as Pete will remember her being). She did all this stuff for them and their dad but she didn't do it graciously or kindly. A part of Pete may have believed she hated them and everything associated with this family. He remembers her saying during this episode to their dad that she was too young to take care of everything in the house all by herself (cooking, cleaning and shopping), being a mother to the boys, going to school. Pete remembers suddenly realizing that Jordie was kneeling in the dark just behind him. He came forward and they looked at each other in surprise.

They'd been in their own world about all this—their mom's refusal to be a mother to them, cheating on their dad. Additionally, Pete realized from this episode how much their dad put on Crys. Pete had vowed he would never forgive their mom, never forget. Crys said during this memory that she hated their mom, screamed it at their father. After the divorce, Jordie was the only one who still loved their mom and wanted anything to do with her.

During this situation with his screaming, sobbing daughter, their dad claimed he was working hard to make money for the family. They all have to do their parts. She'll have to take care of things here while he worked to put food on the table. In this incident, Pete's dad didn't put up with Crystal's complaining long. He told her he worked hard today and he was hungry—wanted his supper. His dad never got on board with a microwave. He wanted a meal, freshly cooked, and he usually had his dinner waiting when he got home because Crys knew better than to defy him. But today she'd obviously intended to put her foot down about it. But it didn't work.

A few minutes later, Pete and Jordie heard Crystal cry out and their dad asked her what the hell was wrong with her. Couldn't she do anything right? They heard the old man getting up and, afraid they would get caught out of bed, they crept away. The next day they found out that Crys had dropped the heavy iron skillet she'd planned to cook Dad's pork chops and potatoes in on her foot. Crys had ugly feet all her life. Pete and Jordie used to tease her about her bride of Frankenstein feet with mismatched toes, yellowed, crooked nails, hairy. But, after this event, that foot was even uglier, so swollen she couldn't wear a shoe on it for days. The bloody, purple toenail eventually fell off and never grew back.

Pete feels broken from this memory. He'd been angry at Crys for years. She took off just a few years after this and she'd only come back once—but none of them had seen her. They'd known she was with their aunt, but after their aunt died, they'd lost touch with Crys. She'd called their dad, but only sporadically. And Pete no longer knows if she stuck around TX, where their aunt lived, or if she took off for parts unknown. Even after hiring a private investigator earlier this year, Pete hasn't been able to locate her.

His cell phone rings. It's Jordie. His tone is dire. When he says, "You better get down to the hospital," Pete is stunned. His dad has end-stage cancer and he's known this would happen for a while now. He's had the time to prepare himself for the eventuality of death, but he doesn't feel even vaguely ready.

Lisa guesses it's his dad.

Pete: "Yeah."

He turns on the flashlight on his cell phone instead of a lamp, gets up, and gets dressed. He has tears in his eyes.

Chapter 2

POV Character: Pete
Date: Tuesday, September 25
Time: Later

When Pete, Lisa and a still-asleep Teddy get to the hospital, there's little time for more than a kiss goodbye (Jordie, his wife MaryEmma and their kids are there along with Pete and Jordie's mom), then Pete's dad wants to talk to Jordie and Pete alone during his last moments. He tells them their sister called him a few months ago. He asked her to come home, told her he was dying.

Pete: "Dad, we've been trying to locate her all this time. You said you'd tell us if she contacted you. Why would you hide it from us?"

Ted: "She doesn't wanna come home. It was obvious then. She'll never forgive me for putting too much on her when she was just a slip of a girl. It's all my fault."

Pete: "Dad … it's not all your fault. You know it's not."

Neither him nor Jordie are willing to point to the obvious person to blame—their mother. But Pete knows they're both thinking it and even their dad probably is. But in the last few years, they've forgiven her; even Ted has forgiven her, and they've all been amicable. This isn't the time to place blame.

Ted: "Find her. Tell her I'm sorry. I wish I'd done everything different."

Pete: "We will, Dad."

Ted: "You're good boys. Both of you. Proud …"

Ted's last word is "Crystal …"

Hard lessons Pete's been learning of late: that a person's identity changes as they get older and priorities shift for better or worse. His grief over his dad's passing.

Pete's sorry he wasn't able to do the one thing their dad needed all this time—to see his daughter one last time and get her forgiveness. Pete wishes he himself hadn't been so angry for so long. With his mom. His sister for running away. He'd been unfair to Crys, though maybe not so much with his mom. But Crys' crimes against him and Jordie were unfair—she'd hurt their feelings when she ran away from the responsibility and burden she saw them as. It'd be hard to imagine she felt any other way because she'd never come back. When their dying father begged her to come home, she'd clearly refused without words. She'd never come back.

Pete: "How could she stay away? When he told her he was dying?"

Jordie: "Why is it so hard to find her? In this day and age, it seems impossible for someone to stay so hidden."

Pete: "There are ways."

Jordie: "I wonder if Dad told her …"

Pete glances at his brother. "Told her what?"

Jordie: "That he reconciled with Mom. I mean, they never got back together. But Dad forgave her. We forgave her. If Crys knew that, maybe it's why she stayed away. She didn't want anything to do with Mom. She said she'd never forgive. If anybody could do that, it's Crys."

Pete knows nothing. Their dad had said Crystal never said much the few times she'd called over the years. She'd asked about Pete and Jordie, maybe implying she felt some concern or maybe even regret about abandoning them. She refused to tell their dad where she was, what she was doing. If she didn't want to come home for whatever reasons before Ted died, why would she want to after?

Chapter 3

POV Character: Pete

Date: Saturday, September 29

Time: Afternoon

His dad's funeral. In the afternoon, the wake is at Jordie's house. Pete feels wrecked. Lisa and Teddy comfort him. Jordie reminds him later of what Pete's barely thought about in the past week. They're paying mega bucks for a private investigator to locate Crystal. Maybe it's time to stop looking and accept that she's not coming back. Pete agrees and says he'll take care of it soon.

When they go home that evening (next door), Pete calls the private investigator, who surprises him when he says he may have his first real lead in finding Crystal. It might pan out, might not—like all the others—but this one is promising. Should he stop his investigation? Pete hesitates, and then says, "No. Follow the lead. If it doesn't go anywhere promising, then we'll call it a done deal." PI says he'll contact him in a few days, hopefully with news one way or the other.

Chapter 4

POV Character: Pete

Date: Monday, October 1

Time: Late morning

The will reading at his dad's lawyer's office. Pete and Jordie are there. They're stunned to find out that their dad's dabbled in the stock market for years and it's left him extremely wealthy. His fortune is being divided between his three children: Pete, Jordie and Crystal. He's left everything to them.

Jordie offers to look into selling their dad's house, car, but they need to go through everything first. Figure out what to keep. Soon. Pete isn't sure he can handle that just yet.

While he leaves, planning to head back to the police department, Pete considers: The money, admittedly, will come in handy. He and Lisa are trying to adopt a newborn baby girl, and that's an expensive process. They've been living on his salary alone since Lisa quit her job at the adoption agency after they adopted Teddy, so she could be a full-time mother to him. The house they moved into (next door to Jordie) is definitely a fixer-upper. He's been trying to renovate it since they moved, but he's been slowed by the lack of money to do much that really needs to be done. Even the new nursery is on hold. He and Lisa don't even have a savings to fall back on anymore. But he thinks he'd still rather have his dad back than get this money.

He's about to call Lisa to tell her about the will reading when his phone rings. It's the PI. He found Crystal …

Stage 4: Setting aside the project

You've probably noticed that three of the nine (four if you use all eleven) stages are setting the project aside. Letting your project sit, out of sight and out of mind, for a couple weeks—or even months—in between stages will provide you with a completely fresh perspective. Distance gives you objectivity and the ability to read your own work so you can progress further with it, adding more layers and dimensions to your characters, plots, and settings. Another reason for setting projects aside between stages is that writers may reach a point where their motivation lags, and they want to abandon the story. Sometimes the author may not feel inspired to write a book he's just spent weeks or even months outlining, just as he may not want to revise something he's spent weeks or months writing.

Setting a project aside between the various stages it goes through also allows your creativity to be at its peak. The process becomes easier, too, and your writing will be the best it can be. Putting a work-in-progress on a back burner for an extended period of time will allow you to see more of the connections that make a story multidimensional.

To set your project aside between stages, return everything to your story folder. Keep this book on a shelf and on the back burner in your mind for as long as you possibly can. Get to work on something else so you won't concentrate too much on this project, making it the center of your attention again.

As a general rule, every book I write gets a few months between stages, a break I really need from each project. I can't imagine going through all the steps in finishing a book back-to-back. I get so sick of a story when one stage carries into the next without pause that I can no longer see whether anything I'm doing is improving or ruining it. When one stage of a work-in-progress is complete, I'm eager to get away from it. Many times I leave a stage certain the whole thing is fit only for burning in the nearest fireplace, but when I come back to it months later, I discover that all my previous hard work was well worth the effort. The layers of the story are building up beautifully into something I know will be even better when it's finally finished.

Stage 5: Writing the first draft

Once you take the project out to begin writing the true first draft of the story, you'll notice that you have everything you need to begin. The outline you created for yourself should contain everything your book will, only on a much smaller scale, and will include a scene-by-scene breakdown of the entire story, rich with dimensions. If your outline was solid when you finished it, that should translate into a book that needs only minor revision and editing to add a few more crucial layers once you write the draft.

When I sit down to write the book months after I've outlined it, I work from my scene-by-scene, "first-draft" outline and always know what's going to happen in the story on a daily basis. This isn't to say that the book doesn't come to life, growing and fleshing out more deeply and vividly as I write. It does immeasurably. So there goes the argument that writing an outline will kill your enthusiasm for the book. If anything, it becomes even more exciting because I'm taking the framework and foundation I set down in an outline and making it powerful, multidimensional, and cohesive with prose. I want to challenge those who say an outline kills your enthusiasm for writing the book to try this method anyway—a couple of times, if you're willing. You really do have to experience this to understand it—but when I write a book based on a first-draft outline, pure magic happens because I watch the outline-skeleton taking on flesh and blood, becoming a walking, talking, *breathing* story right before my very eyes. If anything, it's more exciting this way—and a whole lot easier. I'm adding extra detail and life to my story, exploring possibilities that I may have only just touched on in the outline. It's organic.

When it's time to write a book I've outlined months before, I write two scenes (working from my prepared outline) each weekday, and it doesn't matter how long or short those scenes are. I'll continue writing until they're both written, even if it's well into the afternoon. It's usually more like two to four hours each day. That's definite progress, though.

Generally, I write a novel in a month. You can see the math in how long this process takes here: If I have a novel with forty scenes in the outline and I write two scenes a day for five days a week, at the end of a week, I'll have written ten scenes. Based on those figures, it'll take me four weeks to finish the book. At times, the story overwhelms me and, energized, I may write more than two scenes a day. Sometimes I'll even write on the weekend, allowing myself to finish the work in three weeks instead of four. On my project and annual goals projections (which you can find in Appendix A), I always give myself the maximum amount of time to do the work, in case the magical flow of writing isn't "on" during a particular project, and also because the last thing I want to do is burn out (more about that in Stage 10). If you want to see a time line of how to plan to write a draft of your novel, see Appendix A, the Additional Aids section, for overviews and worksheet templates you can use for scheduling your project goals, and even yearly goals, usually down to an exact date.

One thing I want to note is that at no time during my first draft do I ever, ever, ever go backward and start revising. Writing and revising are two very different processes and a simple need for revising can so easily become an outright overhaul. Not only does this stop your progress in its tracks, but you may not be doing your story a favor by trying to be in two separate mind-sets at the same time. But more about revising later.

With the first draft complete, the story goes back on the shelf for as long as I can leave it. And I go on to another project I'm developing.

Stage 6: Setting aside

Stephen King calls this "recuperation time," and it really is that, considering the blood, sweat, and tears you've expended thus far. (Something that's half done in the writing-in-stages process!) When you take the manuscript down again to begin revisions, followed by editing and polishing, "You'll find reading your book over after a … layoff to be a strange, often exhilarating experience. It's yours, you'll recognize it as yours … and yet it will also be like reading the work of someone else. … This is the way it should be, the reason you waited. …" See Stage 4 for more details about setting a project aside. As I said, I schedule *months* for this particular setting aside.

Stage 7: Revising

Ray Bradbury described this stage as the time, after letting the story cool off, of "reliving" rather than "rewriting." Revision is, ideally, the process of reworking material in an effort to make what's already there better and stronger. If an author jumps directly into writing a story without brainstorming, researching, outlining, setting aside before and after the first draft, this revision will be a mere second layer of the story and, inevitably, the author has left himself with the torturous work of untangling, organizing, reshaping, revising, and searching for three-dimensionality in three hundred or more disjointed pages. Many an author who employs this method of working may need to do *multiple* drafts or revisions to develop an editor-quality manuscript that is consistent, well layered, and mostly coherent. Whether or not it's three-dimensional is up for debate.

In a midway version of best- and worst-case scenarios, revision may mean making significant changes to a draft, such as adding or deleting plot threads, completely rewriting certain sections, or fleshing out characters to make them three-dimensional. In a milder form (usually after the author starts with a solid outline he used to write the first draft), revision could translate into tweaking the three-dimensionality of characters, plots, and settings, maybe incorporating last-minute research.

As I said previously, writing and revision are two completely separate processes that require different mind-sets, and therefore shouldn't be done at the same time. While writing a book, a simple need to polish words, sentences, or paragraphs can become a complete rewrite. This isn't a productive way to work when you're attempting to *finish* the first draft of the book.

An unfortunate side effect of revising, editing, and polishing while you're still writing (and, yes, so many writers attempt to do all four of these at the same time instead of separately, in their own distinct stages) is that you don't get the necessary distance from the project to be able to revise effectively. You need to enter the revision phase with fresh, objective eyes once the first draft of the book is finished. In some ways, you need to view that first draft as if it's not your own work so you can perform the hard work that may be necessary. Only then can you see the story without rose-colored glasses, as it really is.

Let's first talk about the difference between the revision process, and the editing and polishing process, because these are separate jobs that can—but ideally *shouldn't*—take place at the same time. On the road to writing a book, you want to minimize major changes like rewriting an entire story thread; adding, deleting, or revising multiple chapters; and infusing three-dimensionality of characters, plots, and settings. These kinds of major fixes will cost you a lot of time and effort (hence the need for an outline first). If you've utilized your outlined scenes while writing the first draft to make sure your story is progressing, the chance of detecting problems early will allow you to take corrective action in a way that isn't overwhelming. This prevents major revisions at the end of a project, when you've already committed hundreds of pages to a solid structure.

That said, during this time you'll be working on fixing more serious problems, but you probably will be doing some editing and polishing during this stage as well. You're there; it wouldn't make sense not to clean up some minor issue that isn't quite right, yet clearly needs a little elbow grease. However, what you're really looking for during the revision is fixing anything in your story that doesn't work or make sense. When you revise, you evaluate (and fix) any of the following:

- Three-dimensionality of characters, plots, and settings
- Structure
- Character, plot, and setting credibility, and the cohesion of these elements
- Scene worthiness
- Pacing
- Effectiveness of hints, tension and suspense, and resolutions
- Transitions
- Emotion
- Hooks and cliff-hangers
- Character voice

- Consistency
- Adequacy of research
- Properly unfurled, developed, and concluded story threads
- Deepening of character enhancements/contrasts and their relevant symbols

Revision is a necessary, natural part of writing. Every first draft needs it. Revision will help you smooth out any rough edges in your first draft. Information dumps or illogical leaps (or critique partners that point out such things) will alert you to the sections that need to be reworked. You could put the information overload elsewhere in the book, break it up and scatter it throughout several scenes, or cut, condense, and polish so it flows better and makes more sense. As for illogical leaps, you can fill in, tweak, or modify throughout a story to shore up weak areas and provide the justification for a specific element. You'll also add layers as you do this, building on the three-dimensional qualities.

I strongly believe that once an author begins this stage, revision should be done as quickly as possible, with as little interruption from the material as possible. This won't compromise the quality of your revision, I promise—just the opposite, in fact. Ideally, if you can set aside a block of time of about a week to work exclusively on revision, you'll find that your story will be more consistent, and you'll remember details much better. In my case, I remember things photographically—I could argue that I memorize the entire book during this time, and any error will jump out at me as I work. During revision days, I may even be woken from sound sleep because a glaring error in some portion of the book will emerge from my subconscious. The whole book is quite literally laid out in my mind, ready to be accessed at a moment's notice during this short revision period. If revision on a project is broken up by a period of weeks or months, especially if you're working on other projects during this time, the book may suffer from consistency issues and possibly even structural and cohesion problems. If you can set aside a crucial, uninterrupted block of time (preferably one week) to focus on revision, your story will benefit from it immeasurably.

When it's time for me to begin the revision of one of my works-in-progress, I divide the number of scenes in the book by five (weekdays). While I used to do my revisions on a printed copy of the manuscript, the sheer amount of work typing up all those corrections after I was done revising led me to completing this step directly in the Word file. Instead of spending a couple days after a revision typing up corrections in the file, now I can rest and relax, letting my mind analyze the story to be sure I haven't forgotten anything.

In this stage, I revise those scenes I've given myself to work on for the day. I mentioned earlier that I almost always end the first draft feeling like the book isn't as good as I'd hoped when I started. This is the very reason I set aside the project for so long. When the revision stage rolls around, the book is in fact pretty solid (regardless of any feelings I might have had when I put it on a shelf), and I've been away from it long enough that I'm no longer sick of it, so I have distance and objectivity. When I get to the revision stage, it's a rare thing that I'm not pleasantly surprised by how well the story reads for me at this point. I enjoy it, though I'll always find things I want to revise and tweak. In general, I can see how strongly my three dimensions of character, plot, and setting are coming along in the layering process. I tend to add a good 10,000 to 25,000 words to the book during this time (Note: My first drafts tend to be shorter in order to allow for revision and polishing at the proper stage), which is an extremely rich layer of texture and complexity.

This is also almost always the point where I can see the finish line. I know it won't take much more to get the book to the state where I feel it's complete, perfect, and ready to be published—essentially when I'm ready to let it go. I think that's an important part of the writing-in-stages process. Unless and until you feel you're ready to let the book go because it's as flawless as you can make it, *don't* let it go. You'll probably feel the same way as I do at the revision step if you follow the writing-in-stages method in the order I've laid out. Getting to the letting-go point might be much harder if you're not using this process.

This week of revising is easy work for me. I did all the hard work in the outlining. The writing doesn't usually take much out of me because the kinks were worked out in advance, and this revision is affirming my confidence in the strength of the story. When the scenes that I've scheduled to revise each day are complete, I'm done for that day … unless I can't stop reading and want to go on, which I frequently do. In that way, it usually only takes a maximum of three days to complete a revision, but I give myself the full week anyway. Back on the shelf it goes to sit. And I go on to something else.

Stage 8: Setting aside

See Stages 4 and 6, because what I said in those sections is pertinent here as well. This latter setting aside, though, is slightly different in that this is usually a good stage to get critique partners and beta readers involved. Everyone knows writers can get too close to their own work. It's an occupational hazard. While you're hopefully feeling you've got a story beyond compare, it may need a little more work and you simply can't see it (or vice versa—you think it's manure, but it's actually really good, and you're too close to be able to see *that*). That's why it's so important to turn your beloved opus over to a trusted spouse, friend or, preferably, a critique partner (or three) for a critical read. The opinion of others is very important. You're probably not ready to send that book out to a publisher or agent until you've had enough reader reactions to judge the strength of your accomplishment.

During this project downtime, you might be sick of your book and/or stinging from some of the glaring holes others saw that you somehow managed to miss. I highly recommend that you give yourself this "shelf-time" to digest the comments made about your beloved baby. When you return for the final editing and polishing, perhaps for the last time before you submit it, you might even agree with your friend on several points … but you may also disagree. Ultimately, what you decide is best for your book is up to you. You'll hopefully feel confident enough to evaluate, unbiased, what needs to be done to shine it up.

In previous stages of setting aside, I would leave a story alone for months. Unless my schedule is extremely busy, I may only leave it this time for a few weeks. I'm getting closer to deadlines and I also know deep down that I'm heartbeat close to being done with the project. I won't be as negatively critical of the story when I come back to it (because the story is generally really strong at this point), so I can see it a bit more objectively, even though I haven't been away from it as long as previously.

Stage 9: Editing and polishing

What most writers call revising is actually just editing and polishing. Writers get excited about their stories at nearly every stage, since they have a picture in their mind's eye of what will emerge. The "editing" portion of this task is called *copyediting* in publishing circles and entails the correction and enhancement of grammar, vocabulary, and punctuation details. Editing and polishing are a lot like turning a rough gemstone into a finished one. You're cutting the bad, replacing it with the good, and polishing up what remains until it shines. A writer unquestionably needs to remove clutter to make a story understandable, to prevent a reader from tripping over clumsy prose, and to infuse a story with vivid, interesting narration that speaks succinctly to the reader, concurrently bringing the whole story to life. *Editing and polishing* adds a definite extra layer to your story. Without it, your story probably won't read smoothly, nor will it shine. The process of editing and polishing can also involve any or all of the following:

- Ensuring a completeness of three-dimensionality in character, plot, and setting
- Rearranging sentences or paragraphs
- Showing (more frequently) and telling (at times), where these are most needed
- Tightening sentences and individual words (such as changing passive to active and dull to impacting; cleaning up repetition)
- Smoothing out roughness and making your writing more natural or interesting

- Punching up tension and suspense
- Ensuring variation in sentence construction and length
- Diversifying and enriching words

Editing and polishing should be almost as simple as reading through the manuscript and making minor adjustments that allow the words to flow like music to the ears. A solid outline followed by a first draft virtually ensures that. I usually complete this step quickly—within a day (or two) once I take it out for this purpose. The difference between revising, and editing and polishing is generally in the amount of work I do for each. With a revision, there's always more to do, so I need three days to a week to focus on fixing everything. For editing and polishing, I may only mark or fix something every few pages. Also, though I haven't been away from the story quite as long as I was in the previous setting aside, I tend to not want to put the book down during this stage. There's total immersion into the story, the way the amount of work I needed to do previously didn't allow.

Again, this is something I used to do on a printed manuscript, but as I get older I prefer to do less work, and that means completing this step directly in the story file on my computer so I don't have to spend hours after I'm done editing and polishing making corrections to the computer file. I generally add another 5,000 to 10,000 words to the story in this process—again, another pivotal layer.

In the almost twenty years I've been steadily selling books to publishers, writing the book has become the *easy* part of the whole production process. For the most part, my first drafts have been *final* drafts, requiring minimal revision; usually a final edit and polish completes the job. Most of my editorial revisions are basic, commonsense suggestions to refine word usage and smooth out the flow of sentences. I've been very fortunate to regularly enjoy five-star reviews and a warm reception from readers; so I trust my process.

Stage 10: Setting aside (optional)
While I'll get into the in-depth reasons for continuing past Stage 9 in Stage 11, the basic reason for this shelf time for the project is obvious.

You just finished editing and polishing. You'd have to be insane to want to read the book again right after you finished going over it from start to finish. You'll have gained no distance from it if you jump directly into Stage 11 at this point. So give yourself another few weeks or more, if your deadlines allow, before moving on to Stage 11. See Stages 4, 6, and 8 for more details.

One other thing I alluded to earlier is that writers don't want to get burned out when it comes to any specific project. When writers say they're burned out, they mean they've been working too much and not taking the time off to refresh themselves and keep their creative energy flowing. (This is completely different from writer's block, which can stem from situations like a story not being ready to be worked on, not enough brainstorming or inspiration, or sheer laziness usually attributed to a fickle muse.) This is especially true if you're working on one project, doing all these stages back-to-back, without taking a break from the project or from work in general. You bring back your own love for a project each time you set it aside and then come back to it fresh. Don't underestimate the importance of doing that. You and your stories will suffer for it eventually if you skip over the setting-aside stages.

There's another reason for avoiding burnout whenever you can. The soil in your brain is like the soil farmers sow crops in. It needs rest and rotation (writing in stages, for the author) to become fertile and nutrient rich again. When you work up your yearly goals (see Appendix A, Additional Aids for an overview and template worksheet), you're not only deciding what you're going to be working on during that year, but you're also planning your *breaks* from writing. If taking weekends off doesn't refresh you, take a week, weeks, or even a month off during the year. Read, watch movies, relax, and reenergize your creativity. (This doesn't mean you can't be brainstorming or researching for upcoming projects during this time.) By the time your vacation is up, you'll be raring to go on your next writing project. Take your scheduled vacations when you've planned them, unless something wonderful happens (an editor contracts a series from you, you're asked to write a screenplay of your book ... fill in the blank for your own idea of wonderful) in your career or life, and you can't let the opportunity pass you by. As soon as that thing is finished, take the vacation you planned. Reward yourself by allowing your creative soil to become fertile again.

Stage 11: Final read-through (optional)

Following Stage 9, some authors may be ready to send out the story, either to a publisher who's waiting to release it, or in a submission to find a publisher or agent for the book. A couple situations prompted me to add two steps to my original nine-stage process, though, that I think even those savvy, confident authors might want to evaluate before submitting. First, we live in a digital world. Everything is started, managed, and completed on the computer. But the very real and inescapable fact is that human eyes are fallible. They aren't capable of seeing everything on a computer (or something similar to this) screen and frequently what you see on the screen isn't necessarily what's in the hard copy—spacing, formatting, and other issues may crop up from one medium to the other. We need the hard copy to truly catch everything that demands our attention (like typos and Track Changes errors) in the final draft of a manuscript. Our eyes can see only some of these things on the printed version of the book. This is essential, and I guarantee if you're not getting this hard copy (from your own printer of the final proof after edits, directly from you publisher, or from another means like the one I'll describe in a second), you're missing a (possibly) tremendous amount of issues that readers *are* going to catch. Do yourself a favor: Get a hard copy for your final read-through.

Second, the current state of the industry—exploding with indie publishers and authors—requires another stage in which to find the errors that seem to creep into our stories like lice. The fact is, there are very few legitimately professional editors and/or copyeditors working at publishing houses these days—especially at smaller publishers—and authors who are self-publishing their own works may even skip the professional-editor-input altogether. For that reason, it's even more crucial to have a stage where the writer sees his book in this final form (and this is true even if the book is only released as an e-book without a paper companion), where he can catch (probably not all but most) typos. I highly recommend utilizing a publishing service like Lulu or CreateSpace, or any other you like, to set up an inexpensive hard copy of your book to serve as a final read-through hard copy. You may not offer these books for sale anywhere, since the hard copy you want is only for your own use. Some printers offer "value line" versions, which are trade paperbacks that are so inexpensive, they don't qualify for distribution with places like Amazon.com, but the quality is still more than acceptable, especially for your particular task. This is the perfect advanced reading copy for you to use for your final read-through, and you're unlikely to pay more than $5 for it at author-discounted pricing. You can set up this copy at one of these printers during Stage 10, when your book has gone through its last edit and polish, and you shouldn't need to do much beyond catching typos and formatting errors. When you get the copy you ordered for this stage, put it on your desk until you're ready to read with a little distance. Whether or not you have professional artwork book-ending the manuscript pages doesn't matter so much as having that copy to catch as many problems as you can before the book is either self-published or goes to your editor, hopefully exterminating any remaining typos.

As soon as I'm done with the editing and polishing, and the story is as clean as I think it can get "digitally," I'll put the book into a value-priced trade paperback format (what I call my print test paperback) and order a copy. When I'm ready for this final read-through, I like to put myself in the position of being the first reader for this book. As much as possible, I try to ignore the fact that I have a very personal affiliation with the book and I simply read it—both in a critical and savoring mind frame. This isn't easy, but I consider this my very last chance to make changes before my editor sees it. I want her to find the finished product almost perfect. I take my time reading, sometimes lingering for weeks if the deadline I have to submit it to my editor is way out there, to evaluate how the story goes over in this unhurried mode.

When I get to this stage in the process, I usually find very few changes are required, and I may not add more than one thousand words during this time, which is still a nice, "gilding" layer. The story is brimming with life, and there's almost nothing left to stumble over or smooth out. Most important though, in nearly every case, I come out loving the story more than I ever have before. It exceeds the expectations I had for it when it was little more than a spark that incited me to write. Truthfully, I don't consider that conceit. I'd worry if I didn't have that reaction. If you don't love your own work, don't become immersed in the worlds and characters and conflicts contained in your stories, how can you expect readers to?

Summary and Conclusion

Each of these stages is a layer of your story—nine to eleven strong layers that, for career authors, should be the first step in ensuring multidimensional writing. Each time you add something new during these stages, you're creating another vital layer that makes the whole story stronger, richer, and more three-dimensional. As our dictionary definition of *three-dimensional* stated at the beginning of this book, we see another perspective of our story in this process and can fuse in more and more details to forge three-dimensionality of characters, plots, and settings.

All of my projects are done in these eleven stages. I *love* that I'm never doing the same thing in terms of outlining, writing, revising, or editing and polishing a project. I move from outlining one book, to revising a different one, to writing something else altogether, layering and building and developing each project into something wonderfully three-dimensional.

I also love that I rarely have to start from scratch on any project. While I do set the book aside multiple times, the rest of the steps are done *once*. I can't remember the last time I had to outline, write a draft, revise, and edit and polish more than once for each project. I'm always fresh, always enthusiastic, always eager to complete a book a little more at each stage, knowing my work will be solid, lifelike, and ready to send to editors when I'm at last ready to let go.

One other thing I want to point out is that I generally spend each year (though the year isn't necessarily January through December) working on five novels—in some years I also write as many novellas— all in various stages in this process. To give you a point of reference, in 2015 I accomplished what you see in the bulleted list below. I'm using this particular year, though it's not indicative of my norm of writing five novels and a few novellas. The reason my production slowed is because I switched publishers for most of my older fiction titles in 2014, and so I had a lot of books that I revised and reissued with a new publisher. Rereleasing those old titles was and continues to be a focus that's prevented me from finishing and publishing as many brand-new projects as I usually do in a year's time. But, for the most part, this is close to my normal annual accomplishments:

- outlined four novels
- wrote three novels and one writing reference
- revised and edited four novels and one writing reference
- completed editor revisions for five novels, two novel reissues, and nine novella reissues
- had five novels, two novel reissues, and nine novella reissues, and one children's book published
- prepared four novel proposals, one writing reference proposal, and one article proposal

How did I do it? Broken down, this is how I juggled each project through the various stages, month by month, to complete everything. I've included the general work estimates within the discussions we've been having about writing in stages so you can see how I fit it all in:

JANUARY

- Researched and outlined *Shadows of the Night*, Book 2: Angelfire II Quartet (May 2016 release) [two weeks]
- Editor revisions for Adventures in Amethyst Series, Books 1–4 reissue [one hour]

- Prepared and submitted a proposal for *Bridge of Fire*, Book 9: Woodcutter's Grim Series (November 2020 release) [a couple hours]
- Revised *Pretty Fly*, Book 6: Falcon's Bend Series (September 2015 release) [one week]

FEBRUARY

- Editor revisions for *Til Summer Comes Around*, Book 5: Adventures in Amethyst Series [one hour]
- Researched and outlined *Rose and Thorn*, Book 6: Adventures in Amethyst Series (August 2016 release) [two weeks]
- Editor revisions for *Midnight Angel*, Book 2: Angelfire II Quartet [one hour]

MARCH

- Revised *Clumsy Girl's Guide to Having a Baby*, Book 6: Friendship Heirlooms Series (January 2016 release) [one week]
- Wrote *Shadows of the Night* [almost four weeks]

APRIL

- Editor revisions for *Clumsy Girl's Guide to Falling in Love*, Book 1: Friendship Heirlooms Series reissue [one hour]
- Edited and polished *Pretty Fly* [one day]
- Vacation from writing

MAY

- Editor revisions for *First Comes Love*, Book 4: Friendship Heirlooms Series [one hour]
- Prepared proposal for *Once Upon a Cliché*: A Peaceful Pilgrim Novel (January 2021 release) [a couple hours]
- Wrote *Rose and Thorn* [four weeks]

JUNE

- Edited and polished *Clumsy Girl's Guide to Having a Baby* [one day]

- Editor revisions for Woodcutter's Grim Series, Volume I (Books 1–3 and The Final Chapter) reissue [one hour]
- Editor revisions for Woodcutter's Grim Series, Volume II (Books 4–7) reissue [one hour]
- Vacation from writing

JULY

- Revised *Shadows of the Night* [one week]
- Editor revisions for *Michael's Angel*, Book 2: Friendship Heirlooms Series reissue [one hour]
- Vacation from writing

AUGUST

- Researched and outlined *Promises in the Dark*, Book 4: Angelfire II Quartet (November 2016 release) [usually two weeks—finished in about seven days so I had more time this month for all the other things I wanted to complete]
- Revised *Rose and Thorn* [usually one week—this took two days]
- Final read-through *Pretty Fly* [throughout the first part of the month]
- Researched and outlined *Briar's Patch*, Book 7, Adventures in Amethyst Series (January 2017 release) [usually two weeks—again finished in about seven days]
- Editor revisions for *Perfect Reflection*, Book 5: Friendship Heirlooms Series [one hour]
- Final read-through *Clumsy Girl's Guide to Having a Baby* [throughout the second part of the month]

SEPTEMBER

- Wrote *Crooked House*, Book 3: Bloodmoon Cove Spirits Series (September 2016 release) [four weeks]
- Editor revisions for *Pretty Fly* [one hour]
- Edited and polished *Shadows of the Night* [one day]
- Edited and polished *Rose and Thorn* [one day]

OCTOBER

- Wrote *Bring Your Fiction to Life* [four weeks]
- Editor revisions for Cowboy Fever Series (Books 1–5 reissues) [one hour]

NOVEMBER

- Prepared proposals for *Hidden*, Book 7 (September 2020 release) and *Hell Hath No Fury*, Book 8 (July 2021 release): Bloodmoon Cove Spirits Series [a couple hours each]
- Final read-through *Shadows of the Night* [throughout the first part of the month]
- Revised *Bring Your Fiction to Life* [two weeks—nonfiction is more intense]
- Prepared proposal for *Bring Your Fiction to Life* [nonfiction is harder]
- Editor revisions for *The Deep*, Book 8: Woodcutter's Grim Series reissue [one hour]
- Final read-through *Rose and Thorn* [throughout the second part of the month]

DECEMBER

- Revised *Crooked House* [one week]
- Edited and polished *Bring Your Fiction to Life* [one to two days]
- Vacation from writing

Note: Final read-throughs are done the way I read a book normally; so very relaxed, done here and there throughout the course of days or weeks.

Notice several things here:

Release dates are always tentative. You might also wonder about some of the way-out-there release dates. At the time of this writing—the end of 2016—I have thirty-nine contracted releases left to fulfill. Figuring between five to ten brand-new releases a year, it'll take me at least four more years to write them all, hence the very "future" release dates.

Where it says "editor revisions," I worked for under an hour on each project to perform the revisions that were requested by my editor. In every situation, these amounted to fixing typos and clarifying sentence structures. Nothing more and nothing serious. Also, unusual for a publisher, my fiction titles are edited and released within days. If my publisher is putting out a print version of the book, the e-book and print book releases might be staggered by a few weeks or a month. Essentially these edits take no time or effort, and I do them immediately when I receive them.

My vacations are included (most of them amounted to a week or two during the summer months, when I did other writing-related things during that time, but took breaks from my writing, with another vacation at the end of the year). I try to do it this way every year, because it prevents me from becoming overwhelmed and burned out on writing.

I recommend studying my year above to see how I did this with individual projects. For instance, in 2015, I went through all the writing stages with the book *Shadows of the Night*, Book 3: Angelfire II Quartet, which was published in May 2016. In January 2015, I researched and outlined the book, then set it aside until the end of March (almost three months), when I took it out and wrote the first draft. Once the writing was done, I set it aside again until July (another few months), when I revised it. The edit and polish came in September. Immediately after the editing and polishing, I put the book into a print test copy and, at the beginning of November, I did a final read-through before submitting it to my editor in February, which was months in advance of the May 2016 release date. This is how I tend to work, giving each book at least a year for all the stages it needs to go through to be a solid, three-dimensional story with many, many layers. If I didn't put each project through this rigorous schedule, I wouldn't feel it was ready to be published. While it's true you may get the same amount of layers if you write the book without an outline, most authors will need numerous revisions (and possibly multiple overhauls) to get it to full-fledged dimensionality, if it ever does.

You might have noticed the quote at the beginning of this chapter ("The waste of life occasioned by trying to do too many things at once is appalling.") and are now wondering how this fits, since obviously there's a lot I accomplish, despite all the vacations and mini-vacations. People tend to assume I must work twenty-four hours a day based on my high level of production, but you know differently now, don't you? I generally only write weekday mornings, taking the afternoons off at my leisure. I take (most) every weekend off, and schedule vacations or mini-vacations throughout the year to keep myself from burning out. The only way to do this is by knowing how much I can accomplish—as a general rule—for each stage in the process and by working in layers. It's more of a science than a phenomenon now that you see how it works, isn't it? I don't believe in trying to do too much. I've found a way to do all I can without becoming harried, overworked, and overwhelmed.

You can see how I've worked in stages over the course of *many* years here on my Works-In-Progress page at http://www.angelfire.com/stars4/kswiesner/WIP.html. In Appendix A, you'll find an overview of how to do this along with blank worksheets you can use to set up your own schedule for writing in stages.

You can also see another reason for writing in stages and making yearly goals in the monthly listing above: I'm proactively advancing multiple stories at once. As a career author, this is critical. I ensure the future of my career success with many projects in progress over the course of several years. A good rule of thumb for unpublished writers is to stay one to two projects ahead of *submissions*. For a published author, you should stay one to two projects ahead of your *releases*. Six months to a year before the *next* year, you need to either be thinking— or preferably *working*—on the next year's projects. In November 2015, I'd finished four novels scheduled to be published from December 2015 to September 2016, with another three outlined and waiting on a shelf to begin writing in 2016.

These methods came about because of the state of the writing industry. Making a first sale these days is impossibly hard, even if you're a fantastic writer. Making subsequent sales is becoming more difficult, too, as publishers judge you on your very first performance, instead of allowing you to build a following over time. Even more daunting is if you can only write one book a year. In this current state of publishers folding, changing hands, and concentrating mainly on their prolific, best-selling authors, it's essential that writers learn how to finish quality books and do it fast enough to keep the momentum of their careers rolling steadily. Career authors who want to compete in a totally chaotic market need to learn to write fewer drafts because they can sell a proposal "on spec," which basically means that you submit a proposal to a publisher in lieu of a completed manuscript because you've proven to them that you can complete assignments on time and publication ready. That's why it's crucial to become a productive writer, capable of producing multilayered stories as soon as you can—ideally, before you sell your first book. You'll be confident about what you can do, and you'll have more to offer any publisher who contracts for your books. An author who uses outlines, allows for sufficient shelf time, and sets goals will never have to suffer from missed deadlines or low-quality work. In fact, each book may get better than the last, and you may get far enough ahead that you can fit just-for-fun projects into your schedule or take longer breaks from writing.

Finally, what *I* do and what *you* ultimately do will be completely different, and you want to find what works best for you. The point is to make progress. If you want to be a career author, take the steps to make it possible for you to write quality novels indefinitely.

BUILD YOUR THREE-DIMENSIONAL MUSCLES HOMEWORK

If you haven't already done this, create and begin utilizing story folders now that allow you to lay the foundation for years of potential writing material, and the momentum to finish them well in advance of deadlines. If you're a writer with the goal of becoming a professional, career author, learn how to write in stages to ensure the development of multiple layers of story, and to build in three-dimensionality before you dive into writing any book. Develop the habit of using project and multiyear goals sheets that will keep you on track with the necessary structure and discipline. Doing so will set the stage for consistently delivering well-crafted stories, continually.

. . .

With the development of three-dimensional characters, plots, and settings, as well as scenes, and a multilayered storytelling approach in mind, we now have all the ingredients to ensure three-dimensional writing. In the conclusion to follow, we'll sum up what we've learned.

Conclusion

STEP THROUGH THE PAINTING INTO THE WILD JUNGLE

"The key to understanding the answer to any questions about guidance is having a clear grasp of what is three-dimensional."

—ELAINE SEILER, *YOUR MULTI-DIMENSIONAL WORKBOOK: EXERCISES FOR ENERGETIC AWAKENING*

The word *three-dimensional* can easily be defined as solid, realistic, rounded, and lifelike—even *living*. Writing that is three-dimensional seems to have length (the foundation of a story), width (structure), and depth (fully fleshed-out characters, plots, and settings rooted in layers of rich, textured scenes). Three-dimensional writing is what allows a reader to step through the pages of a book and enter the fictional world, where plot and characters are in that realistic realm that starts with little more than a line and progresses into shape, and finally solid form. Once three-dimensionality is grasped, all things are possible: direction, motion, focus, vivid color, texture, harmony, and variety in which change is attainable and value becomes concrete. The possibility of stepping through the painted picture into the wild jungle has become an achievable goal.

In our initial chapters, we explored the three core elements of character, plot, and setting, and how to create three-dimensionality with each. Spend a considerable amount of time with these dimensions. Draw them out slowly. You may need to search for situations and settings that will allow your characters to break free of the barriers that force them to remain one- or two-dimensional. Place them where they can't hide. If necessary, reshape their roles and personalities by giving them strengths and weaknesses, relationships, skill sets, internal and external conflicts, and goals and motivations that (1) provide ways for them to grow organically, and (2) are cohesive with the opposition. (In the back cover blurb breakdown section of the chapter five, we referred to this as "the conflict standing in the way.") Remember, the growth of main characters requires their active participation in the events they're working to resolve. The best way to learn how the P/P/F Dimensions affect the core elements is to read published books and identify each dimension from chapter to chapter. You can use the exercises in Appendix B to help you with that.

We explored the anatomy of three-dimensional scenes, namely opening, resolution, and bridge scenes. We discovered the process of crafting properly set *up* and set *out* scenes that anchor, orient, and lead readers with purpose through your story landscape, looking back in careful increments to fill in realistic layers and always ensure there's a whisper of what's to come. Readers will only be immersed when they have a hope/dread response scene by scene.

We also learned two additional techniques to all but guarantee that your story has the required depth, namely in the construction of back cover blurbs with P/P/F Dimensions, and in our evaluation of an outline or manuscript draft with a P/P/F Dimension Development Chart, which can help you pinpoint the exact scene(s) where a lack of three-dimensionality may riddle your story.

We wrapped up the threefold process of building in three-dimensional writing by focusing on the crucial need for career authors to write in stages to create the layers necessary to achieve depth in every project.

The good news is, the more you practice these techniques and identify them in the published books you read, the better your chances of mastering the fundamentals, and your mind will automatically begin to think in three-dimensional ways. Start by coming into each project with the necessary preparation of crafting three-dimensional characters, plots, and settings. From there, you can translate these dimensions into well setup scenes. If and when you're ready to become a career author, use a multilayered approach of storytelling by writing in stages to produce solid, quality stories. All three of these steps will ensure that you're creating a story so breathtakingly three-dimensional it allows readers to eagerly enter the picture you've painted right alongside the main characters.

APPENDIX A:
THREE-DIMENSIONAL AIDS

Worksheet 1:

THREE-DIMENSIONAL
CHARACTER SKETCH WORKSHEET

Worksheet 2:

THREE-DIMENSIONAL SCENE WORKSHEET

Worksheet 3:

THREE-DIMENSIONAL
BACK COVER BLURB BREAKDOWN

Worksheet 4:

P/P/F DIMENSION DEVELOPMENT CHART

Three-Dimensional Character, Plot, and Setting Sketch Worksheet
(Table Version)

Character:

CHARACTER: PRESENT SELF	CHARACTER: PAST SELF	CHARACTER: FUTURE SELF
Name:	*Name:*	*Name:*

Character Role: (hero/ heroine, other main character, secondary character, villain)
    Physical Descriptions:
    Personality Traits:
    Strengths and Weaknesses:
	Character Role: (hero/ heroine, other main character, secondary character, villain)
	    Physical Descriptions:
	    Personality Traits:
	    Strengths and Weaknesses:
		Character Role: (hero/ heroine, other main character, secondary character, villain)
		    Physical Descriptions:
		    Personality Traits:
		    Strengths and Weaknesses:

Relationships:
    Parents:
    Other important family:
    Friends:
    Romantic interests:
    Enemies:
	Relationships:
	    Parents:
	    Other important family:
	    Friends:
	    Romantic interests:
	    Enemies:
		Relationships:
		    Parents:
		    Other important family:
		    Friends:
		    Romantic interests:
		    Enemies:

Skill Set:
    Occupation(s):
    Education:
    Hobbies:
    Interests:
	Skill Set:
	    Occupation(s):
	    Education:
	    Hobbies:
	    Interests:
		Skill Set:
		    Occupation(s):
		    Education:
		    Hobbies:
		    Interests:

Plot:

CHARACTER: PRESENT SELF	CHARACTER: PAST SELF	CHARACTER: FUTURE SELF
Name:	Name:	Name:
Plots/Subplots for This Character: Internal Conflicts: External Conflicts: Goals and Motivations:	Plots/Subplots for This Character: Internal Conflicts: External Conflicts: Goals and Motivations:	Plots/Subplots for This Character: Internal Conflicts: External Conflicts: Goals and Motivations:

Setting:

CHARACTER: PRESENT SELF	CHARACTER: PAST SELF	CHARACTER: FUTURE SELF
Name:	Name:	Name:
Important Settings for This Character:	Important Settings for This Character:	Important Settings for This Character:

Three-Dimensional Character, Plot, and Setting Sketch Worksheet
(Free-Form Version)

CHARACTER: PRESENT SELF

Name:

Character Role: (circle one: hero/heroine, other main character, secondary character, villain)

Physical Descriptions:

Personality Traits:

Strengths and Weaknesses:

Relationships:

    Parents:

    Other important family:

    Friends:

    Romantic interests:

    Enemies:

Skill Set:

    Occupation(s):

    Education:

    Hobbies:

    Interests:

Plots/Subplots for This Character:

    Internal Conflicts:

    External Conflicts:

    Goals and Motivations:

Important Settings for This Character:

CHARACTER: PAST SELF

Name:

Character Role: (circle one: hero/heroine, other main character, secondary character, villain)

Physical Descriptions:

Personality Traits:

Strengths and Weaknesses:

Relationships:

    Parents:

    Other important family:

    Friends:

    Romantic interests:

    Enemies:

Skill Set:

    Occupation(s):

    Education:

    Hobbies:

    Interests:

Plots/Subplots for This Character:

    Internal Conflicts:

    External Conflicts:

    Goals and Motivations:

Important Settings for This Character:

CHARACTER: FUTURE SELF

Name:

Character Role: (circle one: hero/heroine, other main character, secondary character, villain)

Physical Descriptions:

Personality Traits:

Strengths and Weaknesses:

Relationships:

　Parents:

　Other important family:

　Friends:

　Romantic interests:

　Enemies:

Skill Set:

　Occupation(s):

　Education:

　Hobbies:

　Interests:

Plots/Subplots for This Character:

　Internal Conflicts:

　External Conflicts:

　Goals and Motivations:

Important Settings for This Character:

THREE-DIMENSIONAL SCENE WORKSHEET
Opening Scene

Set Up Opening: (Establish the "When.")

Who:
❏ Who is the POV character in this scene?

Present character dimensions:
Past character dimensions:
Future character dimensions:

❏ What other characters are in this scene? (Important characters are the only ones you need to concern yourself with in the orientation.)

What:
❏ Establish what the main character and other characters, listed above, are doing physically/mentally at the time the scene opens.

Present plot dimensions:
Past plot dimensions:
Future plot dimensions:

Where:
❏ Where are the main character and other characters in the scene? Establish their location in a broad sense, as well as specifically.

Present setting dimensions:
Past setting dimensions:
Future setting dimensions:

Why:
❏ What's going on in this scene in the overall unfolding of story?

Extending the Bridge Toward the Next Scene: (This might be completed closer to the end of each bridge scene. Give the reader some light for the path ahead—not too much so he fully grasps everything; just enough to make him anticipate what's to come.)

THREE-DIMENSIONAL SCENE WORKSHEET

Bridge Scene (a separate sheet is needed for each scene)

Scene #:

Connecting the Bridge to This Scene from the Last: (Establish the "When" by alluding to what's happened previously and get the reader up to speed for what's about to happen in this scene. Give a definable sense of how much time has passed since this POV character's last scene.)

Who:
❑ Who is the POV character in this scene?

Present character dimensions:
Past character dimensions:
Future character dimensions:

❑ What other characters are in this scene?

What:
❑ Establish what the main character and other characters, listed above, are doing physically/mentally at the time the scene opens.

Present plot dimensions:
Past plot dimensions:
Future plot dimensions:

Where:
❑ Where are the main character and other characters in the scene? Establish their location in a broad sense, as well as specifically.

Present setting dimensions:
Past setting dimensions:
Future setting dimensions:

Why:
❑ What's going on in this scene in the overall unfolding of story?

Extending the Bridge Toward the Next Scene:

THREE-DIMENSIONAL SCENE WORKSHEET
Resolution Scene

Connecting the Bridge to This Scene from the Last: (Establish the "When.")

Who:

❏ Who is the POV character in this scene?

Present character dimensions:
Past character dimensions:
Future character dimensions:

❏ What other characters are in this scene?

What:

❏ Establish what the main character and other characters, listed above, are doing physically/mentally at the time the scene opens.

Present plot dimensions:
Past plot dimensions:
Future plot dimensions:

Where:

❏ Where are the main character and other characters in the scene? Establish their location in a broad sense, as well as specifically.

Present setting dimensions:
Past setting dimensions:
Future setting dimensions:

Why:

❏ What's going on in this scene in the overall unfolding of story?

Tie-Ups and Resolutions:

THREE-DIMENSIONAL BACK COVER BLURB BREAKDOWN WORKSHEET

Story Title:

The high-concept blurb, simplified: A character (*who*) wants (*what*) a goal because he's motivated (*why*), but he faces conflict (*why not*).

Fill in the blanks:

_____character (*who*)

_____wants (*what*)

_____a goal because he's motivated (*why*)

_____but he faces conflict (*why not*)

The back cover blurb, simplified:

who _____ (*name of character*)

wants to _____ (*goal to be achieved*)

because _____ (*motivation for acting*)

but who faces _____ (*conflict*)

Fill in the blanks for all main characters:

who _____ (*name of character*)

wants to _____ (*goal to be achieved*)

because _____ (*motivation for acting*)

but who faces _____ (*conflict*)

Tag each element from your formula in the paragraph(s) you come up with, then try to identify the present, past, and future dimensions in the back cover blurb. In the most condensed form, you should weave a main character's three dimensions seamlessly into your back cover blurb.

P/P/F Dimension Development Chart

CHAPTER/ SCENE #	POV CHARACTER	SCENE TITLE	PRESENT DIMENSION	PAST DIMENSION	FUTURE DIMENSION

ADDITIONAL AIDS

Worksheet 5:
COHESION CHECKLIST

Worksheet 6:
SCENE-BY-SCENE OUTLINE
OVERVIEW & TEMPLATE

Worksheet 7:
PROJECT GOALS
OVERVIEW & WORKSHEET

Worksheet 8:
YEARLY GOALS
OVERVIEW & WORKSHEET

Cohesion Checklist

How do you know if your characters, plots, and settings are truly cohesive? Below, circle the answer that best fits your reaction to the question. Remember, anything but a resounding "Yes" to each question means you need to go back to that element and develop more cohesion in your story.

QUESTION	ANSWER	AREAS TO REWORK
Does your outline read like a mini version of the book? Do your beginning, middle, and end follow a progressive, logical course?	Yes No Not Sure	• Characters • Internal and External Conflicts • Goals and Motivations • Plots • Settings
Are conflicts, goals, and motivations defined enough to pinpoint within a high-concept sentence (and/or back cover blurb)?	Yes No Not Sure	• Characters • Internal and External Conflicts • Goals and Motivations • Plots
Do internal and external conflicts, goals and motivations intersect, collide, and impact? Are the character's conflicts, goals, and motivations urgent and causal (can't have one without the other)?	Yes No Not Sure	• Characters • Internal and External Conflicts • Goals and Motivations • Plots
Do characters have believable, identifiable, and compelling internal and external conflicts, goals, and motivations they care about deeply?	Yes No Not Sure	• Characters • Internal and External Conflicts • Goals and Motivations • Plots
Do the characters have the skills to achieve the goal if sufficiently motivated?	Yes No Not Sure	• Characters • Skill Set • Internal and External Conflicts • Goals and Motivations • Plots
Are the main characters directly involved in resolutions of internal and external plot conflicts?	Yes No Not Sure	• Characters • Conflicts • Goals and Motivations • Plots

What are the consequences (i.e., desires met/worst fears realized) to the resolution? Are these story resolutions logical? Predictable? Would a twist ending be more effective and exciting?	Yes No Not Sure	• Characters • Internal and External Conflicts • Goals and Motivations • Plots
Do your settings truly fit the characters and plots, or are they simply there, little more than a sketch you've put a little paint on?	Yes No Not Sure	• Settings • Characters • Internal and External Conflicts • Goals and Motivations • Plots
If the story were set anywhere else, would the setting make the characters and plot less cohesive?	Yes No Not Sure	• Settings • Characters • Internal and External Conflicts • Goals and Motivations • Plots

Scene-by-Scene Outline Overview & Template

The first step in creating a scene-by-scene outline is to complete formatted outline capsules (detailed below) for each scene. These brief scene summaries help you organize your information by scene and allow you to start thinking about your information in an organized, linear manner.

Let's go over the categories that make up a capsule so you have a clear understanding of what to include in each space. Much of this information is necessary for consistency only. You may not actually use it in your outline, or even your story. For instance, the time and day may be simply for your own use. If you don't want to include each section, use the ones that are most effective for you.

- **CHAPTER AND SCENE #:** A chapter or a series of asterisks are visual indicators that tell the reader one scene has ended and a new one is beginning. In this section of the formatted outline capsule, you would include the chapter number, followed by the scene number within that chapter: "chapter 4, scene 3," for instance.
- **DAY:** Jot down either a specific date or just the day the scene takes place.
- **POINT-OF-VIEW (POV) CHARACTER:** List the scene's main character.
- **ADDITIONAL CHARACTERS:** List any other important characters who are in this particular scene.
- **LOCATION:** You can include a location without specifics, or you can determine the location and details about that location here.
- **APPROXIMATE TIME:** Include the time of day when the scene takes place.
- **DRAFT OF SCENE:** Sketch out what happens in this scene in a free-form manner.

Either insert a page break in your electronic file after each scene capsule or use a fresh piece of paper to allow space for expansion of the scene draft. This will always help you to visually note what still needs to be completed in your outline. Do this for every scene in your book. You can revise the outline as much as you need to fine-tune your story.

This listing can be duplicated and cut and pasted into a new page in your story file over and over, depending on how many scenes you project your story will need.

STORY TITLE:

Chapter and Scene #:

Day:

Point-of-View (POV) Character:

Additional Characters:

Location:

Approximate Time:

Draft of Scene:

Project Goals Overview

The purpose of writing out goals for each project is to help you determine how much time you need to spend on each stage in your project. Generally, I use this worksheet for writing and revising. Through many years of experience, I've determined that nearly every story I write takes me two weeks to outline, four weeks to write, one week to revise, and one day to edit and polish—but not in a consecutive time line, as I talked about in chapter six. You'll need to figure out how long each stage in the process takes you. However, if you're working from a scene-by-scene outline, as soon as that's complete, you can work up a project goals worksheet for writing the first draft. The same technique can work for revising a project (and editing and polishing, if you feel you need the structure). When you figure out how long it takes you to perform each of these tasks, you can come up with exact dates to work on them. You can then translate the information from your project goals worksheet directly into your yearly goals (coming up next).

It might sound impossible to accurately predict how long it'll take you to complete a project, especially down to the day (assuming life doesn't throw you any radical curveballs), but there is a trick to doing just that. You need to complete the following steps before you can make your prediction:

1. Develop a solid idea of how much you're able to write per working day. (This method works best if you write scene by scene, rather than page by page.) Writing at least one scene a day—regardless of how long or short the scene—is ideal. If you stick to writing one scene every day, you'll rarely feel you're doing too much or too little. I prefer to write two scenes a day since it allows me to write a full-length novel within a month or less (usually twenty work days).
2. Determine whether you'll work weekends or holidays, and what your schedule is like for the time period you'll be working on this particular book. As a general rule, most months come out to twenty working days if you don't work on weekends.
3. Complete a full outline, with scenes divided numerically.

Using a blank page, make a list of the number of scenes within the book, putting one scene on each line. Obviously, these scenes will come from your outline. You can simply make a sequential list of scenes, such as:

___Scene 1
___Scene 2

Or you can specify chapter and scene number, like:

___Chapter 1, Scene 1
___Chapter 1, Scene 2

Now, get out your calendar or planner—whatever you use to schedule your days. Any standard calendar of the upcoming months will work, but if you have events (dentist's appointment et al) planned during the time you'll be working, you'll want to take those into account on your project goals worksheet.

Decide the date you want to begin writing and mark it on your writing goals worksheet next to the first scene. If you're writing one scene per day, you'll then write the next date by the second scene, etc. Don't forget to skip weekends and holidays if you don't plan to work on those particular days.

By the time you've put a date next to each scene in your book, you'll know exactly when you'll be done with the first draft. So if you have a novel with forty scenes and twenty working days per month, and you're writing two scenes a day, it'll take one month to write. You might want to budget a month to a month and a half for project completion.

If you want to make a revision project goal sheet, the same thing applies: You already know how many scenes are in your book if you've outlined or written the first draft. From there, figure out how many scenes a day you want to revise and how many days you want this to take, and do your calculations based on that. As I said in chapter six, I tend to do all my revisions and editing and polishing tasks in under a week. So let's say my book has forty scenes, I'd give myself five days to revise, which means I'd have to revise at least eight scenes a day to accomplish my goal.

Again, once you've had enough experience to know how long it takes you to complete each stage in the process, you can easily put together a multiyear goals worksheet that can accurately reflect what you plan to accomplish.

PROJECT GOALS WORKSHEET

Title:

Circle One: Writing   Revising   Editing and Polishing

            Date: **Scene #**

Example:

❏   *January 2*   *Chapter 1*
❏   *January 30*   *Chapter 21*

❏   _____   _____
❏   _____   _____
❏   _____   _____
❏   _____   _____
❏   _____   _____
❏   _____   _____
❏   _____   _____
❏   _____   _____
❏   _____   _____
❏   _____   _____
❏   _____   _____
❏   _____   _____
❏   _____   _____
❏   _____   _____
❏   _____   _____
❏   _____   _____
❏   _____   _____
❏   _____   _____
❏   _____   _____
❏   _____   _____

Yearly Goals Overview

One essential tool for developing and maintaining momentum in your writing career is to write out your yearly goals to help you plan the projects you'll work on during any given year. Write your yearly goals in the previous year (or sooner), so when the new year starts you know what you're going to be doing month by month (and hopefully week by week, too, with your project goals projections). Your yearly goals should, above all, be flexible. Feel free to rework your goals worksheet throughout the year to take into account new projects, new sales, and new inspirations or life's curveballs.

Your annual and multiyear goals worksheet will include accurate predictions as to when you'll be researching, creating outlines, writing, revising, editing and polishing, and allowing shelf time for each stage in the writing process. A more in-depth goals worksheet may be necessary if you like to plan further ahead than one year or if you already know you have several books scheduled for publication within the next few years. Writing out multiyear goals with a year-by-year breakdown of your tasks and objectives will allow you to allocate your time intelligently.

You need to plan your vacations as well as your active times. And don't forget to leave a little room for a crisis (personal, career, or family sickness, etc.). I do that by adding a couple extra projects I may or may not finish into my yearly goals. This gives me room to maneuver if I have to. You may prefer making your yearly goals much looser or even more demanding. Find what works for you.

YEARLY GOALS WORKSHEET

Year:

Example:
January
Specific Dates: 2-31
What I Want to Accomplish: ❏ Book 3: Super Series

January
Specific Dates: _____
What I Want to Accomplish: ❏ _____

February
Specific Dates: _____
What I Want to Accomplish: ❏ _____

March
Specific Dates: _____
What I Want to Accomplish: ❏ _____

April
Specific Dates: _____
What I Want to Accomplish: ❏ _____

May
Specific Dates: _____
What I Want to Accomplish: ❏ _____

June
Specific Dates: _____
What I Want to Accomplish: ❏ _____

July
Specific Dates: _____
What I Want to Accomplish: ❏ _____

August
Specific Dates: _____
What I Want to Accomplish: ❏ _____

September
Specific Dates: _____
What I Want to Accomplish: ❏ _____

October
Specific Dates: _____
What I Want to Accomplish: ❏ _____

November
Specific Dates: _____
What I Want to Accomplish: ❏ _____

December
Specific Dates: _____
What I Want to Accomplish: ❏ _____

APPENDIX B
THREE-DIMENSIONAL EXERCISES

Introduction

Exercise 1:

TYRANNOSAUR CANYON,

BOOK 1: WYMAN FORD SERIES
by Douglas Preston

Exercise 2:

PLAGUE LAND,

BOOK 1: A SOMERSHILL MANOR MYSTERY
by S.D. Sykes

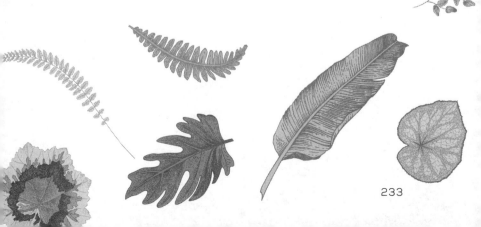

Exercise 3:

A GAME OF THRONES,

BOOK 1: A SONG OF FIRE AND ICE
by George R.R. Martin

Exercise 4:

DIVERGENT,

BOOK 1: DIVERGENT TRILOGY
by Veronica Roth

Exercise 5:

PREY
by Michael Crichton

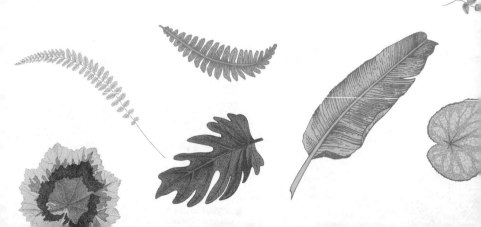

INTRODUCTION

In the following exercises, I've offered the back cover blurb for each of the published novels included, as well as an excerpt from that book. These excerpts are freely available online (so you can do this with any book you'd like, and create your own exercises), but I tried as much as possible to give you excerpts that weren't from the first scene in the book, since the opener, as we've discussed in chapter four, is slightly different than all other scenes in a book. This wasn't always possible, since naturally the first part of a book is usually what's excerpted. For that reason, I deliberately removed the chapter specifics—chapter numbers, for example—for each excerpt. Just assume it's not a first scene and analyze accordingly.

If you're unsure of how to tag the three dimensions in the back cover blurbs, look back in the chapters for a breakdown of how I did this with the examples there, or look at the bonus material available for this book online. Instruction on how to use the P/P/F Dimension Development Chart is included in chapter five.

Exercise 1:
Tyrannosaur Canyon by Douglas Preston
Tag present, past, and future dimensions in this back cover blurb:

> A moon rock missing for thirty years ...
>> Five buckets of blood-soaked sand found in a New Mexico canyon ...
>
> A scientist with ambition enough to kill ...
>
> A monk who will redeem the world ...
>
> A dark agency with a deadly mission ...
>
> The greatest scientific discovery of all time ...
>
> What fire bolt from the galactic dark shattered the Earth eons ago, and now hides in that remote cleft in the southwest U.S. known as ... Tyrannosaur Canyon?

See if you can fill out a P/P/F Dimension Development Chart for this scene:

CHAPTER/ SCENE #	POV CHARACTER	SCENE TITLE	PRESENT DIMENSION	PAST DIMENSION	FUTURE DIMENSION

Excerpt
Forge Books © 2005

Tom Broadbent reined in his horse. Four shots had rolled down Joaquin Wash from the great walled canyons east of the river. He wondered what it meant. It wasn't hunting season and nobody in his right mind would be out in those canyons target shooting.

He checked his watch. Eight o'clock. The sun had just sunk below the horizon. The echoes seemed to have come from the cluster of hoodoo rocks at the mouth of the Maze. It would be a fifteen-minute ride, no more. He had time to make a quick detour. The full moon would rise before long and his wife, Sally, wasn't expecting him before midnight anyway.

He turned his horse Knock up the wash and toward the canyon mouth, following the fresh tracks of a man and burro. Rounding a turn, a dark shape sprawled in front of him: a man lying facedown. He rode over, swung off, and knelt, his heart hammering. The man, shot in the back and shoulder, still oozed blood into the sand. He felt the carotid artery: nothing. He turned him over, the rest of the man's entrails emptying onto the sand.

Working swiftly, he wiped the sand out of the man's mouth and gave him mouth-to-mouth resuscitation. Leaning over the man, he administered heart massage, pressing on his rib cage, almost cracking the ribs, once, twice, then another breath. Air bubbled out of the wound. Tom continued with CPR, then checked the pulse.

Incredibly, the heart had restarted.

Suddenly the man's eyes opened, revealing a pair of bright blue eyes that stared at Tom from a dusty, sunburnt face. He drew in a shallow breath, the air rattling in his throat. His lips parted.

"No ... You bas ..." The eyes opened wide, the lips flecked with blood.

"Wait," said Tom. "I'm not the man who shot you."

The eyes peered at him closely, the terror subsiding—replaced by something else. Hope. The man's eyes glanced down at his hand, as if indicating something.

Tom followed the man's gaze and saw he was clutching a small, leather-bound notebook.

"Take ..." the man rasped.

"Don't try to talk."

"Take it ..."

Tom took the notebook. The cover was sticky with blood.

"It's for Robbie ..." he gasped, his lips twisting with the effort to speak. "My daughter ... Promise to give it to her ... She'll know how to find it ..."

"It?"

"... the treasure ..."

"Don't think about that now. We're going to get you out of here. Just hang in—"

The man violently clutched at Tom's shirt with a trembling hand.

"It's for her … Robbie … No one else … For God's sake not the police … You must … promise." His hand twisted the shirt with shocking force, a last spasm of strength from the dying man.

"I promise."

"Tell Robbie … I … love …"

His eyes defocused. The hand relaxed and slid down. Tom realized he had also stopped breathing.

Tom recommenced CPR. Nothing. After ten futile minutes he untied the man's bandanna and laid it over his face.

That's when it dawned on him: The man's killer must still be around. His eyes searched the rimrock and the surrounding scree. The silence was so profound it seemed that the rocks themselves held vigil. Where is the killer? There were no other tracks around, just those of the treasure hunter and his burro. A hundred yards off stood the burro itself, still packed, sleeping on its feet. The murderer had a rifle and the high ground. Broadbent might be in his sights even now.

Get out now. He rose, caught his horse's reins, swung up, and dug in his heels. The horse set off down the canyon at a gallop, rounding the opening to the Maze. Only when he was halfway down Joaquin Wash did Tom slow him to a trot. A great buttery moon was rising in the east, illuminating the sandy wash.

If he really pushed his horse, he could make Abiquiú in two hours.

Exercise 2:
Plague Land by S.D. Sykes

Tag present, past, and future dimensions in this back cover blurb:

> *When young girls go missing from a medieval English village, Lord Oswald de Lacy must find the killer before tragedy strikes again.*
>
> Oswald de Lacy was never meant to be the Lord of Somerhill Manor. Despatched to a monastery at the age of seven, sent back at seventeen when his father and two older brothers are killed by the Plague, Oswald has no experience of running an estate. He finds the years of pestilence and neglect have changed the old place dramatically, not to mention the attitude of the surviving peasants.
>
> Yet some things never change. Oswald's mother remains the powerful matriarch of the family, and his sister, Clemence, simmers in the background, dangerous and unmarried.
>
> Before he can do anything, Oswald is confronted by the shocking death of a young woman, Alison Starvecrow. The ambitious village priest claims that Alison was killed by a band of demonic dog-headed men. Oswald is certain this is nonsense, but proving it—by finding the real murderer—is quite a different matter. Every step he takes seems to lead Oswald deeper into a dark maze of political intrigue, family secrets, and violent strife.
>
> And then the body of another girl is found.

See if you can fill out a P/P/F Dimension Development Chart for this scene:

CHAPTER/ SCENE #	POV CHARACTER	SCENE TITLE	PRESENT DIMENSION	PAST DIMENSION	FUTURE DIMENSION

Excerpt
Pegasus © 2015

Somershill Manor, November 1350

If I preserve but one memory at my own death, it shall be the burning of the dog-headed beast. The fire blazed in the field beside the church—its white smoke rising skyward in a twisted billow. Its odor acrid and choking.

"Let me through," I shouted to their backs. At first they didn't respond, only turning to look at me when I grabbed at their tunics. Perhaps they had forgotten who I was? A young girl asked me to lift her so she might see the sinner die. A ragged boy tried to sell me a faggot of fat for half a penny.

And then a wail cut through the air. It was thin and piteous and came from within the pyre itself—but pushing my way through to the flames, I found no curling and blackened body tied to a stake. No sooty chains or iron hoops. Only the carcass of a bull, with the fire now licking at the brown and white hair of its coat.

The beast had not been skinned and its mouth was jammed open with a thick metal skewer. I recognized the animal immediately. It was my best Simmental bull, Goliath. But why were they burning such a valuable beast? I couldn't understand. Goliath had sired most of our dairy herd. We could not afford such waste. And then a strange thing caught my eye. Beneath the creature's distended belly something seemed to move about like a rat inside a sack of barley. I tried to look closer, but the heat repelled me. Then the plaintive call came again. A groan, followed by the high-pitched scream of a vixen. I grasped the man standing next to me. It was my reeve, Featherby.

"How can the beast be calling?" I said. "Is it still alive?"

He regarded me curiously. "No, sire. I slaughtered him myself."

"Then what's making such a noise?"

"The dog-headed beast. It calls through the neck of the bull."

"What?"

"We've sewn it inside, sire."

I felt nauseated. "Whilst still living?"

He nodded. "We hoped to hear it beg for forgiveness as it burns. But it only screams and screeches like a devil."

I grabbed the fool. "Put the fire out. Now!"

"But sire? The sacrifice of our best bull will cleanse the demon of sin."

"Who told you this?"

"The priest." These words might once have paralyzed me, but no longer.

"Fetch water." I shouted to those about me. Nobody moved. Instead they stared at the blaze—transfixed by this spectacle of burning flesh. The ragged boy launched his faggot of fat into the fire, boasting that he was helping to cook the sinner's heart. I shook him by the coarse wool of his tunic.

"Water!" I said. "I command it!" The boy backed away from me and disappeared into the crowd, only to sheepishly return with a bucket of dirty water. And then, after watching me stamp upon the flames, some others began to bring water from the dew pond. At first it was but one or two of them, but soon their numbers grew and suddenly the group became as frenzied about extinguishing the fire as they had been about fanning it.

When the heat had died down to a steam, we dragged the sweating hulk of the bull over the embers of the fire to let it cool upon the muddy grass. As we threw yet more water over its rump, their faces drew in about me, both sickened and thrilled as I cut through the stitches in the beast's belly to release its doomed stuffing. It was a trussed and writhing thing that rolled out in front of us—bound as tightly as a smoked sausage.

As I loosened the ropes, the blackened form shuddered and coughed, before gasping for one last mouthful of air.

Then, as Death claimed his prize, I held the wilting body in my arms and looked about me at these persecutors. I wanted them to see what they had done. But they could only recoil and avert their eyes in shame.

And what shame. For the face of their sacrifice is stitched into my memory like a tapestry. A tapestry that cannot be unpicked.

But this is not the beginning of my story.

It began before. After the blackest of all mortalities. The Great Plague.

Exercise 3:
A Game of Thrones by George R.R. Martin
Tag present, past, and future dimensions in this back cover blurb:

> Long ago, in a time forgotten, a preternatural event threw the seasons out of balance. In a land where summers can last decades and winters a lifetime, trouble is brewing. The cold is returning, and in the frozen wastes to the north of Winterfell, sinister and supernatural forces are massing beyond the kingdom's protective Wall. At the center of the conflict lie the Starks of Winterfell, a family as harsh and unyielding as the land they were born to. Sweeping from a land of brutal cold to a distant summertime kingdom of epicurean plenty, here is a tale of lords and ladies, soldiers and sorcerers, assassins and bastards, who come together in a time of grim omens.
>
> Here an enigmatic band of warriors bear swords of no human metal; a tribe of fierce wildlings carry men off into madness; a cruel young dragon prince barters his sister to win back his throne; and a determined woman undertakes the most treacherous of journeys. Amid plots and counterplots, tragedy and betrayal, victory and terror, the fate of the Starks, their allies, and their enemies hangs perilously in the balance, as each endeavors to win that deadliest of conflicts: the game of thrones.

See if you can fill out a P/P/F Dimension Development Chart for this scene:

CHAPTER/ SCENE #	POV CHARACTER	SCENE TITLE	PRESENT DIMENSION	PAST DIMENSION	FUTURE DIMENSION

Excerpt
Bantam Books © 1996

> The morning had dawned clear and cold, with a crispness that hinted at the end of summer. They set forth at daybreak to see a man beheaded,

twenty in all, and Bran rode among them, nervous with excitement. This was the first time he had been deemed old enough to go with his lord father and his brothers to see the king's justice done. It was the ninth year of summer, and the seventh of Bran's life.

The man had been taken outside a small holdfast in the hills. Robb thought he was a wildling, his sword sworn to Mance Rayder, the King-beyond-the-Wall. It made Bran's skin prickle to think of it. He remembered the hearth tales Old Nan told them. The wildlings were cruel men, she said, slavers and slayers and thieves. They consorted with giants and ghouls, stole girl children in the dead of night, and drank blood from polished horns. And their women lay with the Others in the Long Night to sire terrible half-human children.

But the man they found bound hand and foot to the holdfast wall awaiting the king's justice was old and scrawny, not much taller than Robb. He had lost both ears and a finger to frostbite, and he dressed all in black, the same as a brother of the Night's Watch, except that his furs were ragged and greasy.

The breath of man and horse mingled, steaming, in the cold morning air as his lord father had the man cut down from the wall and dragged before them. Robb and Jon sat tall and still on their horses, with Bran between them on his pony, trying to seem older than seven, trying to pretend that he'd seen all this before. A faint wind blew through the holdfast gate. Over their heads flapped the banner of the Starks of Winterfell: a grey direwolf racing across an ice-white field.

Bran's father sat solemnly on his horse, long brown hair stirring in the wind. His closely trimmed beard was shot with white, making him look older than his thirty-five years. He had a grim cast to his grey eyes this day, and he seemed not at all the man who would sit before the fire in the evening and talk softly of the age of heroes and the children of the forest. He had taken off Father's face, Bran thought, and donned the face of Lord Stark of Winterfell.

There were questions asked and answers given there in the chill of morning, but afterward Bran could not recall much of what had been said. Finally his lord father gave a command, and two of his guardsmen dragged the ragged man to the ironwood stump in the center of the square. They forced his head down onto the hard black wood. Lord Eddard Stark dismounted and his ward Theon Greyjoy brought forth the sword. "Ice," that sword was called. It was as wide across as a man's hand, and taller even than Robb. The blade was Valyrian steel, spell-forged and dark as smoke. Nothing held an edge like Valyrian steel.

His father peeled off his gloves and handed them to Jory Cassel, the captain of his household guard. He took hold of Ice with both hands and said, "In the name of Robert of the House Baratheon, the First of his Name, King of the Andals and the Rhoynar and the First Men, Lord of the Seven Kingdoms and Protector of the Realm, by the word of Eddard of the House Stark, Lord of Winterfell and Warden of the North, I do sentence you to die." He lifted the great sword high above his head.

Bran's bastard brother Jon Snow moved closer. "Keep the pony well in hand," he whispered. "And don't look away. Father will know if you do."

Bran kept his pony well in hand, and did not look away.

His father took off the man's head with a single sure stroke. Blood sprayed out across the snow, as red as summerwine. One of the horses reared and had to be restrained to keep from bolting. Bran could not take his eyes off the blood. The snows around the stump drank it eagerly, reddening as he watched.

The head bounced off a thick root and rolled. It came up near Greyjoy's feet. Theon was a lean, dark youth of nineteen who found everything amusing. He laughed, put his boot on the head, and kicked it away.

"Ass," Jon muttered, low enough so Greyjoy did not hear. He put a hand on Bran's shoulder, and Bran looked over at his bastard brother.

"You did well," Jon told him solemnly. Jon was fourteen, an old hand at justice.

It seemed colder on the long ride back to Winterfell, though the wind had died by then and the sun was higher in the sky. Bran rode with his brothers, well ahead of the main party, his pony struggling hard to keep up with their horses.

"The deserter died bravely," Robb said. He was big and broad and growing every day, with his mother's coloring, the fair skin, red-brown hair, and blue eyes of the Tullys of Riverrun. "He had courage, at the least."

"No," Jon Snow said quietly. "It was not courage. This one was dead of fear. You could see it in his eyes, Stark." Jon's eyes were a grey so dark they seemed almost black, but there was little they did not see. He was of an age with Robb, but they did not look alike. Jon was slender where Robb was muscular, dark where Robb was fair, graceful and quick where his half brother was strong and fast.

Robb was not impressed. "The Others take his eyes," he swore. "He died well. Race you to the bridge?"

"Done," Jon said, kicking his horse forward. Robb cursed and followed, and they galloped off down the trail, Robb laughing and hooting, Jon silent and intent. The hooves of their horses kicked up showers of snow as they went.

Bran did not try to follow. His pony could not keep up. He had seen the ragged man's eyes, and he was thinking of them now. After a while, the sound of Robb's laughter receded, and the woods grew silent again.

That was when Jon reappeared on the crest of the hill before them. He waved and shouted down at them. "Father, Bran, come quickly, see what Robb has found!" Then he was gone again.

Jory rode up beside them. "Trouble, my lord?"

"Beyond a doubt," his lord father said. "Come, let us see what mischief my sons have rooted out now." He sent his horse into a trot. Jory and Bran and the rest came after.

They found Robb on the riverbank north of the bridge, with Jon still mounted beside him. The late summer snows had been heavy this moonturn. Robb stood knee deep in white, his hood pulled back so the sun shone in his hair. He was cradling something in his arm, while the boys talked in hushed, excited voices.

The riders picked their way carefully through the drifts, groping for solid footing on the hidden, uneven ground. Jory Cassel and Theon Greyjoy were the first to reach the boys. Greyjoy was laughing and joking as he rode. Bran heard the breath go out of him. "Gods!" he exclaimed, struggling to keep control of his horse as he reached for his sword.

Jory's sword was already out. "Robb, get away from it!" he called as his horse reared under him.

Robb grinned and looked up from the bundle in his arms. "She can't hurt you," he said. "She's dead, Jory."

Bran was afire with curiosity by then. He would have spurred the pony faster, but his father made them dismount beside the bridge and approach on foot. Bran jumped off and ran.

By then Jon, Jory, and Theon Greyjoy had all dismounted as well.

"What in the seven hells is it?" Greyjoy was saying.

"A wolf," Robb told him.

"A freak," Greyjoy said. "Look at the size of it."

Bran's heart was thumping in his chest as he pushed through a waist-high drift to his brothers' side.

Half-buried in blood stained snow, a huge dark shape slumped in death. Ice had formed in its shaggy grey fur, and the faint smell of corruption clung to it like a woman's perfume. Bran glimpsed blind eyes crawling with maggots, a wide mouth full of yellowed teeth. But it was the size of it that made him gasp. It was bigger than his pony, twice the size of the largest hound in his father's kennel.

"It's no freak," Jon said calmly. "That's a direwolf. They grow larger than the other kind."

Theon Greyjoy said, "There's not been a direwolf sighted south of the Wall in two hundred years."

"I see one now," Jon replied.

Bran tore his eyes away from the monster. That was when he noticed the bundle in Robb's arms. He gave a cry of delight and moved closer. The pup was a tiny ball of grey-black fur, its eyes still closed. It nuzzled blindly against Robb's chest as he cradled it, searching for milk among his leathers, making a sad little whimpery sound. Bran reached out hesitantly. "Go on," Robb told him. "You can touch him."

Bran gave the pup a quick nervous stroke, then turned as Jon said, "Here you go." His half brother put a second pup into his arms. "There are five of them." Bran sat down in the snow and hugged the wolf pup to his face. Its fur was soft and warm against his cheek.

"Direwolves loose in the realm, after so many years," muttered Hullen, the master of horse. "I like it not."

"It is a sign," Jory said.

Father frowned. "This is only a dead animal, Jory," he said. Yet he seemed troubled. Snow crunched under his boots as he moved around the body. "Do we know what killed her?"

"There's something in the throat," Robb told him, proud to have found the answer before his father even asked. "There, just under the jaw."

His father knelt and groped under the beast's head with his hand. He gave a yank and held it up for all to see. A foot of shattered antler, tines snapped off, all wet with blood.

A sudden silence descended over the party. The men looked at the antler uneasily, and no one dared to speak. Even Bran could sense their fear, though he did not understand.

His father tossed the antler to the side and cleansed his hands in the snow. "I'm surprised she lived long enough to whelp," he said. His voice broke the spell.

"Maybe she didn't," Jory said. "I've heard tales . . . maybe the bitch was already dead when the pups came."

"Born with the dead," another man put in. "Worse luck."

"No matter," said Hullen. "They be dead soon enough too."

Bran gave a wordless cry of dismay.

"The sooner the better," Theon Greyjoy agreed. He drew his sword. "Give the beast here, Bran."

The little thing squirmed against him, as if it heard and understood.

"No!" Bran cried out fiercely. "It's mine."

"It be a mercy to kill them," Hullen said.

Bran looked to his lord father for rescue, but got only a frown, a furrowed brow. "Hullen speaks truly, son. Better a swift death than a hard one from cold and starvation."

"No!" He could feel tears welling in his eyes, and he looked away. He did not want to cry in front of his father.

"Lord Stark," Jon said. It was strange to hear him call Father that, so formal. Bran looked at him with desperate hope. "There are five pups," he told Father. "Three male, two female."

"What of it, Jon?"

"You have five true born children," Jon said. "Three sons, two daughters. The direwolf is the sigil of your House. Your children were meant to have these pups, my lord."

Bran saw his father's face change, saw the other men exchange glances. He loved Jon with all his heart at that moment. Even at seven, Bran understood what his brother had done. The count had come right only because Jon had omitted himself. He had included the girls, included even Rickon, the baby, but not the bastard who bore the surname Snow, the name that custom decreed be given to all those in the north unlucky enough to be born with no name of their own.

Their father understood as well. "You want no pup for yourself, Jon?" he asked softly.

"The direwolf graces the banners of House Stark," Jon pointed out. "I am no Stark, Father."

Their lord father regarded Jon thoughtfully. Robb rushed into the silence he left. "I will nurse him myself, Father," he promised. "I will soak a towel with warm milk, and give him suck from that."

"Me too!" Bran echoed.

The lord weighed his sons long and carefully with his eyes. "Easy to say, and harder to do. I will not have you wasting the servants' time with this. If you want these pups, you will feed them yourselves. Is that understood?"

Bran nodded eagerly. The pup squirmed in his grasp, licked at his face with a warm tongue.

It was not until they were mounted and on their way that Bran allowed himself to taste the sweet air of victory. By then, his pup was snuggled inside his leathers, warm against him, safe for the long ride home. Bran was wondering what to name him.

Halfway across the bridge, Jon pulled up suddenly.

"What is it, Jon?" their lord father asked.

"Can't you hear it?"

Bran could hear the wind in the trees, the clatter of their hooves on the ironwood planks, the whimpering of his hungry pup, but Jon was listening to something else.

"There," Jon said. He swung his horse around and galloped back across the bridge. They watched him dismount where the direwolf lay dead in the snow, watched him kneel. A moment later he was riding back to them, smiling.

"He must have crawled away from the others," Jon said.

"Or been driven away," their father said, looking at the sixth pup. His fur was white, where the rest of the litter was grey. His eyes were as red as the blood of the ragged man who had died that morning. Bran thought it curious that this pup alone would have opened his eyes while the others were still blind.

"An albino," Theon Greyjoy said with wry amusement. "This one will die even faster than the others."

Jon Snow gave his father's ward a long, chilling look. "I think not, Greyjoy," he said. "This one belongs to me."

Exercise 4:
Divergent by Veronica Roth
Tag present, past, and future dimensions in this back cover blurb:

> In Beatrice Prior's dystopian Chicago, society is divided into five factions, each dedicated to the cultivation of a particular virtue: Candor (the honest), Abnegation (the selfless), Dauntless (the brave), Amity (the peaceful), and Erudite (the intelligent). On an appointed day of every year, all sixteen-year-olds must select the faction to which they will devote the rest of their lives. For Beatrice, the decision is between staying with her family and being who she really is—she can't have both. So she makes a choice that surprises everyone, including herself.
>
> During the highly competitive initiation that follows, Beatrice renames herself Tris and struggles to determine who her friends really are—and where, exactly, a romance with a sometimes fascinating, sometimes infuriating boy fits into the life she's chosen. But Tris also has a secret, one she's kept hidden from everyone because she's been warned it can mean death. And as she discovers a growing conflict that threatens to unravel her seemingly perfect society, she also learns that her secret might help her save those she loves ... or it might destroy her.

See if you can fill out a P/P/F Dimension Development Chart for this scene:

CHAPTER/ SCENE #	POV CHARACTER	SCENE TITLE	PRESENT DIMENSION	PAST DIMENSION	FUTURE DIMENSION

Excerpt
Katherine Tegen Books © 2014

> There is one mirror in my house. It is behind a sliding panel in the hallway upstairs. Our faction allows me to stand in front of it on the second day of every third month, the day my mother cuts my hair.

I sit on the stool and my mother stands behind me with the scissors, trimming. The strands fall on the floor in a dull, blond ring. When she finishes, she pulls my hair away from my face and twists it into a knot. I note how calm she looks and how focused she is. She is well-practiced in the art of losing herself. I can't say the same of myself.

I sneak a look at my reflection when she isn't paying attention—not for the sake of vanity, but out of curiosity. A lot can happen to a person's appearance in three months. In my reflection, I see a narrow face, wide, round eyes, and a long, thin nose—I still look like a little girl, though sometime in the last few months I turned sixteen. The other factions celebrate birthdays, but we don't. It would be self-indulgent.

"There," she says when she pins the knot in place. Her eyes catch mine in the mirror. It is too late to look away, but instead of scolding me, she smiles at our reflection.

I frown a little. Why doesn't she reprimand me for staring at myself?

"So today is the day," she says.

"Yes," I reply.

"Are you nervous?"

I stare into my own eyes for a moment. Today is the day of the aptitude test that will show me which of the five factions I belong in. And tomorrow, at the Choosing Ceremony, I will decide on a faction; I will decide the rest of my life; I will decide to stay with my family or abandon them.

"No," I say. "The tests don't have to change our choices."

"Right." She smiles. "Let's go eat breakfast."

"Thank you. For cutting my hair."

She kisses my cheek and slides the panel over the mirror. I think my mother could be beautiful, in a different world. Her body is thin beneath the gray robe. She has high cheekbones and long eyelashes, and when she lets her hair down at night, it hangs in waves over her shoulders. But she must hide that beauty in Abnegation.

We walk together to the kitchen. On these mornings when my brother makes breakfast, and my father's hand skims my hair as he reads the newspaper, and my mother hums as she clears the table—it is on these mornings that I feel guiltiest for wanting to leave them.

The bus stinks of exhaust. Every time it hits a patch of uneven pavement, it jostles me from side to side, even though I'm gripping the seat to keep myself still.

My older brother, Caleb, stands in the aisle, holding a railing above his head to keep himself steady. We don't look alike. He has my father's dark hair and hooked nose and my mother's green eyes and dimpled cheeks. When he was younger, that collection of features looked strange, but now it suits him. If he wasn't Abnegation, I'm sure the girls at school would stare at him.

He also inherited my mother's talent for selflessness. He gave his seat to a surly Candor man on the bus without a second thought.

The Candor man wears a black suit with a white tie—Candor standard uniform.

Their faction values honesty and sees the truth as black and white, so that is what they wear.

The gaps between the buildings narrow and the roads are smoother as we near the heart of the city. The building that was once called the Sears Tower—we call it the Hub—emerges from the fog, a black pillar in the skyline. The bus passes under the elevated tracks. I have never been on a train, though they never stop running and there are tracks everywhere. Only the Dauntless ride them.

Five years ago, volunteer construction workers from Abnegation repaved some of the roads. They started in the middle of the city and worked their way outward until they ran out of materials. The roads where I live are still cracked and patchy, and it's not safe to drive on them. We don't have a car anyway.

Caleb's expression is placid as the bus sways and jolts on the road. The gray robe falls from his arm as he clutches a pole for balance. I can tell by the constant shift of his eyes that he is watching the people around us—striving to see only them and to forget himself. Candor values honesty, but our faction, Abnegation, values selflessness.

The bus stops in front of the school and I get up, scooting past the Candor man. I grab Caleb's arm as I stumble over the man's shoes. My slacks are too long, and I've never been that graceful.

The Upper Levels building is the oldest of the three schools in the city: Lower Levels, Mid-Levels, and Upper Levels. Like all the other buildings around it, it is made of glass and steel. In front of it is a large metal sculpture that the Dauntless climb after school, daring each other to go higher and higher. Last year I watched one of them fall and break her leg. I was the one who ran to get the nurse.

"Aptitude tests today," I say. Caleb is not quite a year older than I am, so we are in the same year at school. He nods as we pass through the front doors. My muscles tighten the second we walk in. The atmosphere feels hungry, like every sixteen-year-old is trying to devour as much as he can get of this last day. It is likely that we will not walk these halls again after the Choosing Ceremony—once we choose, our new factions will be responsible for finishing our education.

Our classes are cut in half today, so we will attend all of them before the aptitude tests, which take place after lunch. My heart rate is already elevated.

"You aren't at all worried about what they'll tell you?" I ask Caleb. We pause at the split in the hallway where he will go one way, toward Advanced Math, and I will go the other, toward Faction History.

He raises an eyebrow at me. "Are you?" I could tell him I've been worried for weeks about what the aptitude test will tell me—Abnegation, Candor, Erudite, Amity, or Dauntless?

Instead I smile and say, "Not really."

He smiles back. "Well ... have a good day."

I walk toward Faction History, chewing on my lower lip. He never answered my question. The hallways are cramped, though the light coming through the windows creates the illusion of space; they are one of the only places where the factions mix, at our age. Today the crowd has a new kind of energy, a last day mania.

A girl with long curly hair shouts "Hey!" next to my ear, waving at a distant friend. A jacket sleeve smacks me on the cheek. Then an Erudite boy in a blue sweater shoves me. I lose my balance and fall hard on the ground.

"Out of my way, Stiff," he snaps, and continues down the hallway.

My cheeks warm. I get up and dust myself off. A few people stopped when I fell, but none of them offered to help me. Their eyes follow me to the edge of the hallway. This sort of thing has been happening to others in my faction for months now—the Erudite have been releasing antagonistic reports about Abnegation, and it has begun to affect the way we relate at school.

The gray clothes, the plain hairstyle, and the unassuming demeanor of my faction are supposed to make it easier for me to forget myself, and easier for everyone else to forget me too. But now they make me a target.

I pause by a window in the E Wing and wait for the Dauntless to arrive. I do this every morning. At exactly 7:25, the Dauntless prove their bravery by jumping from a moving train.

My father calls the Dauntless "hellions." They are pierced, tattooed, and black-clothed. Their primary purpose is to guard the fence that surrounds our city. From what, I don't know.

They should perplex me. I should wonder what courage—which is the virtue they most value—has to do with a metal ring through your nostril. Instead my eyes cling to them wherever they go.

The train whistle blares, the sound resonating in my chest. The light fixed to the front of the train clicks on and off as the train hurtles past the school, squealing on iron rails. And as the last few cars pass, a mass exodus of young men and women in dark clothing hurl themselves from the moving cars, some dropping and rolling, others stumbling a few steps before regaining their balance. One of the boys wraps his arm around a girl's shoulders, laughing.

Watching them is a foolish practice. I turn away from the window and press through the crowd to the Faction History classroom.

Exercise 5:
Prey by Michael Crichton
Tag present, past, and future dimensions in this back cover blurb:

> In the Nevada desert, an experiment has gone horribly wrong. A cloud of nanoparticles— microrobots—has escaped from the laboratory. This cloud is self-sustaining and self-reproducing. It is intelligent and learns from experience. For all practical purposes, it is alive.
>
> It has been programmed as a predator. It is evolving swiftly, becoming more deadly with each passing hour. Every attempt to destroy it has failed. And we are the prey.

See if you can fill out a P/P/F Dimension Development Chart for this scene:

CHAPTER/ SCENE #	POV CHARACTER	SCENE TITLE	PRESENT DIMENSION	PAST DIMENSION	FUTURE DIMENSION

Excerpt
HarperCollins Publishers © 2002

DAY 6
7:12 A.M.

With the vibration of the helicopter, I must have dozed off for a few minutes. I awoke and yawned, hearing voices in my headphones. They were all men speaking:

"Well, what exactly is the problem?" A growling voice.

"Apparently, the plant released some material into the environment. It was an accident. Now, several dead animals have been found out in the desert. In the vicinity of the plant." A reasonable, organized voice.

"Who found them?" Growly.

"Couple of nosy environmentalists. They ignored the Keep Out signs, snooped around the plant. They've complained to the company and are demanding to inspect the plant."

"Which we can't allow."

"No, no."

"How do we handle this?" asked a timid voice.

"I say we minimize the amount of contamination released, and give data that show no untoward consequence is possible." Organized voice.

"I wouldn't play it that way," said growling voice. "We're better off flatly denying it. Nothing was released. I mean, what's the evidence anything was released?"

"Well, the dead animals. A coyote, some desert rats. Maybe a few birds."

"Animals die in nature all the time. I mean, remember the business about those slashed cows? It was supposed to be aliens from UFOs that were slashing the cows. Finally turned out the cows were dying of natural causes, and it was decomposing gas in the carcasses that split them open. Remember that?"

"Vaguely."

Timid voice: "I'm not sure we can just deny—"

"Yes, deny."

"Aren't there pictures? I think the environmentalists took pictures."

"Well, who cares? What will the pictures show, a dead coyote? Nobody is going to get worked up about a dead coyote. Trust me. Pilot? Pilot, where are we?"

I opened my eyes. I was sitting in the front of the helicopter, alongside the pilot. The helicopter was flying east, into the glare of low morning sun. Beneath my feet I saw mostly flat terrain, with low clumps of cactus, juniper, and the occasional scraggly Joshua tree.

The pilot was flying alongside the power-line towers that marched in single file across the desert, a steel army with outstretched arms. The towers cast long shadows in the morning light.

A heavyset man leaned forward from the backseat. He was wearing a suit and tie. "Pilot? Are we there yet?"

"We just crossed the Nevada line. Another ten minutes."

The heavyset man grunted and sat back. I'd met him when we took off, but I couldn't remember his name now. I glanced back at the three men, all in suits and ties, who were traveling with me. They were all PR consultants hired by Xymos. I could match their appearance to their voices. A slender, nervous man, twisting his hands. Then a middle-aged man with a briefcase on his lap. And the heavyset man, older and growly, obviously in charge.

"Why did they put it in Nevada, anyway?"

"Fewer regulations, easier inspections. These days California is sticky about new industry. There was going to be a year's delay just for environmental-impact statements. And a far more difficult permitting process. So they came here."

Growly looked out the window at the desert. "What a hole," he said. "I don't give a crap what goes on out here, it's not a problem." He turned to me. "What do you do?"

"I'm a computer programmer."

"You covered by an NDA?" He meant, did I have a nondisclosure agreement that would prevent me from discussing what I had just heard.

"Yes," I said.

"You coming out to work at the plant?"

"To consult," I said. "Yes."

"Consulting's the way to go," he said, nodding as if I were an ally. "No responsibility. No liability. Just give your opinion, and watch them not take it."

With a crackle, the pilot's voice broke in over the headsets. "Xymos Molecular Manufacturing is dead ahead," he said. "You can just see it now."

Twenty miles in front of us, I saw an isolated cluster of low buildings silhouetted on the horizon. The PR people in the back all leaned forward.

"Is that it?" asked Growly. "That's all it is?"

"It's bigger than it looks from here," the pilot said.

As the helicopter came closer, I could see that the buildings were interlocked, featureless concrete blocks, all whitewashed. The PR people were so pleased they almost burst into applause. "Hey, it's beautiful!"

"Looks like a hospital."

"Great architecture."

"It'll photograph great."

I asked, "Why will it photograph great?"

"Because it has no projections," the man with the briefcase said. "No antennas, no spikes, no things poking up. People are afraid of spikes and antennas. There are studies. But a building that's plain and square like this, and white—perfect color choice, associations to virginal, hospital, cure, pure—a building like this, they don't care."

"Those environmentalists are messed up," said Growly, with satisfaction. "They do medical research here, right?"

"Not exactly ..."

"They will when I get through, trust me. Medical research is the way to go on this."

The pilot pointed out the different buildings as he circled them. "That first concrete block, that's power. Walkway to that low building, that's the residences. Next door, fab support, labs, whatever. And then the square windowless three-story one, that's the main fab building. They tell me it's a shell, it's got another building inside it. Then over to the right, that low flat shed, that's external storage and parking. Cars have to be under shade here, or the dashboards buckle. Get a first-degree burn if you touch your steering wheel."

I asked, "And they have residences?"

The pilot nodded. "Yeah. Have to. Nearest motel is a hundred and sixty-one miles. Over near Reno."

"So how many people live in this facility?" Growly asked.

"They can take twelve," the pilot said. "But they've generally got about five to eight. Doesn't take a lot to run the place. It's all automated, from what I hear."

"What else do you hear?"

"Not very much," the pilot said. "They're closed-mouthed about this place. I've never even been inside."

"Good," said Growly. "Let's make sure they keep it that way."

The pilot turned the stick in his hand. The helicopter banked, and started down.

I opened the plastic door in the bubble cockpit, and started to get out. It was like stepping into an oven. The blast of heat made me gasp.

"This is nothing!" the pilot shouted, over the whirr of the blades. "This is almost winter! Can't be more than a hundred and five!"

"Great," I said, inhaling hot air. I reached in the back for my overnight bag and my laptop. I'd stowed them under the seat of the timid man.

"I have to take a piss," said Growly, releasing his seat belt.

"Dave …" said the man with the briefcase, in a warning tone.

"It's just for a minute."

"Dave—" an embarrassed glance toward me, then lowering his voice: "They said, we don't get out of the helicopter, remember?"

"I can't wait another hour. Anyway, what's the difference?" He gestured toward the surrounding desert. "There's nothing out here for a million miles."

"But, Dave—"

"You guys give me a pain. I'm going to pee." He hefted his bulk up, and moved toward the door.

I didn't hear the rest of their conversation because by then I had taken off my earphones. Growly was clambering out. I grabbed my bags, turned and moved away, crouched beneath the blades. They cast a flickering shadow on the pad.

I came to the edge of the pad where the concrete ended abruptly in a dirt path that threaded among the clumps of cholla cactus toward the blocky white power building fifty yards away. There was no one to greet me—in fact, no one in sight at all.

Looking back, I saw Growly zip up his trousers and climb back into the helicopter. The pilot pulled the door shut and lifted off, waving to me as he rose into the air. I waved back, then ducked away from the swirl of spitting sand. The helicopter circled once and headed west. The sound faded.

The desert was silent except for the hum of the electrical power lines a few hundred yards away. The wind ruffled my shirt, flapped my trouser legs. I turned in a slow circle, wondering what to do now. And thinking about the words of the PR guy: They said, we don't get out of the helicopter, remember?

"Hey! Hey, you!"

I looked back. A door had cracked open in the white power block. A man's head stuck out. He shouted, "Are you Jack Forman?"

"Yes," I said.

"Well, what you waiting for, an engraved invitation? Get inside."

And he slammed the door shut again.

That was my welcome to the Xymos Fabrication Facility. Lugging my bags, I trudged down the dirt path toward the door.

Things never turn out the way you expect.

INDEX

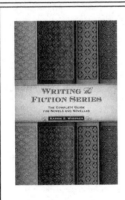